Blacks in East Texas History

Blacks in East Texas History

SELECTIONS FROM THE

East Texas Historical Journal

EDITED BY Bruce A. Glasrud and Archie P. McDonald

FOREWORD BY Cary D. Wintz

WITH CONTRIBUTIONS BY Alwyn Barr, Elizabeth R. Rabe, James Marten, James M. Smallwood, Merline Pitre, Garna L. Christian, Karen Kossie-Chernyshev, Gail K Beil, Stefanie Decker, William H. Wilson, James Conrad, and Theodore M. Lawe

Texas A&M University Press COLLEGE STATION

First edition
This paper meets
the requirements of
ANSI/NISO Z39.48-1992
(Permanence of Paper).
Binding materials have
been chosen
for durability.

Library of Congress Cataloging-in-Publication Data
Blacks in East Texas history : selections from the East Texas historical journal; edited by Bruce A. Glasrud and Archie P. McDonald; foreword by Cary D. Wintz; with contributions by Alwyn Barr . . . [et al.]. — 1st ed.
p. cm.
Includes index.
ISBN-13: 978-1-60344-041-7 (cloth : alk. paper)
ISBN-10: 1-60344-041-0 (cloth : alk. paper)
1. African Americans—Texas, East—History. 2. African Americans—Texas, East—Social conditions—19th century. 3. African Americans—Texas, East—Social conditions—20th century. 4. Slavery—Texas, East—History—19th century. 5. Racism—Texas, East—History. 6. Texas, East—Race relations. 7. African Americans—Texas, East—Biography. 8. Texas, East—History. 9. Texas, East—Biography. I. Glasrud, Bruce A. II. McDonald, Archie P. III. Barr, Alwyn. IV. East Texas historical journal.
E185.93.T4B57 2008
976.4'140496073—DC22
2007052622

Contents

Foreword

The Past and the Future of East Texas and African American History

CARY D. WINTZ

THE HISTORY OF EAST TEXAS AND THE HISTORY of African Americans in Texas are inextricably bound together. Beginning with the settlement of East Texas by Anglo Americans early in the nineteenth century, African Americans, almost all of whom were slaves, provided a significant portion of the labor that cleared the land, planted and harvested the crops, and built the economy, and their presence defined the social and political culture that emerged in antebellum East Texas. Early Texas, by most measures, was an extension of the plantation South. As Randolph "Mike" Campbell established so clearly in his groundbreaking study, *An Empire for Slavery,* in terms of the proportion of slaves and slaveholders in society, slavery was as strongly entrenched in Texas, the newest slave state, as it was in Virginia, the oldest.[1] Through the nineteenth and at least the first half of the twentieth century East Texas remained more Southern than Western in demographics and race relations. Slavery, emancipation, Reconstruction, Jim Crow laws and the struggle against them, the civil rights movement, desegregation, and post-desegregation racial politics were central to the experiences and history of all East Texans, black and white, and the centrality of these events underscores the fundamental connection of African American history to East Texas.

In spite of this reality, through the mid-twentieth century Texas historians paid little attention to the role of African Americans in the state. Prior to 1950 the major texts and monographs in Texas history barely touched upon the African American experience, and what they included largely perpetuated historical myths and inaccuracies. These books discussed slavery but described it as a benign institution. They depicted Reconstruction as an era of travail as Texans suffered under the oppressive rule of Yankees and their corrupt local collaborators but said little about race and rarely mentioned an African American by name. From 1877 on, blacks usually disappeared from these texts. The era of segregation and disfranchisement, as well as the early struggles for civil and political rights, generally did not make it to print.

Two books provide a clear example of the neglect of African American history in the first half of the twentieth century. Near the beginning of the century University of Texas professor Charles William Ramsdell published his classic study, *Reconstruction in Texas.* African Americans and African American issues played an extremely small role in his work. He mentioned black suffrage, but it received much less attention than the effort to disenfranchise former Confederates, and he described the Klan as generally perpetrating "comparatively harmless pranks" to frighten the "superstitious freedmen" into good behavior; he ascribed more serious violence to "reckless and irresponsible persons masquerading under the name of the Ku Klux."[2] Ramsdell mentioned by name only one African American, George T. Ruby, whom he described as a "mulatto carpet-bagger from New England, a man of some ability and fair education" who allied with white "carpet-baggers" in support of "ultra-radical policies."[3]

In 1943 Hardin-Simmons professor Rupert Richardson published the first edition of his influential Texas history text, *Texas: The Lone Star State.* His coverage of African American history was scant. What there was of it continued in the tradition of Ramsdell. Richardson presented slavery in Texas as a relatively mild institution. Slaves, he contended, "fared better in Texas than in the older states," on the whole "slaves were well-treated," especially women and children, and slaves suffered from the "pangs of separation from loved ones far less frequently than did the white people."[4] Richardson mentioned the disfranchisement of blacks at the turn of the century obliquely. He noted that the two Terrell Election Laws "improved the fairness and honesty of both primaries and general elections" and observed that "it has been the policy of the Democratic party in Texas to prohibit Negroes from voting in its primaries."[5] He did mention the legal challenges to the white primary but did not mention the *Smith v. Allwright* case that was pending as his text was published. The second edition of *Texas: The Lone Star State* (1958) left the earlier description of slavery and the Terrell Election Laws intact but did note that in 1944 the U.S. Supreme Court overturned the white primary, opening the Democratic primary to black voters. Richardson also added about two pages discussing the desegregation of higher education, the impact of the Brown school desegregation decision, and other early efforts to dismantle segregation.[6]

It was not until the end of the civil rights era that African American history began to receive the attention from serious scholars that it deserved. While work in this field has involved historians from a number of universities, both inside and outside Texas, two universities deserve much of the credit for bringing the African American experience in Texas to the forefront. The first, Texas Tech University in West Texas, was instrumental in training graduate students in Afro-Texas history.[7] These students produced the dissertations and books that launched the professional study of the history of blacks in Texas. Lawrence D. Rice wrote the first Texas Tech dissertation on African American history in 1967 under the direction of Lawrence Graves. In 1971 Rice published his dissertation with Louisiana State University Press as *The Negro in Texas, 1874–1900*. Bruce Glasrud followed with his 1969 dissertation, "Black Texans, 1900–1930: A History," and three more Tech dissertations came out of the department early in the 1970s. Alwyn Barr joined the faculty at Tech as director of the ethnic studies program. He helped train additional graduate students and also wrote *Black Texans: A History of Negroes in Texas, 1528–1971*, the first survey of African American history in Texas. Other pioneering studies of African Americans in Texas from Texas Tech faculty and former Ph.D. students include James M. Smallwood's *Time of Hope, Time of Despair: Black Texans during Reconstruction* (1981) and Alwyn Barr and Robert Calvert's edited collection of essays, *Black Leaders: Texans for their Times* (1981).

While Texas Tech prepared young scholars to explore African American history in Texas, Texas Southern University prepared African American students to enter the history profession and to focus their scholarship on the African American experience in Texas. Texas Southern offers only an M.A. in history and has a relatively small number of history graduate students. Nevertheless, in the mid-1980s, TSU revamped its graduate history program with the purpose of preparing the most talented of its graduate students for Ph.D. work. Its program emphasized research methods and analytical writing; students were expected to engage actively in research projects, utilizing the archival and historical data available in the Houston area. Most of the work focused on the African American experience in southeast Texas. By the early 1990s TSU M.A. graduates began entering Ph.D. programs, and most of those who matriculated were successful. Today four of these students hold tenured or tenure-track positions at three Texas universities: Texas A&M University, Texas State University–San Marcos, and Sam Houston State University. Three of the four either have published their first books or have a book in press. Ernest Obadele-Starks published his study of black labor on the Texas Gulf coast in 2000, Dwight Watson's study of race and the Houston police department came out in 2005, and Bernadette Pruitt's work on the migration of blacks into early twentieth-century Houston has been accepted for publication.[8]

Texas Southern University's history faculty have also contributed to the study of African Americans in Texas and East Texas. Merline Pitre has authored two books, the first a study of black political leaders in Reconstruction and post-Reconstruction Texas and the second, an investigation of Lulu B. White and her involvement in the struggle for civil rights in Houston. Cary D. Wintz co-edited with Howard Beeth a collection of essays on the history of African Americans in Houston, and in the late 1990s he joined Adrian "Andy" Anderson as one of the two active authors of the revised Rupert Richardson Texas history text. Revisions to the venerable text under Anderson and Wintz's authorship included the full incorporation of the African American experience into the narrative of the Lone Star State's history.[9]

During the last two decades of the twentieth and the first years of the new century both the quantity and the quality of publications in African American history in Texas improved substantially. So many new books appeared and continue to be published each year that it is becoming difficult to keep track of them. In a quick inventory of my personal library at home I counted more than fifty books; my university office contains a few more. Bruce Glasrud and Laurie Champion produced a thorough survey in a bibliography prepared in 2000, but the continuing flow of new scholarship rendered it incomplete within months of its publication.[10] Far more impressive than the numbers of scholarly studies of Afro Texans are the range of topics examined and the growing complexity of the methodology and the interpretation. Topics include a number of studies on the role of African American women in Texas, books and articles on black education and black religion, studies of black communities, and the black struggle for equality and racial justice. There are also studies of black writers and artists as well as black music and black musicians.

While it is not possible to discuss or even mention all of the books that have added to our understanding of African Americans in Texas, there are several that underscore the changes that have transformed the field. For example, Neil Foley's *The White Scourge* and Michael Phillips's *White Metropolis* have added new dimensions to our understanding of race, class, and economic exploitation.[11] Foley discussed the evolution of labor in the production of cotton from the late nineteenth to the early twentieth century, arguing that the racially based labor system in Texas involved a multiplicity of racial and ethnic groups—blacks, Mexican Americans, and poor whites—and was one in which blacks, Mexican Americans, and poor whites were defined as inferior and exploited by a white power elite. Similarly, in his study of race and ethnicity in Dallas, Phillips shattered our traditional view of race as a black-white dichotomy. Instead he argued that whiteness was as much an attitude or an ideology as a complexion. It was the basis of power in a capitalistic society that controlled wealth and dominated and oppressed the underclass—blacks, of course, and Mexicans but also immigrants, the white working class, Jews, Catholics, and often women. Likewise, Julia Blackwelder's *Styling Jim Crow* redefined our image and understanding of African American women in the age of Jim Crow.[12] Blackwelder forced us to examine the beauty industry as a vehicle that provided African American women with an occupation that offered job security and independence, a reasonable income, and entry into a profession that functioned almost completely in isolation from white political and economic control during the era of segregation. By focusing on women as workers in a profession generally ignored or marginalized by historians, Blackwelder, like Foley and Phillips, suggested new areas of historical inquiry.

There are dozens of other books that have explored new topics and provided new insights into the Afro-Texas experience. The three books discussed above are also interesting because they addressed the East Texas African American experience, but not in a traditional sense. Blackwelder's Houston-based study and Phillips's exploration of race in Dallas examined blacks in the two great metropolitan areas that define the northwestern and southeastern boundaries of East Texas; Foley's book followed the cotton culture from the largely black tenant farmers and sharecroppers of northwestern East Texas to the large commercial farms of South Texas. And, as African Americans historically were rooted deeply in East Texas, East Texans have in turn contributed greatly to the study of African American history. A significant part of this contribution came out of the offices of the East Texas Historical Association and the *East Texas Historical Journal.* Archie McDonald became the "provisional" editor of the journal in 1971, a position he holds through 2007. The same year that he took the reins of the journal, it published its first essay on African American history, Fred Robbins's "The Origins and Development of the African Slave Trade in Galveston, Texas, and Surrounding Areas from 1816 to 1836." Over the next thirty-five years another forty-four essays on black Texas history have appeared in the journal—an average of more than one essay per year (see the appendix). All four articles in the spring 1976 issue, designated a Special Issue on Black History, focused on this topic.

To appreciate the impact of the *East Texas Historical Journal,* it is important to place it in the context of the emergence of modern Afro-Texas historiography, which dated from the early work at Texas Tech in the late 1960s. As graduate students in West Texas began their pioneering work in African American history, the *East Texas Historical Journal* began publishing scholarly work on the African American experience. Among the authors it published were three of these early Tech students: James M. Smallwood, Bruce A. Glasrud, and Neil G. Sapper. The journal published its first essay on Afro-Texas history written by an African American in 1988. Texas Southern University history professor Merline Pitre achieved this honor with her article on black political participation in Texas Reconstruction. To date, five of the seven essays in the journal authored by blacks were the work of Texas Southern faculty or former graduate students.

The *East Texas Historical Journal* was not the only Texas historical journal that published work on African Americans in Texas. The state's oldest and most prestigious journal, the *Southwestern Historical Quarterly,* also published this work. Before 1950 the journal contained only a scattered few essays on blacks in Texas. Not until the last quarter of the century did work on this subject appear with any regularity. *The Houston Review*, published by the Houston Public Library Board from 1979 through 1996, also printed a number of scholarly articles on blacks in Houston.[13] In terms of the coverage of Afro-Texas history, the *East Texas Historical Journal* compared favorably to these other journals. Comparing the contents of the *East Texas Historical Journal* with the *Southwestern Historical Quarterly* during the past five years reveals that while each published ten articles on the African American experience, the *East Texas Historical Journal*, which publishes only two issues per year, contained a higher percentage of articles on blacks than did the *Southwestern Historical Quarterly*.

While the quantity and the quality of research and publication on African American history in Texas has improved substantially during the last thirty years, the education of African Americans as historians has not kept pace. Since East Texas has a significant proportion of the state's African American population, we would anticipate that African Americans are well represented in the region at all levels of higher education. According to the U.S. Census of 2000, 16.4 percent of the population of East Texas is African American, while only 11.5 percent of the population of the entire state is black. As expected, the enrollment of blacks in state-funded colleges and universities reflects this distribution of population; statewide 10.8 percent of students in universities are black, while in East Texas the number is 17.6 percent.[14] In contrast to the statewide enrollment data, blacks are enrolled in East Texas institutions of higher education at a rate slightly greater than their numbers in the population. At first glance, these numbers look encouraging. However, if we exclude data from Texas Southern University and Prairie View A&M University, the two state-supported, historically black universities, African American enrollment in the other East Texas state colleges and universities drops to 11.2 percent, a level far below the 16.4 percent of African Americans in the population. The data on the employment of African American faculty at East Texas institutions of higher education reveal an even greater gap. African Americans make up only 7.6 percent of the faculty, less than 50 percent of their distribution in the population; if we exclude Texas Southern and Prairie View, only 3.4 percent of the faculty is black.[15]

An examination of the training of historians in Texas underscores the above data on the employment of black faculty and explains some of the problems encountered in staffing history departments with African American faculty. Texas does not train many African American historians. Data collected from an informal survey of the history Ph.D. granting departments in Texas in 2000 and again in 2003 indicated that the number of black Ph.D. students was small and declining. In 2000 the nine Ph.D. history programs in the state enrolled a total of sixteen African Americans; three years later the number had dropped to eleven. In the ten years from 1994 to 2003 only eight blacks earned a Ph.D. in history in Texas.[16]

As the twenty-first century proceeds, Texans can take pride in the changes that have occurred in the research and writing on our shared history. African Americans, along with women and other ethnic minorities, as well as all social and economic classes, have been brought into our historical narrative. East Texans and the *East Texas Historical Journal* have contributed greatly to this process. However, the improvements in our textbooks, the books we have produced, and the articles in our journals, while impressive, leave problems unresolved. We have brought African Americans into Texas history; we have brought African Americans into Texas universities as students and faculty, although there is still more to be done in this area; but we have not been as successful in attracting African Americans to our profession and especially in recruiting and training young African Americans in our history Ph.D. programs. We have accomplished much, but (with apologies to Robert Frost) we have promises to keep, and miles to go before we sleep.

Notes

1. Randolph B. Campbell, *An Empire for Slavery: The Peculiar Institution in Texas, 1821–1865* (Baton Rouge: Louisiana State University Press, 1989), 2.
2. Charles William Ramsdell, *Reconstruction in Texas* (New York: Columbia University Press, 1910), 232–33.
3. Ramsdell, *Reconstruction in Texas,* 201.
4. Rupert Norval Richardson, *Texas: The Lone Star State* (New York: Prentice-Hall, 1943), 222.
5. Richardson, *Texas* (1943), 369.
6. Richardson, *Texas: The Lone Star State,* 2nd ed. (Englewood Cliffs, N.J.: Prentice-Hall, 1958), 164, 282–83, 405–406.

7. Bruce A. Glasrud and James M. Smallwood, "The Texas Tech School of Black History: An Overview," *West Texas Historical Association Year Book* 82 (2006): 102–119.
8. Ernest Obadele-Starks, *Black Unionism in the Industrial South* (College Station: Texas A&M University Press, 2000); Dwight Watson, *Race and the Houston Police Department, 1930–1990: A Change Did Come* (College Station: Texas A&M University Press, 2005). Bernadette Pruitt's manuscript, a revised version of her dissertation, has been accepted for publication by Texas A&M University Press.
9. Merline Pitre, *Through Many Dangers Toils and Snares: Black Leadership in Texas, 1868–1900* (Austin: Eakin Press, 1985; rev. ed., 1997) and *In Struggle against Jim Crow: Lulu B. White and the NAACP, 1900–1957* (College Station: Texas A&M University Press, 1999); Howard Beeth and Cary D. Wintz, eds., *Black Dixie: Afro-Texan History and Culture in Houston* (College Station: Texas A&M University Press, 1992); Rupert N. Richardson, Adrian Anderson, Cary D. Wintz, and Ernest Wallace, *Texas: The Lone Star State,* 8th ed. (Upper Saddle River, N.J.: Prentice-Hall, 2001; 9th ed., 2005).
10. Bruce A. Glasrud and Laurie Champion, eds., *Exploring the Afro-Texas Experience: A Bibliography of Secondary Sources about Black Texans* (Alpine, Tex.: Center for Big Bend Studies, Sul Ross State University, 2000).
11. Neil Foley, *The White Scourge: Mexicans, Blacks, and Poor Whites in Texas Cotton Culture* (Berkeley: University of California Press, 1997); Michael Phillips, *White Metropolis: Race, Ethnicity, and Religion in Dallas, 1841–2001* (Austin: University of Texas Press, 2006). The first chapter of Phillips's book appeared initially as "White Violence, Hegemony, and Slave Rebellion in Dallas, Texas, before the Civil War," in the fall 1999 issue of the *East Texas Historical Journal.*
12. Julia Kirk Blackwelder, *Styling Jim Crow: African American Beauty Training during Segregation* (College Station: Texas A&M University Press, 2003).
13. The original *Houston Review* ceased publication for financial reasons following the completion of the 1996 edition. In the fall of 2003 the Center for Public History at the University of Houston revived the review in a less scholarly, more popular format and renamed it *Houston History.* The African American experience in Houston has remained a significant feature of the new magazine.
14. Texas Higher Education Coordinating Board, Statistical Report FY 2004—Student Enrollment, Public Universities, Headcount Enrollment by Classification, Gender Ethnic Origin, http://www.thecb.state.tx.us/reports/HTM/0777.HTM.
15. Texas Higher Education Coordinating Board, Statistical Report FY 2004—Faculty Data, Public Universities, Faculty Headcount by Rank, Gender, Ethnic Origin, http://www.thecb.state.tx.us/reports/HTM/0777.HTM.
16. The author conducted an informal telephone survey of the directors of the history graduate programs at the nine Ph.D. granting institutions (University of Texas at Austin, University of Texas at El Paso, University of Texas at Arlington, Texas A&M University, University

of Houston, Texas Tech University, Southern Methodist University, Texas Christian University, and Rice University). Given the informal nature of the survey there could be some errors in the data but not enough to change the fact that African Americans comprise a very small percentage of the enrollment in our history Ph.D. programs.

Acknowledgments

EVERY PERSON WHO EDITS A BOOK ACQUIRES OBLIgations and support. We are no exceptions. First and foremost we wish to thank the authors of these articles; obviously, without them there would be no book. We also wish to thank the Board of Directors of the East Texas Historical Association for their encouragement and acceptance. Cary D. Wintz allowed us to use his ETHA presidential address of 2005 in our work; he also provided us with insight and suggestions. Thanks, Cary.

Texas A&M University Press sent the manuscript out to two readers; their enthusiastic endorsement and valuable suggestions made this a much better book. Mary Lenn Dixon, the editor-in-chief at Texas A&M University Press has been with us since the inception with encouragement and help. Managing editor Thom Lemmons oversaw the process from manuscript to finished book. Last, but absolutely not least, Portia Gordon, secretary-treasurer of the East Texas Historical Association, made journals available to us, scanned copies, and efficiently ensured that we received items when we needed them. Portia, we sincerely thank and appreciate you.

Bruce A. Glasrud
Archie P. McDonald

Blacks in East Texas History

Introduction

East Texas Black History and the East Texas Historical Association

BRUCE A. GLASRUD

AND ARCHIE P. MCDONALD

THE CONCEPTION FOR *BLACKS IN EAST TEXAS HISTORY: Selections from the* East Texas Historical Journal began in September 2006, at the annual meeting of the East Texas Historical Association. There we discussed the feasibility of publishing a book of articles about blacks in East Texas that had been previously published in the *East Texas Historical Journal (ETHJ).* We realized that a significant number of articles had been written by historians of considerable stature in the field of Afro-Texas history and that the published articles would constitute an interesting and well-received anthology.

Subsequently, we examined issues of the *East Texas Historical Journal.* From its beginning through 2007, the *East Texas Historical Journal* published forty-five articles that had a focus on African Americans in Texas, and we considered this a substantial number. As a result of that process, we realized that both the quality and the quantity of articles in the *East Texas Historical Journal* concerning blacks in Texas history were little short of amazing. The East Texas Historical Association had a long, continuing, and vibrant interest in the history of peoples of color as well as other vital aspects of the historical experience in East Texas.

The East Texas Historical Association began in 1962 when, as noted in Archie McDonald's introduction to *The East Texas Historical Journal, General Index,* edited by Donald W. Whisenhunt (1983), "four men breathed life into a new historical association." They were Charles K. Chamberlain, Ralph W. Steen, F. I. Tucker, and F. Lee Lawrence. Others helped, but the aforementioned four "gave much more than anyone else because of their love for history in general, and Texas and Eastern Texas history in particular" (iii). The association's purpose included facilitating research, collecting and preserving historical records and data, and publishing historical scholarship. As a result, that same year (1962) the first issue of the journal was published, with Charles Chamberlain as editor. Chamberlain, a professor of history at Stephen F. Austin State University, continued to edit the journal for nine years. In 1971 Chamberlain stepped down, and the Board of Directors allowed "me [McDonald] to become editor on a provisional basis, and since no one has said anything to the contrary since, I suppose it has worked out" (iii). Following a year at Murray State University, McDonald had arrived at Stephen F. Austin State University in 1964 with a master's degree from Rice University. He received his Ph.D. in U.S. Southern history from Louisiana State University in 1965.

It is probably no surprise, but an interesting circumstance nonetheless, that the same year Archie McDonald agreed to edit the journal (1971), the first article in the *East Texas Historical Journal* focusing on African American history in Texas was published: Fred Robbins's "The Origin and Development of the African Slave Trade in Galveston, Texas, and Surrounding Areas from 1816 to 1836." Four articles on black Texas history followed: two in 1972, one in 1973, and one in 1975. Then, in an exciting and critical moment for a small regional historical journal in the South, the *East Texas Historical Journal* in the spring of 1976 published a Special Issue on Black History, with articles by James A. Burran ("Violence in an 'Arsenal of Democracy': The Beaumont Race Riot, 1943"), Rebecca W. Palm ("Protestant Churches and Slavery in Matagorda County"), James M. Smallwood ("Black Texans during Reconstruction: First Freedom"), and Gerald Gaither ("Blacks and the Southern Farmers' Alliance Movement"). The following year, 1977, the journal published its tenth article on black Texas history: "Child or Beast? White Texas' View of Blacks, 1900–1910," by Bruce A. Glasrud.

Since the publication of that article by Glasrud, thirty-five additional scholarly articles on black Texas history have been published by the journal under McDonald's editorship. The overall total of forty-five articles (see the appendix) on such a significant topic is important, and doubly so in the South, where some journals refused to accept, publish, or encourage the study of black history. The total is also significant since the *East Texas Historical Journal* publishes only two issues per year. One need only compare the number of articles published in other state and regional journals to understand the significance of this achievement. To our knowledge, few historical journals published as many articles on black history as did the *East Texas Historical Journal;* one would have to turn to *Phylon* or the *Journal of Negro History* to find more articles on this topic. In Texas, especially since the Texas State Historical Association's publication of Alwyn Barr and Robert A. Calvert's edited volume, *Black Leaders: Texans for Their Times* (1981), the *Southwestern Historical Quarterly* has played a major role in disseminating minority history as well.

The forty-five articles published from 1971 to 2007 in the *East Texas Historical Journal* cover a variety of topics and are evenly balanced. For example, twenty-two of the articles focus on the nineteenth century, twenty-two on the twentieth century, and one, Alwyn Barr's "Advancing from History's Hollow to History's Mountain: Sources on African American History in Texas," covers both centuries. Nine articles are about slavery, six cover Reconstruction, and six discuss the civil rights era. Eleven of the articles focus on black women, six analyze white/black violence, four look at education, and six deal with religion. Other topics include the Southern Farmers' Alliance, buffalo soldiers, black Texas politicians, the first Ph.D. earned by a black Texan, the NAACP, Dallas municipal policy, the Greenville sign ("the blackest land, the whitest people"), one of the Tuskegee airmen, and World War II hero Doris "Dorie" Miller. In other words, varied aspects of black East Texas history have been covered exceedingly well by these articles. For the purposes of this book, twelve of the articles have been assembled into a collection that is representative, readable, and significant.

The present volume includes not only the foreword, this introduction, and the aforementioned twelve articles but also an appendix listing the forty-five articles on black Texas history the journal has published, and a list of contributors. This anthology is meant to be a showcase for the quality, quantity, and variety of works published by the East Texas Historical Association over a period of thirty-five years. It also showcases authors who either wrote early introductory expositions of some of their later studies or parts of lengthier works. These are authors who either made a career of researching and writing about black Texas history or who wrote about black Texans while pursuing other avenues of inquiry. Among these contributors are younger authors who, at the time of their articles' original publication, were just beginning their journey to additional important contributions.

By compiling this anthology/collection, we demonstrate that these studies remain significant. They have not been refuted by recent scholarship, though such work has shown how important these studies were and has filled gaps left by the earlier studies. For example, Elizabeth R. Rabe's article on slave children and James Marten's study of blacks in Civil War Texas address aspects of slave experiences not usually studied, and Stefanie Decker's treatment of black women in the civil rights era examines an important element of the struggle for equality in Texas. It should be added that the civil rights movement in Texas also influenced the state's history and historians. Certainly Alwyn Barr, Bruce A. Glasrud, Merline Pitre, and James M. Smallwood were influenced by this struggle. The *ETHJ* editor's receptivity to black Texas history is in part explained by McDonald's awareness of and sympathy for the regional, state, and local stirrings.

If there is one topic not covered specifically by an article in this anthology, that topic would be racial violence. However, articles by James M. Smallwood, Garna L. Christian, and Bruce A. Glasrud document racial violence during Reconstruction, the late nineteenth century, and the early twentieth century, respectively. Other *ETHJ* articles on the issue of racial violence include the previously mentioned "Violence in an 'Arsenal of Democracy': The Beaumont Race Riot, 1943," by James A. Burran, along with Michael Phillips's "White Violence, Hegemony, and Slave Rebellion in Dallas, Texas, before the Civil War," Kenneth R. Durham Jr.'s "The Longview Race Riot of 1919," and Edward Hake Phillips's "The Sherman Courthouse Riot of 1930.")

Cary D. Wintz's foreword to this anthology is a revision of his East Texas Historical Association presidential address, which he delivered in September 2005. In it the Texas Southern University history professor reviews some of the significant studies of black East Texas history, outlines the major themes of black Texas history, and discusses the authors responsible for analyzing those themes. Naturally, a number of them are included in this anthology. Wintz also mentions the universities, such as Texas Southern University and Texas Tech University, that have been involved in teaching and training students and scholars in black Texas history.[1]

The twelve anthologized articles are in chronological historical order. Two articles bookend the volume, and in between are five articles covering the nineteenth century and five on the twentieth century. The articles were selected on the basis of readability, scholarship, balance, and topic. We decided to use no more than one article per author, which affected four scholars: Gail K Beil, Karen Kossie-Chernyshev, Merline Pitre, and James M. Smallwood. However, each of them is represented with a first-rate article in the collection.

Alwyn Barr's previously mentioned article, "Advancing from History's Hollow to History's Mountain: Sources on African American History in Texas," begins the collection. Barr, undoubtedly the dean of scholars of the black experience in Texas, focuses on the types of primary sources that are available to students and scholars of African American history in Texas. Though none of the resources will surprise anyone (hopefully), it is important to remember that these sources must be used with care. For example, the dominant newspapers were published by whites, and the bias is sometimes overwhelmingly negative and stereotyped; still, a careful investigator can derive data from those newspapers. Barr, a former president of the Texas State Historical Association, has published the standard work on blacks in Texas—*Black Texans: A History of African Americans in Texas, 1528–1995*. Readers should also understand, and utilize, resources that have become available over the past decade via easy access to the Internet. One example stands out: the incredible resource of the Slave Narratives, now available digitally, along with relevant photographs, via the Library of Congress Web site. Secondary sources, too, are easier to retrieve; students, scholars, and readers may turn to JSTOR, the online journal archive, or have ready access to inter-library loans via the OCLC's ArticleFirst database.

The final essay in the book, the other bookend, is a co-authored study by James Conrad and Theodore M. Lawe, "Preserving Rosenwald Schools in East Texas: The Sand Flat and Richland School Project." We use it as a bookend because it is current, discussing historic preservation issues and needs in the black community, and at the same time discusses the importance of the Rosenwald schools to the black community earlier in the twentieth century. The essay focuses on rural East Texas and the role that two communities played in preserving Rosenwald schools in their areas. Multimillionaire Julius Rosenwald and Booker T. Washington worked to upgrade black education in the South, and the result was the Rosenwald schools. Some were established in Texas.

The nineteenth-century experience for African American Texans begins with slavery. The choice of which article on black slavery to use was a difficult one since there were several excellent offerings. We chose Elizabeth R. Rabe's "Slave Children of Texas: A Qualitative and Quantitative Analysis" because she focused on an aspect of Texas slavery not previously studied, and she did so by using primary sources as well as recognizing the secondary literature. Hers is a path-breaking work.

Sometimes it is easy to forget that slavery continued until 1865; James Marten, in "Slaves and Rebels: The Peculiar Institution in Texas, 1861–1865," discusses the status of black slaves during the Civil War and how they adjusted to the changing conditions. His work leads us to the Reconstruction era. The dominant scholar of the black experience during the years of Reconstruction in Texas is James M. Smallwood. He published three articles on that topic in the *East Texas Historical Journal,* any one of which could have been used in this anthology. We selected "Black Texans during Reconstruction: First Freedom" because of its significance in detailing what Reconstruction meant to black Texans and how they responded to their "first freedom." His other articles, one on religion and one on education, deal with topics that are covered in other essays in our anthology, though not during Reconstruction.

The two remaining articles on nineteenth-century topics also reflect choices from an array of significant possibilities. However, we wished to use one of Merline Pitre's articles and decided that "The Evolution of Black Political Participation in Reconstruction Texas" covered a topic of considerable importance, and some of the black politicians she discusses held office beyond Reconstruction. Pitre, one of the first of a new generation of black African American scholars (including Darlene Clark Hine) and an acknowledged specialist in black Texas history, produced a worthy and significant article. The final article on nineteenth-century topics is Garna L. Christian's "The Violent Possibility: The Tenth Cavalry at Texarkana." The Tenth Cavalry was one of two black cavalry units in the West in the years after 1866. For a time they were stationed in Texarkana; Christian explicates the deep-seated fear with which some whites viewed armed blacks, even though the soldiers were there to protect them. Christian is author of the award-winning *Black Soldiers in Jim Crow Texas, 1899–1917*.

The five essays that were selected to represent twentieth-century topics describe white attitudes that led to violent treatment of black Texans via riots and lynching; an African American religious community and its endeavors in East Texas; an author, teacher, and man of the Harlem Renaissance; women in the civil rights movement; and the rural-to-urban odyssey of eight black families during the twentieth century. The first of these five articles, "Child or Beast? White Texas' View of Blacks, 1900–1910," by Bruce A. Glasrud, notes that white Texans were either paternalists, who viewed blacks as childlike, or racists, who viewed blacks as beastly. As a result of these views, at least one hundred black Texans were lynched, while others faced instances of "whitecapping" (forcible removal) and race riots during the first decade of the twentieth century. Despite such circumstances, as Karen Kossie-Chernyshev argues in "Constructing Good Success: The Church of God in Christ and Social Uplift in East Texas, 1910–1935," not all black Texans gave up, left the state, or despaired. Members of the Church of God in Christ developed ways to help through efforts at social uplift over the next, albeit difficult, twenty-five years.

The rigid, discriminatory nature of Jim Crow society in twentieth-century Texas had other effects on black Texans. Prominent poet, scholar, and Wiley College professor Melvin Tolson became a radical, as Gail K Beil illustrates in her persuasive article on Tolson, "Melvin B. Tolson: Texas Radical." Tolson also became acquainted with prominent national literary leaders such as Langston Hughes, wrote the first major scholarly study of the Harlem Renaissance (his master's thesis), and later moved to Langston University in Oklahoma.

Black Texas women resisted and became radicals as well. Stefanie Decker, in "Women in the Civil Rights Movement: Juanita Craft versus the Dallas Elite," describes the means by which black women, especially Juanita Craft, became involved in the African American struggle for civil rights in Texas. Black Texans survived many adverse situations in the state, as William H. Wilson relates in "Growing Up Black in East Texas: Some Twentieth-Century Experiences," which details the experiences of eight black families in twentieth-century Texas. What became especially noticeable to Wilson was the centrality of three values—family, work, and education (religion was associated with the family)—to their lives, whether in a rural or urban setting. Wilson is a prize-winning historian who published a well-received history, *Hamilton Park: A Planned Black Community in Dallas.*

These twelve articles reflect solid scholarship, vital information, arresting interpretations, and crucial issues of the black experience(s) during the nineteenth and twentieth centuries in East Texas. They provide an overview of the history of black Texans, as well as examples of critical writing from authors interested in that experience. The major chronological divisions have been covered, as well as the principal themes and topics of African American history in the eastern portion of the Lone Star state—slavery, freedom, segregation, and the struggle for civil rights.

By showcasing these articles in *Blacks in East Texas History,* we demonstrate the consistent commitment that the *East Texas Historical Journal* has made over the years to publish quality, original scholarship on the lives of black Texans. The articles chosen indicate also that for many years the East Texas Historical Association has been interested in and supportive of the investigation of Afro-Texas life in East Texas.

Note

1. See also Bruce A. Glasrud and James M. Smallwood, "The Texas Tech School of Black History: An Overview," *West Texas Historical Association Year Book* 82 (2006): 102–19.

Advancing from History's Hollow to History's Mountain

Sources on African American History in Texas

ALWYN BARR

During a conference on Civil Rights in Austin at the Lyndon Johnson Presidential Library in 1972, former President Johnson declared:

> Until we overcome unequal history, we cannot overcome unequal opportunity. But to be black in a white society is not to stand on equal and level ground. While the races may stand side by side, whites stand on history's mountain and blacks stand in history's hollow. It's time we get down to the business of trying to stand black and white on level ground.[1]

These words of Lyndon Johnson provide the theme of this essay: advancing from history's hollow to history's mountain. An important contribution to that advance will be the writing of more and better articles and books on African Americans in Texas. To produce those studies it is necessary to know about the source materials that are available and what additional materials should be collected.

Two essays offer starting points. In a bibliographical chapter on "Black Texans" in *A Guide to the History of Texas* (1988)[2] I described what had been written at that time. My historiographical essay, "African Americans in Texas: From Stereotypes to Diverse Roles," in *Texas Through Time: Evolving Interpretations* (1991)[3] provides an analysis of books and articles as well as suggestions about topics in need of further research.

To pursue new research, writers must make full use of a wide range of original sources. Major newspapers of most cities and towns are useful, although they usually reflected bias against blacks until the mid-twentieth century. A good example of their effective use is Lawrence D. Rice, *The Negro in Texas, 1874–1900* (1971). African American newspapers began to appear in the larger towns after the Civil War. Few copies from the late nineteenth century have been found; the discovery of others would be most enlightening. For the twentieth century the most valuable black newspapers are the Houston *Informer* and the Dallas *Express,* since extensive runs of each have been microfilmed and are available in major city and university libraries. The Galveston *City Times* and the San Antonio *Register* are available on microfilm for briefer periods. National black papers, such as the Washington *New Era* during Reconstruction, the Indianapolis *Freeman* late in the nineteenth century, and the Chicago *Defender* early in the twentieth century, contain accounts of events, persons, and communities in Texas. They, too, may be found on microfilm. Tuskegee Institute kept files of newspaper clippings from 1899 to 1966 on events involving African Americans, including those in Texas, that may be viewed on microfilm.

Several national African American magazines have published articles on Texas in the twentieth century. *Crisis,* the voice of the National Association for the Advancement of Colored People, has carried discussions of civil rights issues and activities. In *Opportunity,* the National Urban League has mentioned economic and social concerns. *Ebony* has explored social events and focused on rising leaders, as did *Sepia,* published in Fort Worth for readers across the nation. The newspapers or magazines of various religious denominations are valuable for comments on churches and religious leaders.[4] Two topics that deserve further exploration through newspapers and magazines are literary efforts and sports activities.

Books and pamphlets also represent important printed sources. A few autobiographies have been written by black Texans, including Jeff Hamilton, *My Master* (1940; reprint 1993), by a slave of Sam Houston; J. Vance Lewis, *Out of the Ditch: True Story of an Ex-Slave* (1910), who became an attorney; Henry Flipper, *Negro Frontiersman* (1963; expanded edition 1997), by an army officer; and James Farmer, *Lay Bare the Heart: An Autobiography of the Civil Rights Movement* (1985), by one of its leaders. City directories provide useful information on individual occupations, businesses, churches, and schools. The directories for Dallas, Galveston, and San Antonio are on microfilm through 1900. Some volumes privately printed by blacks remain elusive but are extremely valuable for research. The *Red Book of Houston* (1915) offers sketches of individuals and institutions in the black community of that city. Other examples are H. T. Kealing, *History of African Methodism in Texas* (1885), W. A. Redwine, *Brief History of the Negro in Five Counties* (1901, reprinted in the *Chronicles of Smith County, Texas,* 1972), and Ira Bryant, *Negro Church of Houston* (1936). The centennial histories of many churches appeared in the 1960s and 1970s, but are little known outside the local community. Other volumes that fall into these categories need to be located, preserved, and possibly reprinted for wider use.

Related to printed sources are photographs that offer important insights about individuals, groups, homes and institutions, and clothing. Major collections are in the Institute of Texan Cultures at San Antonio, the Center for American History at the University of Texas in Austin, the Houston Metropolitan Research Center, the Rosenberg Library in Galveston, and the archives at Texas A&M University. The Museum of African American Life and Culture in Dallas recently obtained the *Sepia* Magazine Collection of over 40,000 photographs that span 1945 to 1983.[5] Visual materials have not been published extensively, but good presentations are Lynne Adele, *Black History/Black Vision* (1989) and *Behold the People: R. C. Hickman's Photographs of Black Dallas, 1949–1961* (1994) which offer illustrations of work by African American artists and a photographer. A history of photographers and examples of their work appear in Alan Govenar, *Portraits of Community: African American Photography in Texas* (1996).

Studies of black material culture provide important insights into the clothing, furniture, and daily lives of people in earlier periods. Museums with valuable collections and exhibits include the Institute of Texan Cultures in San Antonio, the George Washington Carver Museum in Austin, and the Museum of African American Life and Culture in Dallas. Archaeological work can supplement material culture collections with artifacts or careful restoration of historic sites. One possible example may be the work conducted at the Freedman's Cemetery in Dallas.[6] A study that clarifies the value of such efforts is Terry Jordan, *Texas Graveyards: A Cultural Legacy* (1982).

Oral history interviews have been gathered during the twentieth century to provide information not available in written records. The Federal Writers' Project during the 1930s collected narratives of former slaves who also offered information on emancipation and Reconstruction. Selections from these interviews were published by Ron Tyler and Lawrence Murphy as *The Slave Narratives of Texas* (1974, reprinted 1997). A multi-volume series edited by George Rawick, *The American Slave* (1972–1977), contains eleven volumes of interviews with former slaves in Texas. Their value is reflected in two important studies by Randolph B. Campbell, *An Empire for Slavery: The Peculiar Institution in Texas* (1989), and by James M. Smallwood, *Time of Hope, Time of Despair: Black Texans During Reconstruction* (1981). Other projects have focused on twentieth-century events and people. Ruth Edmonds Hill has edited *The Black Women Oral History Project* (1992) in eleven volumes that include interviews with Christia Adair of Houston and Juanita Craft of Dallas. The Oral History Collection at Baylor University has gathered unpublished interviews with black teachers, sports figures, and political leaders. East Texas State University and Texas Tech University have taped personal accounts by local black leaders in education, farming, and politics. Texans, including James Farmer of CORE and Juanita Craft of the Dallas NAACP, are among those who were interviewed for the Civil Rights Documentation Project at Howard University in Washington, D.C.[7] Probably the most extensive published example of a modern oral history project is Ruthe Winegarten, *I Am Annie Mae* (1983), based on interviews with a Dallas woman about her range of economic and civic activities. There is a need for additional oral history interviews, especially with African American musicians, such as those edited by Glen Alyn in *I Say Me for a Parable: The Oral Autobiography of Mance Lipscomb, Texas Bluesman* (1993).

Researchers also should be aware of a variety of unpublished manuscript sources. First, there are public records at the local level. These include tax rolls, deed records, probate records, as well as county court and district court records—all useful for the history of slavery and for individuals and events after the Civil War. Campbell employed them skillfully in *Empire for Slavery.* For the post-1865 period, the records of city councils, health departments, and school boards are valuable sources for studies of topics such as education and law enforcement.[8]

State records are equally important. The Archives Division of the Texas State Library in Austin has several collections that relate to black history. There are lists of voters who registered during Reconstruction, records of the legislatures and constitutional conventions that had black members, and letters to governors from black leaders and citizens. The papers of the Texas adjutant general provide material on the state police during Reconstruction and the militia that included black members, as well as on lynching, segregation, and voting rights. Civil rights cases are among those in the records of the Texas Supreme Court. The Archives and Records Division of the Texas General Land Office holds information on land grants to free blacks who served in the Texas Revolution.[9] George Woolfolk used state records in his account of *The Free Negro in Texas* (1976). Further study could explore African American land acquisition in a state that controlled its public lands.

Records of the federal government are crucial for many African American topics. The primary depository, the National Archives in Washington, D.C., has a branch in Fort Worth that holds some original records for the South Central region as well as microfilm of several record groups in Washington. These include United States manuscript census returns, presently available up through 1920, which can provide biographical information on individuals and families such as occupation, age, place of birth, education, and, from 1850 to 1870, property holdings. Microfilm of these census returns also may be found in larger city and university libraries. The Federal Records Center in Fort Worth also contains military records of black soldiers and several rolls of microfilmed Freedmen's Bureau papers on Texas which offer insights into labor, violence, and education during Reconstruction. Barry Crouch elaborates on "Hidden Sources of Black History: The Texas Freedmen's Bureau Records as a Case Study," in the *Southwestern Historical Quarterly* (January 1980). Other valuable records include those of the Federal Extension Service, which contain information on black and white farming and rural living conditions from 1909 to 1944. Records of the Fair Employment Practices Committee reveal job discrimination during World War II. Federal court records include civil rights cases from Texas. Another branch of the National Archives, the Lyndon B. Johnson Presidential Library in Austin, holds papers on the civil rights movement in the 1960s and the political career of Barbara Jordan, the first black member of Congress from Texas.[10] A study partially based on federal records is Robert V. Haynes, *A Night of Violence: The Houston Riot of 1917* (1976).

Private papers of individuals and groups form another significant type of manuscript source. Public libraries and local historical societies contain several valuable collections. For example, the Metropolitan Research Center of the Houston Public Library has the papers of black businesses and churches, such as the Antioch Baptist Church materials, in the Vanita Crawford collection. The center also has papers of social organizations, including the City Federation of African American Women's Clubs. In the library are records of the Colored Trainmen of America and other labor unions, as well as papers of prominent families and individuals such as Christia Adair, a leading civil-rights advocate in Houston.[11] The Museum of African American Life and Culture in Dallas has collections on the political and social history of the community as well as the Bishop College Archives and a collection on black women in Texas. At the Dallas Public Library are some papers of Juanita Craft, a Dallas city council member, and the records of the Dallas Negro Chamber of Commerce. In the Dallas Historical Society may be found records of fraternal, educational, and business institutions, especially the Crawford Funeral Home. The Rosenberg Library in Galveston holds the papers of Leon Morgan, a black educator who was also active in cultural and religious endeavors. Records of slavery, schools, churches, and individuals, such as writer Ada Simonds, are available in the Austin Public Library.[12] Local history journals, especially the *Houston Review,* the *Chronicles of Smith County, Texas,* and *Legacies* in Dallas, have begun to publish more on these topics, but the need remains for further studies, especially of women's activities.

Universities and colleges also hold important collections of manuscripts. For example, the Center for American History at the University of Texas in Austin recently acquired the papers of James Farmer, a Texan who became the national leader of the Congress of Racial Equality. Other collections in the Center for American History include the papers of J. B. Rayner, a Populist political leader and later a college president; musician Mance Lipscomb; material on desegregation of the University of Texas at Austin; and some papers of Dallas civil-rights and political leader Juanita Craft.[13] A fine study based on such materials is Gregg Cantrell, *Kenneth and John B. Rayner and the Limits of Southern Dissent* (1993).

The Texas Collection at Baylor University holds the papers of nationally prominent singer Jules Bledsoe, the Farmers Improvement Society of Texas and its founder R. L. Smith, and various Waco political and civil-rights leaders. In the archives at the University of Texas at Arlington are the Lee Lewis papers, which include records of the Texas Federation Club, a black union group. The papers of Joseph Chatman, a president of the Lone Star Medical Association, are in the Southwest Collection at Texas Tech University.[14]

The several colleges originally founded for black students are important because of their own archives and publications, including catalogs. Prairie View A&M University also holds the records of the Interscholastic League and the Agricultural Extension Service for African Americans. Texas Southern University in Houston has established a Barbara Jordan Archive. The papers of W. R. Banks, a former president of both Texas College and Prairie View, are at Texas College in Tyler.[15] The best use of these materials has been by George Woolfolk in a study of *Prairie View* (1962) and by Michael Heintze in *Private Black Colleges in Texas* (1985).

Universities and libraries outside the state hold several manuscript collections on Texas topics. For example, the Bennett College library in Greensboro, North Carolina, holds the papers of N. W. Cuney, the late nineteenth-century Republican leader. The Fondren Library at Rice University has microfilm of the Cuney materials. Records of schools, churches, and ministers in Texas are among the records in the Disciples of Christ Historical Society in Nashville, Tennessee. Texas materials also are available in the records of the General Board of Christian Education for the Christian Methodist Episcopal Church in Memphis, Tennessee. The Library of Congress in Washington, D.C., has two collections important to Texans. The Booker T. Washington papers, now partially published, contain letters from state leaders such as Emmett J. Scott. The papers of the NAACP, some portions of which have been microfilmed, include materials on local chapters and leaders as well as significant legal cases such as *Nixon, Smith,* and *Sweatt.*[16] The best study based on those records is Darlene Hine, *Black Victory: The Rise and Fall of the White Primary in Texas* (1979).

Finally, many important manuscripts remain in private hands, including the papers of individuals, major fraternal organizations such as the Masons, local chapters of civil rights groups, women's clubs, labor unions, businesses, and church congregations. Some of these records need to be located. Other materials could be better preserved and used if they were placed in libraries. Papers that cannot be transferred to a library because of individual or group restrictions might be copied or microfilmed for greater use. All of these topics deserve further study.

The more extensive use of available sources and the discovery and preservation of new materials should lead to additional books and articles, especially on previously unresearched topics. Those publications in turn will help answer the call to advance studies of the African American community in Texas from history's hollow to history's mountain.

Notes

1. *Life* (December 29, 1972), 16D.
2. Light Townsend Cummins and Alvin R. Bailey Jr., eds., *A Guide to the History of Texas* (New York, 1988), 107–121.
3. Walter L. Buenger and Robert A. Calvert, eds., *Texas Through Time: Evolving Interpretations* (College Station, 1991), 50–80.
4. Some of the magazines have been microfilmed and should be available in major city and university libraries, or through interlibrary loan.
5. *Dallas Morning News,* December 15, 1990; Eugene C. Barker Texas History Center, *Black Dallas in the 1950s: Photographs from the R. C. Hickman Archives* (Austin, 1987); Charles R. Schultz to A. B., March 27, 1986 (Texas A&M University Archives).
6. Paula Eyrich Tyler and Ron Tyler, *Texas Museums: A Guidebook* (Austin, 1983); *Dallas Morning News,* October 5, 21, 1990 (Freedman's Cemetery).
7. Jim Conrad to A. B., March 26, 1986 (East Texas State University); Rebecca Sharpless Jimenez and others, eds., *Baylor University, Institute for Oral History: A Guide to the Collection, 1970–85* (Waco, 1985).
8. Some county records are available on microfilm through interlibrary loan from the Local Records Division of the Texas State Library in Austin.
9. Michael R. Green to A. B., March 26, 1986 (Archives, Texas State Library); Michael Q. Hooks, "The General Land Office: Preserving Texas History Through Land Records," *Heritage* 2 (Summer 1985), 8–11, 17.
10. National Archives, *Black Studies: A Select Catalog of National Archives Microfilm Publications* (Washington, 1984).
11. Howard Beeth to A. B., March 27, 1986 (Houston Metropolitan Research Center); Cummins and Bailey, *Guide to the History of Texas,* 223; Texas State Historical Association, *Women and Texas History: An Archival Bibliography* (Austin, 1990), 19–21.
12. W. Marvin Dulaney to A. B., December 17, 1990 (Museum of African American Life and Culture); Museum of African American Life and Culture, *Preserving and Sharing a Precious Legacy;* Donald Payton to A. B., April 6, 1986 (Dallas Historical Society); Casey Edward Greene to A. B., April 5, 1986 (Rosenberg Library); May Schmidt, "Sources of Information Relating to Blacks in the Austin-Travis County Collection of the Austin Public Library" (1979); Cummins and Bailey, *Guide to the History of Texas,* 200–201.

13. Don E. Carleton to A. B., April 1, 1986 (Barker Texas History Center); Eugene C. Barker Texas History Center, *Newsletter* (Fall 1985; Spring 1988); University of Texas at Austin, *Library Resources for the Study of African American History and Culture;* John Slate, "Sources for Black History at the Barker Texas History Center" (1991).
14. University of Texas at Arlington, "Texas Black History Sources in the Archives;" Texas State Historical Association, *Women and Texas History,* 66; Ellen Kuniyuki Brown to A. B., April 21, 1986 (Baylor University).
15. Esther H. Baker, "Preliminary Inventory of the Records of the Prairie View Interscholastic League of Texas" (1974); Texas Southern University Library, *The Special Collections.*
16. Walter Schatz, ed., *Directory of Afro-American Resources* (New York, 1970).

Slave Children of Texas
A Qualitative and Quantitative Analysis

ELIZABETH R. RABE

"DO YOU THINK I COULD EVEN FERGIT THEM SLAVE days?" testified Susan Merritt of Rusk County when questioned by Alex Hampton of the Federal Writers' Project (FWP) in 1937. Merritt was one of the more than 2,000 former slaves—more than 600 of whom endured slavery in Texas—who were interviewed between 1936 and 1938 by federal employees. Historians have concluded that this collection of narratives, *The American Slave: A Composite Autobiography,* represents an invaluable source for the study of slavery.[1] Randolph B. Campbell made significant use of the narratives in his authoritative study of slavery in Texas, *An Empire for Slavery.*[2]

George Rawick, the general editor of the slave narratives, has contended that the Texas narratives are "probably one of the two most powerful and useful state collections." But for four decades, historians were not fully aware of the value of the Texas narratives. In the late 1930s, FWP workers deposited the 600 original interviews at the Barker Library at the University of Texas at Austin, then sent 181 of these, heavily edited, to the Library of Congress. The interview of Rosina Hoard of Travis County, for example, was reduced from nine pages to three, and FWP workers removed information that they found to be inappropriate. They deleted comments like "I know dat de slaves was glad to be free."[3] Rawick, however, has compiled the original interviews for scholars.

Both Susan Merritt (b. 1851) and Rosina Hoard (b. 1859) witnessed slavery as children. In 1860, approximately 40 percent of the four million slaves in the United States were children under twelve years of age. Children were also numerous on Texas slave plantations. Richard Bennett Hubbard, the father of a future governor of Texas, owned 18 children on his Smith County plantation.[4] But studies of slave life and culture by scholars like John Blassingame and Eugene Genovese have not emphasized the experiences of slave children. Randolph Campbell devoted only a few pages of analysis to slave children in Texas.[5]

Three scholarly studies have focused on young slaves. In *Deep Like the Rivers,* Thomas Webber explored the methods that slave parents used to educate their children. Wilma King, in *Stolen Childhood,* offered a comprehensive history of slave children in the antebellum South. King argued that "enslaved children had virtually no childhood," suffering fates similar to the horrors borne by children in times of war. In *Born in Bondage,* Marie Jenkins Schwartz differed with King, holding that, despite the rigors of slavery, slave children had childhoods, albeit peculiar ones. As children, slaves learned their complex roles on the plantation and in the slave community. Both King and Schwartz relied on the FWP slave narratives in conducting their research. But neither author investigated the lives of slave children in Texas.[6]

This article addresses a gap in the history of slavery in Texas by analyzing the interviews with 304 former Texas slaves, born between 1850 and 1863, conducted by the Federal Writers Project. The choice of these birth dates ensured that the narrators' primary memory of slavery was a childhood memory. By the age of fifteen, slave children worked like adults, laboring as field workers, servants, or craftsmen. Excluded from this sample were those former slaves born in 1864 and 1865, who could not possibly have had any recollection of slave life. The median birth date of the 304 slaves was 1855—ten years old at the time of emancipation. When interviewed in the late 1930s, these former slaves were in their seventies and eighties but retained strong memories of their childhoods.

This study is not only qualitative but also quantitative. Former slaves' answers to specific questions were entered in a database. The 304 former slaves represented a fair sample of the Texas slave population in 1860. Most resided in East or Central Texas before 1865, 123 of them growing up in Travis, Harrison, Jasper, McLennan, Rusk, Washington, Tyler, Bastrop, or Cherokee counties. As Campbell demonstrated, almost half of Texas slaves lived on plantations with twenty or more slaves.[7] Of the former slave children who responded to the question of residency, 59 percent lived on plantations; 31 percent resided on farms with five to nineteen slaves; and only 10 percent lived on small farms with between one and four slaves.

Texas was the frontier of slavery. When the Lone Star State joined the Union in 1846, its population began to expand rapidly. Southerners migrated to Texas, bringing their bondsmen with them. Between 1846 and 1860, the slave population of Texas grew from 30,505 to 160,467 and continued to grow during the Civil War. Allen Manning of Coryell County made the trip from Mississippi to Texas, remembering that "it look like everybody in the world was going to Texas."[8] Indeed, 94 of the 304 FWP interviewees traveled to Texas with their owners, and 60 percent stated that their parents were born outside of Texas. These slaves walked or rode in covered wagons from southern states.

Upon arriving in Texas, virtually all slave children settled on farms or plantations in East or Central Texas. Slave masters put children to work at a young age. In the Texas slave narratives, 75 percent of the former slaves stated that they worked as children. Starting at about the age of four or five, a child began doing simple chores. Laura Ray's first job in Cherokee County was "totin water from the spring, sweepin yards an seein atter the chickens." Like Ray, young slave children often labored in and around the main house, with over 40 percent reporting that they worked indoors as well as out. Young children ran errands, cleaned the house, swept the yard, fetched water, minded the chickens, and fanned away flies. Fannie Norman of Travis County had to "chase flies w'en de Marster an' de Misse eat meals." Norman would "stand thar wid a big fan an' shoo de flies dat come 'round dem an' de table." Older female slave children frequently cared for the plantation owner's children. Lucy Barnes of Harris County recalled that "I min's the chillun fo' my missie. Dat's my job. Wherever those chillun go, I go—sleep with 'em at night an' keep de cover on 'em."[9] Barnes had a substantial responsibility for a twelve-year-old girl.

Slave children usually ended up working in the fields, producing cotton, corn, and wheat. Over 50 percent of slave children who worked toiled in the fields. Between the ages of eight and thirteen, children began training to become field hands. They tended the livestock, carried water to the field, hoed and plowed the crops, and picked cotton and corn. Jacob Branch of Chambers County commented that "by the time us good sprouts us pickin cotton and pullin cane. Us ain't never idle."[10] By the age of fifteen, almost all children labored in the fields. A few gained skilled positions, working as servants, cooks, carpenters, blacksmiths, or craftsmen.

Children too young to work spent their days in the nursery. Nelson Hogan of Fort Bend, Texas, recalled that "dey keeps us chillen in de quatahs while de old ones is working in de fields." Mothers dropped their children off at the nursery on their way to the fields. The nursery was an enlarged cabin consisting of cradles, a playroom, and a fenced-in yard that allowed toddlers to crawl and walk around outside safely. Older female slaves tended these one-month to four-year-old children, and at the end of the day mothers retrieved their children from the nursery.[11]

When not working, slave children found ways to amuse themselves. They were often left to their own devices without adult supervision. They explored the plantation's fields and woods while playing with one another. Slave children enjoyed games of marbles, house, hide and seek, and "shoo turkey," an adaptation of the game of tag. While playing, children liked to sing jingles. Smith Wilson of Smith County chanted jingles like "I'm a farmer man, Jing, Jang" and "Turn back your head and turn to the one you love." Some owners allowed slave children to socialize with white children. Anderson Jones of Limestone County recalled that Dr. Bedwell, his master, "had a boy named Horace, he wuz about de same age as myself, we played, rode horses, went huntin' and fishin' together."[12]

Although the majority of the ex-slaves reported enjoying games, not all slave children had time to play. Aunt Carolina Houston of Nacogdoches County declared, "I never played a game in all my life. Never had time to play." Houston spent her days in the main house working as a maid.[13] All slave children ultimately shared in Houston's deprivation, for games and playtime ended early in a slave's life.

After work or play, children returned to the slave quarters in the evening to relax and sleep. Sixty percent of the interviewees noted that they had lived in the slave quarters, which served as the center of the slave community. The quarters consisted of a row of cabins, usually set behind the main house. Each slave family had its own one-room cabin constructed of logs, furnished with beds nailed to the walls and boxes and benches for seats. "We lived in cabins made of logs and chinked with mud mortar. We had beds that had only one leg; they fit in each corner of the walls," recalled Hagar Lewis of Smith County.[14] The cabins had dirt floors, holes for windows, and offered little protection from the cold in winter or from mosquitoes in the summer.

Slave children wore rough clothing. Boys and girls alike donned "long shirts slit up the side" made from homespun cotton in the summer and "linsey" wool in the winter. A child only received one or two "shirts" a year. At the age of ten to twelve, a child received trousers and a shirt or a dress. Children did not wear underwear beneath their clothing. Fortunate children had brogan shoes with brass toes in winter, but many went barefoot. John Wells of Hunt County stated that in winter "the snow cracked my feet open."[15] Children like John Wells also suffered from frostbite and colds.

Texas slave children had abundant sources of food. A slave child's diet consisted of foods similar to those that made up an adult slave's diet. "Ash cakes" were a staple, made by "putting co'n meal batter in [corn] shucks and baking it in the ashes" of the fireplace.[16] Texas slaves also consumed fresh or salted pork, molasses, and vegetables like sweet potatoes, greens, and black-eyed peas. Plantation cooks served these foods, mixed together, out of a big wooden bowl. Milk or parched-corn coffee accompanied these meals.

Slaves often supplemented their diets with fresh game and fish. On weekends, young boys accompanied their fathers or other male relatives on hunts. They hunted opossums, raccoons, deer, turkeys, squirrels, and rabbits in the woods and fields of East Texas. Lizzie Farmer reminisced that "when we cooked possum dat was a feast. We'd boil him with red pepper and take him out and put him in a pan and slice sweet 'taters and put round him and roast him." During their free time, both male and female slave children also fished. Fishing was Maggie Jackson of Cass County's favorite activity. She remembered that "most all the chillens use to go fishin' on Saturday. We would bend straight pins and use [them] for hooks."[17]

Slave children reported being well fed, because their owners wanted them to develop into healthy, productive workers. Some, however, did not receive adequate amounts of food and stole to ease their hunger pains. Annie Row of Nacogdoches County remembered that "once w'en Ise jus a chile, Ise was hongry so Ise takes some ob de food f'om de dawg. Deys catched me adoin' dat, an' 'stead ob givin' me some food, deys give me de whuppin's."[18] Row never forgave her master for her degrading treatment nor for forcing her to steal food from a dog to survive.

Like Annie Row, Texas slave children both witnessed and experienced cruelty and brutality early in their lives. Over 70 percent of the interviewees witnessed a beating or whipping. According to George W. Harmon of Lamar County, slaves were "whipped for any misdemeanor dislikable." Slaveholders, overseers, and patrollers beat and whipped slaves to assert and maintain their control. Children were encouraged to observe the punishments of their elders. On the Stevens plantation in Upshur County, the master required that all children witness the whippings of disobedient slaves. Callie Shepherd, a slave on the Stevens plantation, recalled that "dey used to tell us little childers to look. Dey buckled 'em down on de groun' and laid it on dey backs. Sometimes dey laid on with a might heavy han.'"[19]

Slave owners and overseers had few reservations about inflicting corporal punishment on children. Seventy-nine of the 304 interviewees testified to experiencing physical cruelty as children. They received whippings for talking back to their masters, for stealing food, for not completing an assigned task, for playing or sleeping instead of working, and for running away. Anna Miller of Palo Pinto had trouble staying awake through a full day of work. She often fell asleep early in the evening while hoeing or picking cotton. She remembered that "as sho as I does dat, Ise gits a whuppin." Alex Jackson of Upshur County enjoyed running and playing outside. One day he collided with his sister, Nancy, who was carrying a pail of milk to the main house. The milk spilled. For this misdeed, Jackson received "one of the worst whippings I ever got."[20]

To survive, slaves developed close-knit families and communities. Historians have long debated whether slaves could maintain meaningful family relationships. The Texas slave narratives suggest that slave families were, in fact, resilient.[21] Most Texas slave children lived with both their parents and their siblings. In fact, 217 of the FWP interviewees noted that they interacted daily with both their mother and father. A grandparent, an aunt, an uncle, or a cousin often resided with this nuclear family unit.

Slave parents had the difficult job of raising their children to survive under servitude. They taught their children to respect their slave elders, to maintain the confidentiality of the slave quarters, and to obey slave owners so as to avoid harsh punishments. Mary Glover of Sumpter, Texas, shared with interviewer Alfred Menn what her mother had taught her. Mary's mother advised her children that "I ain't goin' to be wid yo' always. Yo' mind yo' boss man. Be good and he won't have to whoop yo. Don't take nothin' dat don't belong to yo.' Trust in de Lawd, and he will take care of you." Besides offering good advice, slave adults also spanked misbehaving children when necessary. But Mollie Dawson of Navarro County remembered that parents just had to "look out the corner of the eye at kids and they got good right now."[22]

Slave parents, like all parents, loved their children. As a young boy, Will Adams of Harrison County looked forward to nighttime, when his father returned to the family cabin. Adams recalled that his father "would come in from the fiel' at night and take me out of bed, dress me, feed me, then play with me for hours." Adams's father must have been tired from working from dawn to dusk in the fields. But he always made time to spend with his son. Ninety-four percent of the former slaves spoke of having a close relationship with one of their parents. Sam Meredith Mason of Travis County spoke for many ex-slaves when he declared that "the memory of my mammy is one of the sweetest memories that I have. I had a very sweet mammy. She give all that she could give."[23]

Mulatto slave children with white fathers and black mothers did not have close relationships with their fathers. When questioned about her father, Betty White Irby of Burleson County replied that "I couldn't tell yo' much about my fathaw, 'cause I never did git to see him." All that she knew of her father was what her mother had told her. Irby's father was a Scots-Irishman named Harper. Mulatto children, like other slave children, could be sold or punished, and they generally lived in the slave quarters. But both blacks and whites viewed mulatto children as peculiarities. Because of the light-brown color of her skin, neither white nor black children would play with Sarah Allen. White FWP interviewers, like Fred Dibble, seemed compelled to comment about the physical features of mulattos. In the introduction to Ellen Nora Ford's interview, Dibble remarked that "Negro blood and characteristics are absent for she is the daughter of a white master."[24] Twelve of the 304 former slaves stated that they had white fathers.

Slave children valued their extended families—over 25 percent of the former slaves mentioned a grandparent, an aunt, or an uncle who helped raise them. Grandparents transmitted slave culture and religion to members of the younger generation. Patsy Moses of Fort Bend, Texas, noted that "my ole gran-dad wuz de one dat tell us so many things, 'specially 'bout what de niggers did an believed."[25] As Thomas Webber pointed out, grandparents typically taught children stories and songs about religion, about Africa, and about plantation history.[26] Grandparents also doted upon their grandchildren, lavishing upon them attention or providing an extra piece of food. If a parent died or was sold, grandparents or other family members could be relied upon to care for the children left behind. When she was just a baby, Ellen Thomas's mother died and her grandmother reared her.[27]

Slave children had occasional opportunities to learn outside the boundaries of the slave community. Unlike other slave states, Texas did not prohibit the education of slaves—consequently, 11 percent of the interviewees asserted that they learned to read or write while slaves. By comparison, Webber estimated that only about 5 percent of American slaves learned how to read.[28] Most literate slaves in Texas were taught by whites, particularly the sons and daughters of their owners. Sallie Wroe's master, Mike Burdette of Travis County, permitted his children to teach the slave children. "Massa Burdette 'low us nigger chillen come to de big house at night and his chillen larn us to read. Dey had blue-black spellers," related Wroe. Other slave owners, however, generally opposed their slaves becoming literate. Slaves who attempted to learn to read or write were severely punished. Maggie Matthews of Gonzales County remembered that "I was caught lookin' at a piece of paper wid writin' on it and I got a whoopin' fo' it. I had told 'em dat I could read whut was on it." Matthews actually lied about her reading abilities.[29]

Slaves were chattel property that could be bought or sold at any time. Fifty of the 304 former slaves were sold as children. An additional fifty-two witnessed fellow slaves being auctioned. James Jackson of Bastrop County recalled that "dey sold an' traded de darkies lak dey do hoss's and mules. Dey would carry dem to de court house an' put dem on de block an' auction dem off to de highest bidder." Auctioneers sold parents apart from their children. Slave owners "didn't mind separatin' children from mothers anymore than a calf from a cow," declared

William Green of Wilson County. Frank Sparks of Nacogdoches County bought Willis Easter at the age of two, but did not purchase the little boy's mother or father.[30]

Slave auctions proved traumatic experiences for both children and parents. On the day of a sale, children and parents alike shrieked and cried. Some children would never see their parents again. Fannie Moore Walker of Travis County was about two years old when her mother was sold. For years afterward, Walker questioned her father about her mother's whereabouts. She remembered, "when I was a little girl I used to cry and ask my papa 'Don't I have a mama? Where is she?' Papa would say, 'Aw, she's gone. She'll be back, don't you worry.'" But Walker was never reunited with her mother.[31]

The slave community adopted these forlorn children. Most of the interviewees enthusiastically spoke of a supportive slave community, reinforcing the theories of scholars like Blassingame and Genovese who have written about the vibrant nature of the slave community. The community centered on the slave quarters, where most slaves ate and slept. In order to survive, slaves realized that they needed to support each other and to stay together. Community members felt a familial bond toward one another, often addressing one another as brother or sister.

Everyone, including children, contributed to the community. Able-bodied adults hunted for fresh game, raised vegetable gardens, and labored around the quarters. Elder slaves accepted the responsibility of teaching and protecting the children. Children helped with the washing, sewing, gardening, and furniture repair. Throughout the day, they also toted drinking water to the fields. Children sometimes aided their elders with field work, particularly at harvest time. Each day slaves had work quotas that required them to pick a certain amount of cotton or weave a certain amount of cloth. Slaves could not stop working until they reached this goal; punishment for doing so was typically a whipping. To prevent this, children would pitch in and help. Henry Hence Smith of Smith County aided his mother in the fields. Smith remembered that "I stayed in front and helped her up when she got behind."[32]

After a hard day of work, community members enjoyed spending time together in the slave quarters. Green Cumby of Rusk County recalled that "at night the slaves would gather 'roun' the cabins and talk 'til bed time. Sometimes we'd dance while some would knock out time for us by snappin' de finger and slappin' de knee."[33] Community members would share the news of the day with one another. At these informal gatherings, elders sometimes sang songs and told stories.

Texas slave children paid close attention to these stories and tales, many of which reaffirmed the values and attitudes held by the slave community. Storytellers continually reminded children to listen to their parents and to other slave adults. Darcus Barnett of Dresden, Texas, heard many "stories 'bout de Indians scalping people and they toll us dat dey [the Indians] would git us if [we] didn't be good chillins and mind." Storytellers also imparted lessons of courage, cunning, and heroism to children like Jack Dresso of Orange County, who was thrilled by the exploits of "Bre'r Fox" and "Bre'r Rabbit." In these "Animal Trickster" tales, a smart but weak animal like a fox deceives a strong oppressor. These trickster tales symbolized the lowly slave outwitting his powerful master.[34]

Children also learned the songs of the community from their elders. While toiling in the fields or relaxing in the quarters, slaves sang together. One person would begin a hymn, and another would pick up the tune. In this way, the song spread until everyone, including children, was singing. Slaves sang spirituals, work songs, love songs, and lullabies. Many songs promised a better life in the next world. On the Dunn Plantation in Dallas County, slaves chanted:

> Masse sleeps in de feathah bed,
> Nigger sleeps on de flooah.
> Whin we'ns all git to Heaven,
> Dey'll be no slaves no mo.'[35]

In other songs, slaves communicated with one another. Slaves on the Washington plantation in Travis County warned each other when the master was coming by singing "Ole hog 'round de bench—Ole hog 'round de bench." The workers would make sure that they were toiling hard by the time Master Pratt Washington reached their row.[36]

Children learned to maintain the confidentiality of the slave community at a young age. Slave adults taught children that what was said or done in the quarters should never reach white ears, even when slave owners tried to coax children into betraying their elders. Betty Power's mistress, Mrs. Perry, would have

Betty spy to see if all of the house servants were working. Powers, of Harrison County, remembered that "once she sends me to de sewin' room to see if de womens am wo'kin.' Some dem am, an' some of dem aint. W'en Ise returns Ise says 'Deys all wo'kin'.' Yous see, Ise raised by my mammy to tell nothin' Ise sees."[37] Betty Powers had undoubtedly protected female members of the community from a severe reprimand or worse.

Slave children looked forward to holidays. Former slaves told of celebrating Christmas, the Fourth of July, Easter, and New Year's Day. Slave masters furnished their bondsmen a large feast on these days of rest. Slaves ate delicacies like turkey, chicken, fruit, cake, white-flour biscuits, and "cracklin" bread. After this special dinner, the slave community sponsored a large dance. According to Jack Bess of Goliad County, these holiday dances were joyous. Bess declared that at Christmas "we jes' tears up de country. Lawdy! Lawd! Dat fiddlin' went on all night, and we dance awhile den lay down and sleeps, den gits up and dances some mo'e." On Christmas day, slave children also received small presents. Slave masters played Santa Claus and gave candy, fruit, and nuts to slave children. On the Moody plantation in Orange County, children received "a pair 'r' stockin's 'n' a stick 'r' sugah candy" on Christmas day.[38] Slaves did not, however, celebrate their birthdays. Only 18 percent of the ex-slaves even knew the exact date of their birth.

Slave owners sponsored large celebrations at the conclusion of the fall harvest, which typically ended with a "hog killing" and a "corn shucking." At a "hog killing" the slaves slaughtered the plump hogs then salted, cured, and dried much of the meat in the smokehouse. Children helped "wid grindin' de meat fo' sausages." At the conclusion of the "hog killing," slaves held a party at which they ate fresh pork. "Corn shucking" was also "a big occasion them days." At a corn shucking, slaves of all ages would remove the husks from ears of corn while socializing. When all the corn was shucked, the slaves feasted and danced all night.[39] These two working holidays provided food for the slaves for the entire year.

For both slave adults and children, the best time of the week was Saturday evening. Slaves finished work on Saturday afternoon and did not resume work until Monday morning. Slave communities held parties or dances on Saturday nights. Dave Byrd of Houston County recalled that there was "banjo picking, tin pan beating and negro dance" almost every Saturday night. Sometimes slaves from neighboring or nearby plantations attended. At these gatherings, children danced, sang, and played games with one another. Children also loved to watch jig contests, in which two slaves "put a glass of wauter on deir heads an' den see who can dance de hardest wid out spillin any water."[40]

After a festive night, slaves reserved Sunday for doing chores around the quarters and attending church in the afternoon. Slaves held church in a slave cabin in winter and in a grove of trees in summer. According to Mose Hursey of Red River County, these gatherings were "right fine meetin's, too. They'd preach and pray and sing—shout, too." Slaves sang spirituals like "Roll, Jordan, Roll," "Sing Low Sweet Chariot," and "Come We that Love the Lord." Participants also listened to sermons that their black preachers, personally chosen by slave owners, delivered. Often, such mandatory sermon topics as loyalty, honesty, and obedience reinforced the owners' wishes that members of the slave congregations defer to their earthly masters. As Simpson Campbell of Harrison County observed, "in slavery time the colored preachers had to preach what they was told to preach . . . obey your Master and Mistress."[41] On other plantations, slave owners themselves, or less frequently a white minister, preached or read the Bible to slaves on Sunday afternoons.

Slave communities also organized their own clandestine congregations. Susan Merritt remembered, "at night the slaves would gather round the fireplace on their knees and pray, and sing, and cry, but they darsn't let the white fo'ks know anything about it." Like Merritt, seventy-eight other interviewees spoke of attending worship services without white authorities present. William Moore of Limestone County prayed for freedom. Moore and his elders would moan low and gentle "Some day, some day, some day—this yoke going to be lifted off'n our shoulders—some day, some day, some day."[42] Slaves placed large pots in the centers of their congregations to absorb their cries for emancipation.

In addition to participating in clandestine congregations, children resisted slavery in small, numerous ways. Historians like Lawrence Levine have argued that American slaves understood that they lacked the power to overthrow the slave system through a mass uprising or rebellion. Still, slaves resisted slavery by forming sustaining communities and by secret acts of defiance.[43] Approximately 25 percent of the slave children told of trying to undermine the slave system. Slaves stole food like fresh hog meat, chicken, white flour, and fruit. When she served dinner at the main house, Ida Henry of Harrison County stole food. Henry remembered that "I would put biscuits and pieces of chicken in a sack under de dress dat hung from my waist." Later Henry would slip off and eat this food herself or deliver it to the quarters. Slave children also brought food to runaway slaves hiding in the woods. Catharine Green's father ran to the woods whenever he knew that he was going to receive a punishment. But her father could only stay in the woods as long as Green, of Bastrop County, brought him food.[44]

Slave children did not often attempt to run away. Mose Smith of Lamar County was the only interviewee who tried to escape slavery permanently. Children understandably did not want to leave the security of their parents or the community. If a child ran away, it was usually only for a few hours or days hiding in surrounding fields or woods. Some simply wanted to take a break from work, others to postpone an imminent whipping or to recover from a punishment. The first and only time Calvin Kennard ran away was "de furst time my ole mistress got atter me to whup me." Kennard stayed away for four days, but snuck to "de house an' eat all I wanted den I would git out an' hide 'roun in de lot an' fodder stacks."[45] Six other interviewees ran away for short periods of time.

During their preteen years, slave children may not have always grasped the meaning of slavery. Their parents tried to shield them from the realities of bondage. Guy Stewart cherished his childhood in Travis County. "Dem whar de happy days ob my life," professed Stewart.[46] Children like Stewart assumed that they were safe and secure. They had the precious love of their parents and the camaraderie of the slave community.

But one brutal event in a child's life—be it receiving a whipping, watching the beating of a parent, witnessing the lashing of an elder, or experiencing the sale of a family member—could immediately destroy this sense of security. More than one hundred former slaves told about experiencing a dreadful, life-altering event that caused them to realize that they were chattel property, subject to the commands of their masters. Their parents, grandparents, and elders were not in control. These dire experiences also left indelible imprints on the consciousnesses of slave children. When interviewed more than seventy years after emancipation, former slaves described traumatic incidents in vivid detail. Ida Henry saw a plantation cook's eyes poked out because the dinner potatoes had not been thoroughly cooked. Anthony Christopher of Brazoria County watched as an overseer held "bacon over a fire and let de hot grease drop on de bare hide" of a field worker who had not completed his task fast enough. Wesley Burrell of Washington County observed the lashing of a pregnant woman. Laura Cornish discovered Lodge and Baldo, two highly regarded community members, hiding in the woods with slashed backs. After looking at Lodge and Baldo's lacerated backs, Cornish never ate watermelon again, because "de red meat look jes' like de bloody shirts of old Lodge an' Baldo an jes' to think of it 'bout makes me sick to my stomach."[47] Children, like Cornish, experienced helplessness and rage when they saw the humiliation of a respected elder.

Most painful for children to view was the punishment of a parent or family member. The slave family was the center of any child's world. Anthony Lacy of Jasper County recounted that observing his mother being whipped "skeert me and mek my heart so' [sore]." For Ellen Nora Ford of Colorado County, the day that her owner beat her mother "was a cryin' day for me." Walter Rimm of San Patricio County could only "stand dere and cry" when he saw his father thrashed for the first time.[48] The sharpest memory of most interviewees was witnessing the beating or whipping of a family member.

Every time a parent received a punishment, the slave master asserted his power over the family. Smith Wilson stared as his mother was whipped until she could not walk, then helped carry her to the field to pick cotton. Because of this cruelty, Wilson and his playmates became "so afraid of master Hyns that when us nigger kids seen him coming we would run like turkeys and hide." Corporal punishment left visible reminders for children as well. Anthony Lacy declared that "you couldn' lay yo han' on my mudder' back but you would hit a stripe."[49] These scars confirmed the authority of slave masters.

Parents could not protect their children from experiencing or watching these brutalities. Sallie Wroe saw her sister beaten by the overseer because she did not complete all of her assigned work. Nellie Hill's master made her hold a candle as he lashed her brother Mose one night. Hill, who lived in Gay Hill, Texas, asserted that "when I 'members dat night, I gets de shivers yet."[50]

Viewing the punishment of a family member caused some young children to react violently. While minding the hogs, William Moore heard a scream. He discovered his mother tied to a tree and Master Tom Waller with a bullwhip in his hand. Moore begged Waller to stop lashing his mother. Waller instead hit Moore, who remembered, "I goes crazy . . . I see a big rock and I take it and I throw it and it ketches Marse Tom in the skull." Moore and his mother then had to hide in the woods for three months. Julia Williams of Marion County adored her aunt, who lived on the next plantation, and abhorred watching her being whipped. Whenever Mr. Pruitt, the plantation owner, beat her aunt, Smith would "git chunks of dirt an' throw at him to make him stop."[51]

Most children, however, realized that they could not physically overpower the person administering a punishment. But the humiliation of a family member still incensed them. When he heard his mother cry "Pray Missus" in the middle of a lashing, seven-year-old James Barber of Brazoria County became distressed and grabbed the whip to give his mother a short respite from the agony of the lash. Like Barber, Jacob Branch could not stand to watch the pain on his mother's face during a "cowhiding." Branch, of Chambers County, remembered "many's de time I edges up and take some dem licks off my mama."[52]

Often the most memorable event was the first beating or serious punishment that a child received. It could be for playing instead of working, not completing a task, talking back, or stealing. Many children experienced their first punishment at a young age. When he was four years old, Tob Davis of Nacogdoches received his first beating. The plantation owner, Jack Turnipseed, caught Davis trying to eat a stolen raw egg in the chicken house. Turnipseed paddled Davis hard, threatening "I'se 'test de egg suckin' dawg, an don't lake de egg suckin' nigger any bettah. Ise kills de dawgs dat suck eggs, so youse bettah be careful."[53] Davis told his FWP interviewer that he took Turpinseed's death threat seriously.

Several former slaves could not remember why they received punishments. Susan Merritt told of being hit on numerous occasions by her mistress. “Lots of times she tied me to a stob out in the yard and ‘cowhide’ me till she give out, then she leave me and go rest and come back and beat me some more,” noted Merritt. These “cowhidings” drew blood. Merritt’s mother had to “grease” Merritt’s back to ease the pain. These lashings often caused Merritt to spend a week in bed with fever, and the beatings later ran together in Merritt’s mind. Other slaves asserted that they had been beaten brutally for no reason. President Wilson of McLennan County maintained that “dey’d whip us without no excuse lots of times.”[54] Some former slaves were willing to describe cruelties in chilling detail; others could not even relate what had happened to them, for their memories were too painful. Martin Ruffin remembered that when he was punished “the blood would fly.” But when an FWP interviewer asked Ed Jackson of Travis County about his life as a slave child, Jackson replied, “I jest rathah not talk about it.” Jackson explained “my life back there wa’nt so sweet. They was ha’d on you—got some scars I’m carrin right down to my grabe.”[55]

Slave owners knew that these punishments affected children and other members of the slave community. The town of Jasper had a public whipping post where all members of the town could watch the punishment of a slave. Public whippings of runaways occurred “so’s the slaves could see what happens when theys tries to get away,” noted Esther Easter of Fannin County. Slave masters thought that the more graphic the punishment the less likely other slaves were to perpetrate the same crime. But these whippings did not always have the intended effect. While watching the lashing of the run-away, Easter remembered being “full of misery when I see the lash cutting deep into the boys skin. He swells up like a dead horse.”[56] Easter’s first reaction was sympathy for the boy, not fear of running away.

Former slaves carried these memories into the twentieth century. The cruelties of slavery still infuriated and angered them. Smith Wilson declared that his master “was one of the meanest men I ever knowed . . . he is dead and gone to the devil and I hope he is getting just what he give to his nigger slaves.” Incensed at the suffering of his mother, Wilson hated the man who hurt her for seventy years. Letha Hatcher, the FWP worker who interviewed Anthony Lacy, noted that “his spirit seems to revolt yet at his master’s unjust and cruel treatment of his slaves.”[57] Lacy, like Wilson, had witnessed the beating of his mother.

Not all of the FWP interviewees retained the rage of Smith Wilson and Anthony Lacy. About 15 percent of the 304 interviewees spoke fondly of slavery. Aleck Trimble informed his listener that "I warn't so glad when freedom come . . . I t'ought I was jis' as near hebben as I want to be."[58] Statements like Trimble's have troubled historians.[59] But the FWP interviews must be read and analyzed in a historical context. These interviews took place in segregated Texas in the midst of the Great Depression. Most former slaves lived in poverty, surviving on a meager state pension of between eight and twelve dollars per month. Many actually begged their interviewers for money. These former slaves remembered, of course, that their former owners had provided for their basic material needs. They may have also wanted to please their white interviewers. Nonetheless, those who spoke favorably of the past constituted a distinct minority. Carter Jackson of Rusk County typically asserted: "If youse want to know 'bout slavery, it was Hell!"[60]

After emancipation, freed slaves moved on with their lives. Some pardoned and absolved those who had mistreated them. Louiviana Pleasant Young of Washington County told her interviewer that everything was "all right now, 'cause I'se done prayed and forgive ebberbody fo' whut dey done to me." Betty Powers agreed that placing trust in God was the best course, for "de Lawd tooks care of slavery." But Susan Merritt, who vowed to leave things to God, foresaw a tumultuous doomsday, predicting "there sho' is going to be lots of soul cry against them in judgement."[61]

Slave children led hard lives, but they believed that they belonged to a community. The Federal Writers Project interviews demonstrate that the slave children of Texas remembered their parents, family members, and elders, all of whom showered them with love and attention, fondly. Children also knew that they were valued members of a larger slave community. They completed chores, joined in songs, listened to folklore, and attended social gatherings, all of which provided happy memories for former slaves. Nonetheless, slavery was a devastating experience for children. These young Texans realized that they were chattel property. They knew that they could be arbitrarily punished or sold. They witnessed the humiliation of their parents, family members, and elders. And they carried the physical and mental scars of slavery with them for the rest of their lives.

Notes

1. George Rawick, ed., *The American Slave: A Composite Autobiography,* Series 1, 19 vols.; Supplement, Series 1, 12 vols.; Supplement, Series 2, 10 vols. (Westport, Connecticut, 1972–1979). Hereafter cited as AS with series, volume, page number, and name of interviewee.
2. Randolph B. Campbell, *An Empire for Slavery: The Peculiar Institution in Texas* (Baton Rouge, 1989).
3. AS, Supplement, Series 2, 2, xxviii–xxxix.
4. Elizabeth R. Rabe, "Richard Bennett Hubbard, Jr., and the African Americans on the Hubbard Plantation," *Texas Historian* 56 (September 1995): 4–7.
5. John W. Blassingame, *The Slave Community: Plantation Life in the Antebellum South* (New York, 1972); Eugene D. Genovese, *Roll, Jordan, Roll: The World the Slaves Made* (New York, 1974); Campbell, *Empire for Slavery,* 119, 160, 162–164.
6. Thomas L. Webber, *Deep Like the Rivers: Education in the Slave Quarter Community, 1831–1865* (New York, 1978); Wilma King, *Stolen Childhood: Slave Youth in Nineteenth-Century America* (Bloomington, Indiana, 1995), xx–xxi; Marie Jenkins Schwartz, *Born in Bondage: Growing Up Enslaved in the Antebellum South* (Cambridge, Massachusetts, 2000), 1–18.
7. Campbell, *Empire for Slavery,* 194.
8. AS, Series 1, 7, Part A, 221 (Allen Manning).
9. AS, Supplement, Series 2, 8, 3263 (Laura Ray); AS, Supplement, Series 2, 8, 2928 (Fannie Norman); AS, Supplement, Series 2, 2, 178 (Lucy Barnes).
10. AS, Series 1, 4, Part A, 178 (Jacob Branch).
11. AS, Supplement, Series 2, 5, 1756 (Nelson Hogan); AS, Supplement, Series 2, 7, 2875 (Hannah Mullins); AS, Supplement, Series 2, 2, 104 (George Austin).
12. AS, Supplement, Series 2, 10, 4271 (Ruth Wood); AS, Supplement, Series 2, 10, 4233 (Smith Wilson); AS, Supplement, Series 2, 6, 2064 (Anderson Jones).
13. AS, Supplement, Series 2, 5, 1804 (Aunt Carolina Houston).
14. AS, Supplement, Series 2, 6, 2331 (Hagar Lewis).
15. AS, Series 1, 7, Part A, 263–65 (Red Richardson); AS, Supplement, Series 2, 7, 3718 (Peter Mitchell); AS, Supplement, Series 2, 8, 3088 (Lee Pickett); AS, Series 1, 11, Part A, 85 (John Wells).
16. AS, Supplement, Series 2, 4, 1261 (Minerva Edwards).
17. AS, Series 1, 7, 98 (Lizzie Farmer); AS, Supplement, Series 2, 5, 1901 (Maggie Jackson).
18. AS, Supplement, Series 2, 8, 3370 (Annie Row).
19. AS, Supplement, Series 1, 12, 142 (George W. Harmon); AS, Supplement, Series 2, 9, 3507 (Callie Shepherd).
20. AS, Supplement, Series 2, 7, 2683 (Anna Miller); AS, Supplement, Series 2, 5, 1877 (Alex Jackson).
21. Herbert G. Gutman, *The Black Family in Slavery and Freedom* (New York, 1976).
22. AS, Supplement, Series 2, 5, 1515 (Mary Glover); AS, Supplement, Series 2, 4, 1125–1126 (Mollie Dawson).
23. AS, Supplement, Series 2, 2, 11 (Will Adams); AS, Supplement, Series 2, 7, 2597 (Sam Meredith Mason).

24. AS, Supplement, Series 2, 5, 1856 (Betty White Irby); AS, Supplement, Series 2, 2, 44–47 (Sarah Allen); AS, Supplement, Series 2, 4, 1354 (Ellen Nora Ford).
25. AS, Supplement, Series 2, 7, 2780 (Patsy Moses).
26. Webber, *Deep Like the Rivers,* 175.
27. AS, Supplement, Series 2, 9, 3791 (Ellen Thomas).
28. Campbell, *An Empire for Slavery,* 175; Webber, *Deep Like the Rivers,* 131.
29. AS, Series 1, 5, Part B, 223 (Sallie Wroe); AS, Supplement, Series 2, 7, 2624 (Maggie Matthews).
30. AS, Supplement, Series 2, 5, 1898 (James Jackson); AS, Supplement, Series 2, 5, 1595 (William Green); AS, Series 1, 4, Part B, 1 (Willis Easter).
31. AS, Supplement, Series 2, 10, 3925 (Fannie Moore Walker).
32. AS, Series 1, 10, Part B, 196 (Henry Smith).
33. AS, Supplement, Series 2, 4, 1004 (Green Cumby).
34. AS, Supplement, Series 2, 2, 190 (Darcus Barnett); AS, Supplement, Series 2, 4, 1998 (Jack Dresso).
35. AS, Supplement, Series 2, 10, 4114 (Millie Williams).
36. AS, Supplement, Series 2, 5, 1732 (Rosina Hoard).
37. AS, Supplement, Series 2, 8, 3138 (Betty Powers).
38. AS, Series 1, 4, Part A, 74 (Jack Bess); AS, Supplement, Series 2, 7, 2723 (Andrew Moody).
39. AS, Series 1, 5, Part A, 266 (Martin Ruffin); AS, Supplement, Series 2, 4, 1428 (Rosanna Frazier); AS, Supplement, Series 2, 5, 1885–1886 (Carter J. Jackson).
40. AS, Supplement, Series 2, 3, 566 (Dave L. Byrd); AS, Supplement, Series 2, 2, 468 (Fred Brown).
41. AS, Series 1, 4, Part B, 170 (Mose Hursey); AS, Supplement, Series 2, 3, 615 (Simpson Campbell).
42. AS, Supplement, Series 2, 7, 2642 (Susan Merritt); AS, Supplement, Series 2, 7, 2766 (William Moore).
43. Lawrence W. Levine, *Black Culture and Black Consciousness: Afro-American Folk Thought from Slavery to Freedom* (New York, 1977).
44. AS, Series 1, 7, Part A, 136 (Ida Henry); AS, Supplement, Series 2, 5, 1572 (Catharine Green).
45. AS, Supplement, Series 1, 12, 276–279 (Mose Smith); AS, Supplement, Series 2, 6, 2179 (Calvin Kennard).
46. AS, Supplement, Series 2, 9, 3733 (Guy Stewart).
47. AS, Series 1, 7, Part A, 134–137 (Ida Henry); AS, Supplement, Series 2, 3, 719 (Anthony Christopher); AS, Supplement, Series 2, 3, 534–538 (Wesley Burrell); AS, Series 1, 3, Part A, 941 (Laura Cornish).
48. AS, Supplement, Series 2, 6, 2254 (Anthony W. Lacy); AS, Supplement, Series 2, 4, 1354 (Ellen Nora Ford); AS, Series 1, 5, Part A, 248 (Walter Rimm).
49. AS, Supplement, Series 2, 10, 4229 (Smith Wilson); AS, Supplement, Series 2, 6, 2253 (Anthony Lacy).
50. AS, Series 1, 5, Part B, 223 (Sallie Wroe); AS, Supplement, Series 2, 5, 1727 (Nellie Hill).
51. AS, Supplement, Series 2, 7, 2769 (William Moore); AS, Supplement, Series 2, 10, 4091 (Julia Williams).
52. AS, Supplement, Series 2, 2, 150–152 (James Barber); AS, Series 1, 4, Part A, 139 (Jacob Branch).

53. AS, Supplement, Series 2, 4, 1080 (Tob Davis).
54. AS, Supplement, Series 2, 7, 2643 (Susan Merritt); AS, Supplement, Series 2, 10, 4206 (President Wilson).
55. AS, Series 1, 5, Part A, 266 (Martin Ruffin); AS, Supplement, Series 2, 5, 1888 (Ed Jackson).
56. AS, Supplement, Series 2, 7, 2479 (Bill McCray); AS, Series 1, 7, Part A, 89 (Esther Easter).
57. AS, Supplement, Series 2, 10, 4227 (Smith Wilson); AS, Supplement, Series 2, 6, 2253 (Anthony Lacy).
58. AS, Series 1, 5, Part B, 109 (Aleck Trimble).
59. C. Vann Woodward, "History from Slave Sources," *American Historical Review* 79 (April 1974), 475.
60. AS, Supplement, Series 2, 5, 1883 (Carter Jackson).
61. AS, Supplement, Series 2, 8, 3099 (Louiviana Pleasant Young); AS, Supplement, Series 2, 8 3142 (Betty Powers); AS, Supplement, Series 2, 7, 2645 (Susan Merritt).

Slaves and Rebels

The Peculiar Institution in Texas, 1861–65

JAMES MARTEN

THAT THE CIVIL WAR CHANGED THE LIVES OF southern blacks forever is a truism that tends to obscure the drama that slaves experienced during the war. The Confederate surrender dealt the institution of slavery its final blow, but the war years already had seen drastic changes in the lives and status of slaves. All over the South thousands of slaves flocked to areas occupied by Northern armies seeking long-denied education in missionary schools, proving themselves in the federal army, and broadening their economic opportunities.[1] Far from the liberating Union lines, Texas slaves endured a different kind of war than did blacks east of the Mississippi River. "White man," said a former Texas slave to a WPA interviewer long after the Civil War had ended, "we 'uns didn't know dere am de war. We seed some sojers at de star[t], but dat all." Indeed, although many black Texans extended the boundaries of their bondage, they usually had no choice but to wait out the war with their masters, while the masters had no choice but to rely on their slaves even more than they had in peace time.[2]

This may have been difficult in light of the Lone Star State's recent history. Six months before Texas seceded from the Union, the "Texas Troubles"—a wave of arson and alleged poisonings—convinced white Texans that meddling Northern preachers and peddlers had instigated a massive slave insurrection. Most of the business district of Dallas burned down on July 8, 1860, and fires broke out in a number of other north Texas towns. Rumors flew around the state that the slaves had planned a general uprising for August 6 and town meetings hastily organized vigilance committees to patrol rural areas and keep an eye on suspicious strangers. Members of the Chatfield Vigilance Association pledged to defend their families, as well as their "honor and property" against the "robbers, murderers, assassins, traitors . . . and thieves" at large in the land. To that end, vigilantes hanged at least ten white men and nearly thirty blacks. Relative peace returned to Texas by early autumn.[3]

Texans did not often discuss the faithfulness of their slaves during the next five years; perhaps the latent but ever-present potential for violence within the slave system caused them to reassure themselves with silence. "The negroes, as a general thing," reported the *Marshall Texas Republican* after the shooting had stopped, "have acted very well towards their owners and the white residents of the South, during the disturbed condition of the country for the last four years." A few joined "the invaders," but only because of their "ignorance and the superior control of the white man." With a confidence that belied whites' later reactions to blacks during Reconstruction, the *Republican* asserted that the "war has demonstrated . . . that the idea of negro insurrections, once so prevalent, is a humbug."[4]

The war-time behavior of many Texas slaves supported the editorialist's assertion. Slave members of a Marshall Methodist Church hosted a supper for the minister and other guests early in 1865, while blacks in Houston raised $40 for sick soldiers with a "grand ball" in July 1862. James Hayes, a slave on a plantation near Marshall, validated the popular image of the faithful slave after his master marched off to the army. Whenever Hayes returned from town with the mail, his mistress "run to meet me, anxious like, to open de letter, and was skeert to do it." One day he "fotcher a letter and I could feel it in my bones; dere was trouble in dat letter." Young Master Ben—the oldest son, who had gone off to war with his father—had been killed in action; "all de ole folks, cullud and white, was cryin' . . . When de body come home, dere's a powerful big funeral and after dat, dere's powerful weepin's and sadness on dat place."[5]

Many slaves went to war as horse-tenders, nurses, or personal servants to their masters. Rube Witt enlisted in the Confederate army but reached Mansfield, Louisiana, after Confederate forces had turned back General Nathaniel Banks' Yankee troops, while James Cape helped rob a Yankee train and suffered a shoulder wound while fighting in Tennessee. Some slaves went to great lengths to prove their loyalty. William Byrd walked all the way from Virginia to Texas after his master became a Federal prisoner and waited until after the war to be freed. Henry Smith marched beside his master's son in the Texas Brigade until the latter was killed at Petersburg, then buried him and carried his belongings back to his family in Texas.[6]

Slaves who remained at home frequently demonstrated their loyalty when they "kept de work on de plantations going, for dey had to keep on livin' an' some one had to do dis work." The slaves on Burke Simpson's plantation "jis stayed an' took keer of things for de Master while [he] wuz away to de war." When Union troops invaded South Texas and tried to entice slaves away from the King Ranch, a Houston newspaper proudly reported, they "remained with their mistress . . . proving true to the last." Few blacks considered escaping from the Bexar County ranch on which Felix Haywood worked, because "we was happy." Life "went on jus' like it always had before the war . . . We get layed-onto time on time, but gen'rally life was . . . just as good as a sweet potato." Slaves were not unaware of the threat they posed to Southern society, however. "If every mother's son of a black had thrown 'way his hoe and took up a gun to fight for his own freedom along with the Yankees," Haywood believed, "the war'd been over before it began." Nevertheless, "we couldn't help [but] stick to our masters. We couldn't no more shoot 'em than we could fly."[7]

Life did not continue unbroken on every Texas plantation. James Hayes recalled that although day to day life went on "like always . . . some vittles was scarce." The war "sho' did mess us up," according to Mollie Dawson of Navarro County. Since much of the plantation's produce went toward feeding and clothing Confederate soldiers, "we did'nt have as much ter eat as we had been having and our clothes and shoes had ter last us longer." Masters bound for the army often found overseers to take their place. Andy Anderson's master hired a man named Delbridge, and "after dat, de hell start to pop." Delbridge "half starve us niggers," Anderson remembered, "and he want mo' work and he start de whippin's . . . I guess dat Delbridge go to hell when he died, but I don't see how de debbil could stand him." The fighting reached other slaves, as well. Philla Thomas' father, laboring on Confederate breastworks, died during a Yankee bombardment of Galveston, and when Federal gunboats lobbed shells into Corpus Christi, "all de folks . . . takes to de woods and sev'ral am still gone." Slave children were warned against going into the woods by themselves. Manuel Armstrong, a young boy during the war, recalled that deserters from the Confederate army hid in a nearby forest. Fearing that "de chillen would tell on 'em," the fugitives would "ketch dem an' whip dem an' scare dem an' sen' dem home so they wouldn't come back no mo!"[8]

In the face of these hardships, Texas slaves could hardly ignore the war, although whites tried to prevent them from hearing news from the front. One plantation mistress remembered that "the white men didn't talk the situation around where the niggers could hear . . . knowing that the nigger is a natural news ferret, and the biggest gossiper that ever was." Nevertheless, she recalled, "they knew that everything they said finally reached the niggers' ears." Few slaves "in the whole South ever let on that they knew anything . . . They just kept their mouths shut, and their eyes and ears open." Former slave J. W. King said that "some of de men on de plantation would slip up to a open winda at de big house at night and . . . lissen whut was read f'om a letter." Bad news for the Confederacy fueled the slaves' hopes. Despite their distance from the battlefields, they instinctively grasped what was at stake in the white men's war. Around late night fires, Abram Sells recalled, the older men would crouch, "stirrin' the ashes with the pokes and rakin' out the roas' taters. They's smokin' the old corn cob pipe and homemade tobacco and whisperin' right low and quiet like what they's gwineter do and whar they's gwineter go when Mister Lincoln, he turn them free."[9]

Despite the fairly normal war-time relations between whites and blacks in Texas, those whispered conversations around late-night fires—combined with the absence of a large percentage of the white adult male population—helped inspire the surliness that some Texans detected in their slaves. A Houston newspaper complained in January 1865 about the insolence of the city's blacks. They uttered obscenities in the presence of children, refused to yield roads or sidewalks to white ladies, and bought illicit liquor from white merchants. The editor declared that local slave owners were "altogether too lenient . . . and too regardless of their [slaves'] behavior." Likewise, the *San Antonio News* reported in mid-1864 that blacks were "pulling on important airs" on that city's streets. A "general negrow row" ensued in Nueces County when a female slave stole about $2000 and distributed it among her black and Hispanic friends. Authorities recovered only $700. A Harrison County black allegedly plundered the home of a Mrs. Manson, whose husband was off fighting the war, then burned it down to escape detection. A few whites also reported aberrant behavior among slaves on their plantations. Jack, a slave on John B. Walker's plantation, ran away three times during the summer of 1864. Once he left after having "refused Authority," and on another escapade he "borrowed" a mule.[10]

Mrs. Lizzie Neblett recorded the deterioration of slave behavior on her Grimes County plantation in a series of letters to her husband Will, who was away in the army for much of the war. She complained late in 1863 that most of the slaves would not do anything unless they were told, and that "*I find I must think continually for them.*" Several slaves resisted whippings from the overseer or ran away, part of a disturbing trend of insolence and misbehavior among slaves in the neighborhood. The situation had gotten so bad that many owners were afraid to flog their slaves. One slave, threatened with a beating by one of Mrs. Neblett's elderly neighbors, "cursed the old man all to pieces, and walked off in the woods." He came back only after his master promised not to punish him. Another neighbor's slaves rode his horses all over the county during their nocturnal adventures, and she doubted whether her own slaves were much better: "I believe if I was to tell [the overseer] to whip one of the negroes they would resist & it would make matters no better so I shall say nothing, and if they stop work entirely, I will try & feel thankful if they let me alone." Fear had also entered her relationship with the slaves: "I won't sleep with my doors open, any more, & if they break open either door or window I'll have time to be better prepared for them & will fight till I die." She continued in this vein in a later letter when she wrote, "I would not care if they killed me, if they did not do worse."[11]

The large migration of blacks into Texas from other states added a unique dimension to the story of slavery in Civil War Texas. Thousands of them were shipped from more distressed portions of the Confederacy during the course of the war. Many came from nearby Louisiana and Arkansas, but planters from as far away as Virginia also brought their slaves to Texas. Late in the war, Elvira Boles came to Texas with her master, "a dodgin' in and out, runnin' from de Yankees" all the way from Mississippi. Somewhere along "dat road," Elvira's baby died and was buried in an unmarked grave. Tempe Elgin was a toddler when her master brought her mother and sister to Texas from Arkansas; her father, who belonged to a different owner, followed them for sixty miles, imploring his wife to escape with him. She refused, "so pappy rode away on his hoss and mammy never did see him again." The odyssey of Josh Miles began when his owner decided to leave Virginia early in the war. They reached Texas two years later after lengthy stays in Nashville, Memphis, and Vicksburg were interrupted by invading Yankee armies. Another former slave told of moving to Texas from Franklin, Louisiana, with about 300 other slaves, while Van Moore, who grew up in Texas, recalled his mother's stories of how, as a band of slaves and their masters set out for Texas from war-torn Virginia, the "white folks" encouraged the slaves by telling them that in Texas "de lakes [were] full of syrup and covered with batter cakes, and dey won't have to work so hard." Other masters showed less concern for their slaves' states of mind. Litt Young journeyed west from Vicksburg in 1863 under an armed guard who tied the male slaves to trees at night.[12]

Some Texas slaves, reversing the migratory process, hurried the day of freedom by escaping from their masters and a handful—forty-seven—joined the Union army. Some slaves on a Williamson County plantation ran away—despite the nearly automatic "whippin' at de stake" that would greet them if caught—when a cruel overseer took over for their master, who had gone to fight in the war. Susan Ross' brother, after refusing to go to the army, fled his master's plantation after a beating so severe that "you couldn't tell what he look like." Although the war years did see an apparent escalation in the number of runaway slaves, escape held little chance of success, at least according to one Burleson County ex-slave. "I never seen any slaves that tried to run away until after the war," said John Mosley, "but . . . they never got very far at that." At least one master had "all de quarters move up close to de big house, so if we tries to make de run for it in de night he can catch us." Punishment was sure and swift for captured escapees. Lee McGillery saw "a few slaves try to run away to the north after the war started and when the white folks of the south find them they would most of the time jest shoot them. Some few they never did find."[13]

Most of the slaves attempting to escape exploited the traditional sympathy between Mexicans and blacks by making their way to Mexico. Felix Haywood declared that "in Mexico you could be free. They didn't care what color you was, black, white, yellow, or blue." Haywood claimed that hundreds of slaves fled to Mexico, and "got on all right," becoming in effect, Mexicans, and raising their children to speak only Spanish. At one point Mexicans on the south bank of the Rio Grande rigged up a flatboat in the middle of the river. Once a fugitive reached the boat he could easily pull himself across to freedom. Jacob Branch reported that slave patrols "rid[e] de Mexican side [of] dat river all de time, but plenty slaves git through, anyway." Sallie Wroe's father hauled a load of Travis County cotton to the border. Upon reaching his destination, he and a number of other drivers paddled a bale of cotton over the river to Mexico. When he returned to his family after the war, he told them "he done git 'long fine with Mexico. He learnt to talk jes' like them." Similar instances led the *Houston Tri- Weekly Telegraph* to warn its readers against taking even "their trusty negroes" to Matamoros on business. The booming border town was "overrunning with these trusty, now insolent negroes." "Loose colored women" and escaped slaves with plenty of spending money would lure otherwise faithful slaves into the welcome anonymity of the city.[14]

As a non-citizen, even the least faithful slave legally could not be charged with disloyalty. A Confederate district judge ruled in May 1863, that since slaves "are not members of the body politic—& do not owe allegiance to the Govt.," they could not be tried for treason. Nevertheless, the state legislature responded to the potential threat of rebellious slaves and Northern invaders by passing several laws aimed at preventing slave insurrections—especially those instigated by marauding Yankee troops or their emissaries. An act passed on March 5, 1863, condemned persons convicted of selling, giving, or loaning any sort of weapon or ammunition to a slave to up to five years' hard labor, while another established a penalty of from five to fifteen years for any officer of the United States armed services guilty of "inciting insurrection or insubordination." In addition, "any person of color" captured while invading Texas could be enslaved, a fate suffered by at least a few black Yankees, and it was illegal to leave slaves alone without "free white" supervision or to allow a slave to pretend to own or to control property. Other "disloyal" slaves fell outside the bounds of the law. Late in 1864, three railroad workers took eight hours to beat a black man to death for allegedly stealing three yards of homespun cloth, while another slave suspected of murdering his master was captured in Rusk County, brought home to Tyler, and burned at the stake. Vigilante Texans near La Grange hanged an escaped slave named Yorick—two weeks after General Robert E. Lee surrendered at Appomattox—when he was found "endeavoring to accomplish a purpose too horrid to mention" upon a "German girl."[15]

Despite the problems caused by some Texas slaves during the Civil War, neither the war nor the behavior of their chattel property led Texas Confederates to question the desirability of retaining the peculiar institution. Some masters hurried to the frontier of Texas late in the war, hoping to outrun the Yankees and establish themselves far beyond the effective boundaries of emancipation. A Travis County slave owner relocated in Robertson County, according to one of his bondsman, "cause he done figured de Yankees can't git up dere." As late as May 1865, owners of runaway slaves still offered rewards of up to $500 in Confederate currency, and J. L. Maxwell of Collin County offered to exchange his small farm for "Negro property" that same month. Even after the remnants of the Confederate presence in Texas had been surrendered, the *Marshall Texas Republican* confidently predicted that Southerners would be allowed to keep their slaves in some form of perpetual servitude. Emancipation "naturally" would be followed by "vagrancy, filth, disease, and crime" among the freedmen; masters should be kind to their servants, motivated by "an attachment for the race, by a grateful remembrance for past services."[16]

The experiences of masters and slaves in Texas during the Civil War flowed out of two conflicting pre-war situations: the general faithfulness of most slaves counterpointed to the constant threat that they posed to the institution. While some Texas slaves confirmed Southern fears of that threat by taking advantage of war-time tumult to expand the boundaries of their lives, most did not, in any meaningful way, challenge the restrictions placed on their lives by the peculiar institution. In fact, at least one free black voluntarily gave up his freedom during the war. George, a "free man of color," petitioned the Collin County District Court to become the slave of James B. Thomas. As Martin Jackson's father told him, "the War wasn't going to last forever, but . . . our forever was going to be spent living among the Southerners after they got licked." Reconstruction would, in many ways, fulfill Jackson's prophecy.[17]

Notes

1. See Benjamin Quarles, *The Negro in the Civil War* (Boston, 1953); Harvey Wish, "Slave Disloyalty Under the Confederacy," *Journal of Negro History* (October 1938), 435–450; C. Peter Ribley, *Slaves and Freedmen in Civil War Louisiana* (Baton Rouge, 1976); Clarence L. Mohr, *On the Threshold of Freedom: Masters and Slaves in Civil War Georgia* (Athens, 1986); Robert Francis Engs, *Freedom's First Generation: Black Hampton, Virginia, 1861–1890* (Philadelphia, 1979), 3–79; Ronald L. F. Davis, *Good and Faithful Labor: From Slavery to Sharecropping in the Natchez District, 1860–1890* (Westport, Conn., 1982), 60–73; Willie Lee Rose, *Rehearsal for Reconstruction: The Port Royal Experiment* (New York, 1964); and James H. Brewer, *The Confederate Negro: Virginia's Craftsmen and Military Laborers, 1861–1865* (Durham, 1969).
2. George Rawick (ed.), *The American Slave: A Composite Autobiography* (Westport, Conn., 1972), 140. Despite the spelling errors and phonetic exaggerations inflicted upon black oral testimony by 1930s researchers, I have retained them as they appear in Rawick's splendid compilation of interviews of former slaves.
3. William W. White, "The Texas Slave Insurrection of 1860," *Southwestern Historical Quarterly* (January 1949), 259–276; *Navarro Express*, August 11, 1860. See also Wendell G. Addington, "Slave Insurrections in Texas," *Journal of Negro History* (October 1950), 408–434; Bill Ledbetter, "Slave Unrest and White Panic: The Impact of Black Republicanism in Antebellum Texas," *Texana* (1972), 342–348; and Donald E. Reynolds, "Smith County and Its Neighbors During the Slave Insurrection Panic of 1860," *Chronicles of Smith County* (Fall 1971), 1–8.
4. *Marshall Texas Republican*, June 2, 1865.
5. *Marshall Texas Republican*, January 6, 1865; *Houston Tri-Weekly Telegraph*, July 30, 1862; *The American Slave*, v. 4, pt. 2, 126–129.
6. *The American Slave*, v. 5, pt. 4, 20; v. 4, pt. 1, 194–196 and 182–184; suppl. 2, v. 9, pt. 8, 3609–3623.
7. *The American Slave*, suppl. 2, v. 9, pt. 8, 3561; *Houston Tri-Weekly Telegraph*, January 11, 1864; *The American Slave*, v. 4, pt. 2, 131–134.
8. *The American Slave*, v. 4, pt. 2, 116–119; suppl. 2, v. 4, pt. 3, 1141; v. 4, pt. 1, 14–16; v. 5, pt. 4, 92; v. 5, pt. 3, 249; suppl. 2, v. 2, pt. 1, 64.
9. *The American Slave*, suppl. 2, v. 10, pt. 9, 4335; suppl. 2, v. 6, pt. 5, 2213–2214; v. 5, pt. 4, 14.
10. *Houston Tri-Weekly Telegraph*, January 24, 1865; quoted in Robert L. Kerby, *Kirby Smith's Confederacy: The Trans-Mississippi South, 1863–1865* (New York, 1972), 401; Rufe Byler to Martha Byler, May 15, 1863, Dobie-Byler Family Papers, Barker Texas History Center; *Marshall Texas Republican*, March 5, 1863; John B. Walker Plantation Book, March 30, and August 13, 14, 16, 1864, Barker Texas History Center.
11. Lizzie to Will Neblett, November 4, August 13 and 18, 1863, Lizzie Neblett Papers, Barker Texas History Center.
12. Kerby, *Kirby Smith's Confederacy*, 255; *The American Slave*, v. 4, pt. 1, 108; suppl. 2, v. 4, pt. 2, 1292–1294; v. 5, pt. 3, 79–80, 29–31, 129; v. 5, pt. 4, 227–231.
13. Frank Smyrl, "Unionism, Abolitionism, and Vigilantism in Texas, 1856–1865" (Master of Arts thesis, University of Texas, 1965), 146–160; *The*

American Slave, v. 4, pt. 1, 14–16; v. 5, pt. 3, 256; suppl. 2, v. 7, pt. 6, 2801; v. 5, pt. 3, 249; v. 7, pt. 6, 2495. In Tennessee, where Union lines were always relatively close and where masters had far more to worry about than a few unruly bondsmen, slaves aggressively forced a relaxation of controls and often ran away. See John Cimprich, *Slavery's End in Tennessee, 1861–1865* (University, Ala., 1985).

14. *The American Slave,* v. 4, pt. 2, 132; v. 4, pt. 1, 141; v. 5, pt. 4, 224; *Houston Tri-Weekly Telegraph,* December 29, 1864. For the best survey of racial tension between Hispanic and Anglos in Texas—including Mexican attitudes about slaves—see Arnoldo DeLeon, *They Called Them Greasers: Anglo Attitudes Toward Mexicans in Texas, 1821–1900* (Austin, 1983).

15. H. P. N. Gammel (comp.), *The Laws of the State of Texas,* v. 5 (Austin, 1898), 601–603, 608–610, 484, 762–763; Gary Wilson, "The Ordeal of William H. Cowdin and the Officers of the Forty-Second Massachusetts Regiment: Union Prisoners in Texas," *East Texas Historical Journal* (Spring 1985) 16–26; May 30, 1863, William Pitt Ballinger Diary, Barker Texas History Center; *Marshall Texas Republican,* December 23, 1864; Kerby, *Kirby Smith's Confederacy,* 257; *San Antonio Herald,* copies in the *Marshall Texas Republican,* May 19, 1865. Slaves' liability under the Confederate treason laws rarely came up during the war. The only opinion issued by the Confederate Attorney General that dealt with slaves established the parameters of the government's financial liability for damage to slaves working on government projects. Rembert W. Patrick (ed.), *Opinions of the Confederate Attorneys General, 1861–1865* (Buffalo, 1950), 51–53.

16. *The American Slave,* v. 5, pt. 4, 125; *Marshall Texas Republican,* May 19 and June 16, 1865.

17. Collin County District Court, Civil Minutes, 1858–1864, vol. B, 466; *The American Slave,* v. 4, pt. 2, 189. The Seventh Legislature passed a law allowing free blacks to select their own masters and become slaves early in 1858. Gammel, *The Laws of Texas,* v. 4, 947–948. The most useful surveys of blacks in Reconstruction Texas are James Smallwood's *Time of Hope, Time of Despair: Black Texans During Reconstruction* (Port Washington, New York, 1981), and Jesse Dorsett's "Blacks in Reconstruction Texas, 1865–1877" (Doctoral Dissertation, Texas Christian University, 1981).

Black Texans during Reconstruction

First Freedom

JAMES M. SMALLWOOD

AFTER THE DEFEAT OF THE CONFEDERACY, TEXAS became a scene of confusion for whites and blacks alike, but civil government resumed in the state on July 21, 1865, when Andrew Johnson's appointee, Unionist A. J. Hamilton, arrived in Galveston to assume the governorship. In August he began appointing fellow Unionists and some ex-Confederates to state, district, county, and precinct offices. By the end of the month, civil government functioned in eighty counties, but major adjustments remained.[1] Authorities found themselves confronted with many problems of which the most enduring involved the question of black status. Although most white Texans hoped this would not be the case, Union victory in war carried with it emancipation for slaves. Many questions arose: How would African Americans respond to their new "condition"? How would whites react? What degree of control over black labor, if any, would the national government allow native Anglos? Would blacks have the same political rights and legal status as whites? These issues absorbed Texans in the post-war era.

After General Gordon Granger delivered the Texas Emancipation Proclamation in Galveston on June 19,[2] the immediate reaction of the slaves varied. A minority temporarily became confused. Will Adams reported that on the James Davis plantation in San Jacinto County, "there was lots of crying and weeping when they were set free. Lot's [*sic*] of them didn't want to be free because they knew nothing and had nowhere to go."[3] On other plantations and farms, after masters made the emancipation announcement, some ex-slaves, shocked and unsure of their new status, still asked for passes when they left.[4]

For some freedmen joy replaced temporary confusion. Blacks turned many plantations into scenes of jubilation and alternately sang, danced, and prayed.[5] Some became overjoyed simply because they believed freedom meant "no more whippings."[6] The reaction of Harriet, a domestic slave hired out to Amelia Barr of

Austin, perhaps typified that of many African Americans. After the local sheriff read Granger's proclamation, Amelia informed Harriet that she was free. Afterwards, Harriet

> darted to her child, and throwing it high, shrieked hysterically, "Tamar, you are free. You are free, Tamar!" She did not at that supreme moment think of herself. Freedom was for her child; she looked in its face, at its hands, at its feet. It was a new baby to her—a free baby.[7]

Like Harriet, most slave parents probably thought of their children first, wanting them to have the same benefits as slaveholders' children—schooling, attractive clothes, sufficient food, and exemption from work. A majority of the bondsmen, however, suffered no great confusion as a result of emancipation, and if they felt joy, they restrained their enthusiasm. Most quietly planned to leave their masters as soon as possible.

To the slaves, emancipation had many potential meanings. Generally, blacks expected the same freedoms that Anglos enjoyed, with the same prerogatives and opportunities. In terms of priorities, educated African Americans emphasized the importance of full and immediate political and civil rights while the masses advocated land redistribution and educational opportunity. Blacks believed that political rights would help protect them from social and economic discrimination and that land redistribution would provide a stable base for future progress. On a more common level, blacks also hoped that emancipation meant a new home, a new job, a new social life, complete religious freedom, and the right of unrestricted travel—to seek better employment or to locate lost family members. Emancipation had yet another definition for black women who had been field hands. They believed that they, like white mistresses, should now be exempt from field labor, that they should engage in housework only, reserving free time for visiting and for shopping.[8]

Early in 1865, even before the army and the Freedmen's Bureau could provide assistance, blacks began trying to reorder their lives and fulfill the aspirations of freedom. Wishing to secure an education for themselves and their children, for example, many freedmen bought primers and writing slates and tried to learn how to read and write. Then they organized makeshift schools and supported teachers with moderate tuition and presents of food after the harvest. Just as they began establishing schools, blacks quickly began founding their own religious institutions. They withdrew from native white churches and joined the "northern wing" of established Anglo churches or organized their own services. African Americans also developed a more diversified social life which usually centered around their schools and churches. Church and school-sponsored picnics, dances, and fairs along with regular Sabbath services represented a few of the limited recreational outlets available to blacks. Equally important to the new freedmen was their search for lost relatives which usually began at first opportunity. In most cases, however, blacks had to wait for the aid of the bureau before they could locate family members who had been "lost" because of family splitting before emancipation.[9]

Accepting the aid of sincere Unionists, blacks who successfully made the transition from slavery to freedom tried to help those more unfortunate. In Houston Reverend Elias Dibble organized a mutual aid society to help sick or distressed blacks. With members paying a rather large $2.50 initiation fee and $.25 weekly dues, the society quickly collected an $80 relief fund. In San Antonio Nace Duval, preacher and barber, performed a valuable service for fellow blacks when he established an employment bureau. Many newly emerging black congregations also founded benevolent agencies to assist destitutes. Likewise, some Unionists, particularly Germans, took an interest in African American welfare. In addition to offering protection to hunted freedmen, Louis Constant ran a combination boarding house, relief station, and employment service for ex-slaves.[10]

To test their new freedom and to escape hated reminders of slavery, those blacks who had a place to go gathered their belongings and left their former masters quickly after emancipation. Usually domestics and artisans left first while the aged and infirm tended to leave last. On the William Ballinger farm three younger slaves immediately left, but six who had no place to go continued to work for Ballinger for monthly wages. Only freedmen who had had kindly owners voluntarily remained at their old jobs because most ex-slaveholders tended to treat blacks as if they were still slaves. Rather than accept this, blacks left. Further, those who remained usually did so only for a few months. Yet comparisons of the 1860 and 1870 census statistics reveal that no massive shifting of African American population occurred. The percentage of black population remained relatively stable in all parts of the state. Many blacks who left old masters went only a few miles before hiring out to a new employer. Others, particularly those whom whites brought to Texas during the war, left the state to return to old homes and to rejoin their families.[11] Still others flocked to the nearest town.

According to one witness of what appeared to be a mass black migration to urban centers, the ex-slaves wanted "to get closer to freedom, so they'd know what it was—like it was a place or a city."[12] Migrants became so numerous that they filled the roads to such towns as Houston, San Antonio, Gonzales, and Jefferson. Austin suffered temporary problems in public health and sanitation because of overcrowding. In the urban centers some blacks passed their time in idleness or in gaming, trying to enjoy their new freedom. But historians who have argued that "all" or "most" blacks refused to work and led a wayward type of existence in the cities probably exaggerated. Rather, what whites called laziness usually amounted to a typical worker's rebellion against unreasonable hours and wages and became a way of demanding rest and enjoyment. Whites nevertheless expected the worst from freedmen, and this general attitude allowed them to believe almost any rumor directed against blacks. In 1866 a Freedmen's Bureau agent in Bastrop heard reports that blacks in Austin refused to work and simply wandered around. Austin agent Byron Porter, however, wondered how his counterpart in Bastrop received such misinformation. The great majority of African Americans in Austin, Porter maintained, had jobs. In urban centers, then, most blacks sought employment. Some hired out as domestics or day laborers. Catering to the new black population in the towns, some opened business establishments such as barbershops, grocery stores, and shoe shops. Others found benevolent military commanders like those in Houston who created jobs by instigating temporary relief projects.[13]

Black population growth in urban areas continued through the late 1860s to outstrip white increases, but many freedmen soon discovered that towns were not the havens they sought. Urban Anglos feared blacks, believing that their increased numbers would cause more crime. Further, white employers, believing absolutely in black inferiority, refused to allow freedmen the dignity accorded Anglo labor. Still, blacks found themselves treated as slaves. Refusing to hire the new freedmen, other employers replaced them with white labor even though Anglos demanded higher wages.[14] White politicos applauded this trend. The growth of an Anglo mechanic class was necessary, said the editor of the *Houston Telegraph,* or "the ignorant race" would swamp Houston and retard its development. Later, the editor noted with satisfaction that whites had replaced blacks as drivers of a majority of the city's drays. The editor of the *Huntsville Item* noted similar trends occurring in his town and expressed approval.[15]

Trying to encourage their removal, some city governments also discriminated against freedmen. The Galveston mayor harassed blacks whenever they tried to gather for social events. Although military authorities always gave blacks permission to conduct meetings or hold balls, the mayor broke up any gatherings and fined supposed organizers, justifying his action with an apparently little-used local permit ordinance.[16] Victims of white discrimination and of what became a glutted labor market, many blacks returned to the rural area which they regarded as home because they knew it well. But most found that conditions in the countryside were in many ways worse than in the cities.

Some blacks in rural areas found the transition to freedom particularly difficult because of the immediate reactions of their masters. Despite the fact that most farms and plantations needed laborers, a minority of owners—on first hearing of Granger's proclamation—took action that defied economic logic, relieving slaves of their jobs and telling them to get off the land. Ex-masters dismissed some blacks because they were purported to be bad influences on other freedmen. Thomas Greer of Madison County told his slaves to get out, saying that he would horsewhip any "nigger" he found on his place after the next sunrise.[17] Many freedmen, such as Toby Jones, reported that "they turned us out like a bunch of stray dogs, with no homes, no clothes, no nothing."[18] The blacks who had been turned out had no choice but to wander around, looking for work.

Some ex-slaves became victims of early Klan-like conspiracies. A large group of white citizens in Freestone County emphatically passed a general resolution in late 1865 vowing to hire no blacks and to whip any freedman who tried to contract with Anglos. Whites who violated the resolution might first only be warned but, on second offense, would be whipped or hanged.[19] Some ex-masters, extremely disturbed by emancipation and not content to deny blacks work, decided that slaves would be better off dead than free. By poisoning slave water wells, those masters reportedly killed scores of African Americans before they could escape from the old plantations.[20]

Slaves who were driven from the land found the first steps toward freedom painful. Some joined the migration to towns where they sought not just work but military protection from further abuse. Others relied solely on themselves and resorted to a most primitive type of existence. Unable to buy land, unwilling to accept semi-slavery under white employers, some squatted on unworked land and, using sticks as tools, planted crops. They supplemented their diet by fishing and by hunting—with bows and arrows—and made clothes from animal skins. Despite black efforts to provide for themselves, starvation became rife in some Texas counties, particularly in the north and northeast; to get food, some blacks resorted to thievery.[21] So difficult was the plight of freedmen that Elige Davison could only comment, "if the woods were not full of wild game, all us Negroes would have starved to death."[22] And blacks like Davison could expect little help. The Freedmen's Bureau, the agency Congress established to aid blacks, did not begin to function in Texas until September 1865 and remained hopelessly undermanned until it finally was removed from the state in 1870.

Most former slave owners did not turn the new freedmen off the land, but they, like most other whites, maintained an attitude not conducive to black freedom. Only briefly, just after the South's defeat, did white Texans adopt an apparently moderate attitude, one encouraged perhaps by their uncertainty regarding the kind of treatment that federal forces of occupation would mete out. Further, if they acted in a conciliatory manner, they believed that President Andrew Johnson's lenient Reconstruction policy would yet allow them to control the freedmen. Correspondents for various Texas newspapers reported that most planters and farmers quietly resigned themselves to the Union victory and black emancipation, freeing slaves and coming to terms with them. The citizens of some towns even passed resolutions vowing full cooperation with the federal government. Yet such mass displays of loyalty proved misleading. If a majority of whites at first appeared conciliatory, if newspapers advocated moderation, they did so only because they wanted to remove the necessity of a lengthy military occupation of the state.[23]

Even after the Union government made known its determination to end slavery, a majority of white Texans quickly reaffirmed their belief in white supremacy. As William Ballinger asserted even before Kirby Smith's surrender, Anglo Texans would always "remain Southern in their feelings."[24] After the war, whites clung to the "lost cause," sometimes making up new "Rebel ditties" like "Conquered Banner" and "Faded Gray Jacket" to glorify the Old South.[25] Whites feared that freedom for blacks implied equality of the races, an idea that most refused to accept. Many believed the black race so inferior that amalgamation represented the only way to uplift it; thus arguments against black equality often focused on the question of racial mixing. Whites feared that granting African Americans political and legal rights ultimately would lead to social equality which in turn would lead to amalgamation; hence many Anglos opposed giving any rights to African Americans.[26] If freedmen received any rights, "then kinky hair," lamented one editor, "the mellow eye, the artistic nose, the seductive lips, the ebony skin and bewildering odor will be ours, all ours, ours, ours."[27] Like most white Texans, the editor of the *San Antonio Daily Herald* joined the critics, telling the black man that "this is our government and country, and not his, if he don't like it, he is at liberty to seek another."[28]

In addition to objecting to black freedom for racial reasons, most Anglos stressed economic arguments, using the complaint that unless compelled, freedmen would not work. Whites attributed this alleged reluctance about work to the irresponsible, lazy, and ignorant "nature" of blacks and to the "foolish" notion that Yankees would give blacks land. Anglos apparently failed to remember that the hot summer, even in the antebellum period, traditionally had been a time of less work. Moreover, blacks moved about immediately after emancipation to test their freedom, to escape hated masters, and to find new jobs or lost family members. Whites attributed the migration to pure wanderlust which, they believed, proved their point: free black labor was unstable.[29]

Whites resisted black emancipation for yet other reasons. Some believed that unless blacks were controlled they would take revenge on the society which had enslaved them. This fear became especially pronounced in areas of large African American population. In Harrison County, where freedmen numbered about 60 percent of the total population, Anglos around Marshall set up contingency plans to protect themselves from a rebellion. Even in areas of smaller black population, whites did not feel safe unless they placed some restrictions on freedmen. In San Antonio the city council adopted a nine o'clock curfew for any type of black meeting.[30] The belief that blacks committed most crimes further stimulated white fears of rebellion. Anglo criminals helped reinforce this belief by committing night robberies while disguised as blacks. A group of whites in blackface beat and robbed a German named Homeyer in his home near Brenham, but they proved to be inept for Homeyer later identified them as Anglos.[31]

So strong was the white desire to "keep blacks in their place" that when they realized abolition to be a fact, Anglos took overt action which necessitated strong countermeasures by the federal government. A one-sided guerrilla war with strong racial overtones developed in Texas and continued to influence the entire course of events in the attempted Reconstruction of the state. The war took many forms, with black people the usual targets for violence perpetrated by whites. The violence sometimes seemed casual, with Anglos having no apparent motive except to chastise "uppity" blacks who were guilty of nothing more than exercising their new freedom. At other times the violence became well directed, with planters using force to keep blacks in illegal bondage. Disgruntled whites did not confine their wrath to blacks but also identified Anglo Unionists as targets because to varying degrees they supported black rights. Most white Texans committed no outrages, but many actively conspired with those who did, by hiding them from the authorities and by refusing to testify against them. Violence against blacks and Unionists erupted sporadically throughout the state. Although outrages occurred more frequently in the interior at isolated points unprotected by federal forces, white men murdered and whipped blacks even in areas of military occupation. Federal officials reported that at times entire counties went out of control.[32]

In many areas trouble began with early military occupation. Whites immediately demonstrated their hostility for the government. In Millican when Unionists raised the United States' flag, Col. W. B. Lowery pulled it down. At Weatherford ex-Confederates took the flag from the courthouse and tore it to pieces. Through 1865 reports came to Governor Hamilton from all over the state informing him that disloyal factions just waited for their "chance" to "get at" freedmen and Unionists.[33]

While demonstrating contempt for the Union, some Anglos also inflicted barbarities on freedmen. Whites killed blacks for the most trivial offenses. In Huntsville during a celebration of emancipation by freedmen, one local white rode into the midst of a jubilee and, wielding a knife, disemboweled a black woman whose body was then pitched into a wagon and taken away.[34] An historian listed other "reputedly assigned reasons" for murder:

> freedman did not remove his hat when he passed him (a white man); negro would not allow himself to be whipped; freedman would not allow his wife to be whipped by a white man; he was carrying a letter to a Freedmen's Bureau official; kill negroes to see them kick; wanted to thin out niggers a little; didn't hand over his money quick enough; wouldn't give up his whiskey flask.[35]

Anglos beat blacks for almost any offense, including indications of freedmen that they were in fact emancipated. If blacks did not show due deference in all matters involving whites, they faced punishment. Beginning after emancipation and continuing throughout Reconstruction, Anglos complained about impudent behavior by blacks, failing to understand that blacks needed to test their freedom. Further, white men clung to the sexual mores of the antebellum period, which included exploitation of black women. Freedmen's Bureau records contained frequent complaints of rape or attempted rape of black women by white men.[36]

The congressional investigation of 1866 produced statistics and testimony proving that such violent acts had become a common theme of early postwar race relations in Texas. From mid-1865 to early 1866, authorities issued 500 indictments for the murder of blacks by Anglos, but because of white attitudes, no convictions resulted. Additionally, whites committed many murders that brought no indictment. Two Anglos killed a black domestic servant in Harrison County because she would not punish her child for stealing money. Lucy Grimes explained that the young child only played with the money, as one would with a toy. After hearing what they regarded as a "fishy" story, the men took the woman to a wooded area outside of Marshall, stripped her, and beat her to death. The murder went unpunished because the county judge refused to hear a complaint brought by an African American, Lucy's older son.[37]

Some slaveholders who desperately wanted to control their labor force added to the violent atmosphere by refusing to free their chattels. Other owners merely followed a policy of drift, informing bondsmen of Granger's proclamation only after rumors of freedom became so strong that they could not be denied. Still others determined to get summer crops in before telling slaves of emancipation. This group usually tricked the freedmen into remaining at their jobs. Unscrupulous masters promised blacks full rations and a share of all crops—some even promised to give them small plots of land and livestock. After the harvest, most refused to honor their agreements and drove blacks from the land.[38]

Some owners refused to free their bondsmen even after the harvest. Anderson Edwards remained a slave on the Rusk County plantation of Major Matt Gaud for one full year after Granger's proclamation. Saying that God "never did intend to free niggers," Gaud ignored the emancipation order until federal soldiers discovered his illegal actions and forced him to release Edwards and other slaves. One mistress kept a black woman chained to a loom to prevent her escape and continued to work her for "about" a year. In statements corroborated by white Unionists, other slaves reported similar experiences.[39]

In other instances, which occurred more frequently than many historians previously have supposed, owners kept blacks in illegal bondage not for just a few months but for years. After Union forces occupied Galveston, John E. Chisholm retreated deep into East Texas, settled, and worked his bondsmen as late as December 1866. On July 4, 1867, a group of freedmen in Austin encountered a black couple traveling with a white man who still held them in slavery. The freedmen's hostile protests influenced the immediate release of the couple. In the same month, the Freedmen's Bureau agent in Austin reported that he recently had freed two girls whom planter William Greenwood had maintained in bondage. No one released the slaves of Alex Simpson, a horse thief, until he was hanged in 1868.[40] Certainly, most owners freed their slaves before 1868, but six months after Granger's proclamation, *Flake's Daily Bulletin* reported that some openly bragged that they continued to hold freedmen.[41]

Not all blacks submitted to illegal enslavement. When they learned that by right they should be free, they attempted to escape. As before the war, however, some whites used as much force as necessary to return escapees. Of his own personal knowledge, one Freedmen's Bureau agent indicated that in the counties around Houston with considerable black population Anglos still used dog packs to capture runaways.[42] Further, whites sometimes killed escapees to discourage attempts by others. In Harrison County, most slaveholders freed their bondsmen before owners in neighboring Rusk County. Impatient for emancipation, slaves in Rusk County frequently ran away, trying to get over the county line, but many were killed in the attempt. "You could see lots of niggers hanging to trees in Sabine bottom right after freedom," asserted ex-slave Susan Merritt, "because they [white men] caught them swimming across the Sabine River and shot them."[43]

The Harrison County murders did not represent infrequent occurrences. A correspondent for *Flake's Daily Bulletin* reported that in "Middle Texas" as late as August, whites behaved in the same manner as those in Harrison. "More than twenty dead Negroes," he said, "have [of late] drifted down the Brazos."[44] Moreover, four separate reports made by army officers in December 1865 indicated that suppression and continued enslavement of blacks remained common throughout East and Central Texas. One federal official asserted that in the interior ex-masters still conducted their plantations as if the South had won the war. Gen. E. M. Gregory, first commissioner of the Freedmen's Bureau in Texas, and Gen. William E. Strong, inspector general of the bureau, held similar views. Gregory toured the region between the lower Colorado and the Brazos, while Strong toured the area between the Trinity and the Neches. They found that wherever government troops were stationed Anglos behaved themselves but that where troops were absent some whites held blacks in bondage and treated them with utmost cruelty. Strong, who gave the more pessimistic report, recommended a military campaign to correct the situation. In conjunction with the tours of Gregory and Strong, I. J. W. Mintzer, surgeon-in-chief for the bureau, visited over 100 plantations along the Brazos and the Colorado and disgustedly reported that at will planters broke oral and written contracts with blacks. Whites who did not continue to hold blacks in bondage sometimes exercised a more subtle type of control which proved equally effective. Anglos banded together and agreed not to hire any laborers without the consent of their previous employer.[45] While some ex-slaveholders circumvented federal laws by continuing to hold blacks after June 19, 1865, others re-enslaved those who had been emancipated. Operating along the Texas coast, some whites gifted with beguiling stories convinced blacks to board ships that would carry them to "a better place." Ship captains then took them to Cuba to sell them into slavery. In late 1865 some planters, like David F. Portis of Austin County, decided to leave the United States and tried to force their ex-slaves to go with them. Leading a party of sixteen men, Portis confronted Louis Constant, German Unionist, and asked the whereabouts of a certain teenaged black male whom Portis intended to carry with him to Brazil. Constant knew where the freedman was hiding but refused to allow a search.[46]

As late as 1867 some white entrepreneurs evolved an elaborate plan that one witness called the "Brazilian emigration scheme." Allegedly, Anglos from the coast went into Smith County offering blacks work as boat hands. Eventually, the businessmen transported several hundred freedmen to the coast and divided them into crews. Ships then sailed, bound for New Orleans. Before reaching the port, whites put the blacks in chains. Captains then loaded the "cargo" aboard vessels bound for Brazil where the captives again would be enslaved.[47] As was obvious from the attitudes and actions of white Texans, the first few months of the new freedom found most blacks in a difficult situation.

Although the myth developed that the white South cared for the ex-slaves' welfare, kindness and concern may have been the exception rather than the rule. Yet freedmen could expect little relief from the still disorganized state government. Hamilton filled offices slowly and unknowingly appointed many unreconstructed rebels. Although other southern states held their constitutional conventions in the fall of 1865, he postponed the Texas convention until February 1866, explaining to President Johnson that he could not act more rapidly because whites refused to give freedmen their rights. In the interim, Hamilton took no positive action to settle the outstanding issues involving blacks. He appealed publicly for racial conciliation, but in his November proclamation to freedmen he put little emphasis on their rights and instead stressed order, told blacks to work, and tried to discourage rumors of land redistribution.[48]

The Texas Emancipation Proclamation guaranteed freedmen absolute equality in personal and property rights, but confusion resulted regarding the legal status of blacks. Many state judges like Hiram Christian, chief justice of Bell County, wrote Hamilton inquiring about the judicial rights of African Americans—could freedmen sue, complain against, or testify against whites? The governor ruled that these were judicial questions to be settled by the courts. Some justices like C. C. Caldwell of Harris County instructed juries that perfect equality prevailed in all cases, but most judges in the state, following the old antebellum codes, refused to hear black complaints or testimony against Anglos. Furthermore, blacks usually faced exclusion from jury service. Even if courts accepted their testimony, white juries generally refused to convict fellow Anglos. So unfair was the system of justice that ranking federal officers labeled proceedings involving freedmen as complete farces.[49] Denied the protection of the Hamilton administration and the state courts, blacks continued to place faith in the federal government. Most African Americans believed that the Johnson government would implement a land redistribution program to give them economic security and that the army and the Freedmen's Bureau would protect them from further abuse. Blacks were disappointed on all counts.

Because the bureau did not enter the state until late 1865, the army shouldered the early responsibility for helping African Americans adjust to freedom and for settling racial disputes. When General Granger issued the emancipation order, he initiated Texas Reconstruction. By his order blacks received equality in personal and property rights. At the same time, however, the general established a trend that later federal officials would follow. He showed more concern for order, stability, and the black labor "problem" than for black rights. He advised freedmen to sign labor contracts and to remain with their old masters. He warned that he would not allow blacks to collect at army posts nor would he support them in idleness. He also forbade blacks to travel without passes from their employers.[50]

The attitude of a majority of military personnel limited the effectiveness of the army. White soldiers in the ranks felt prejudice against blacks and did little to help or protect them.

Occasionally, elements of the occupation force committed depredations on those who most needed protection. Blacks sometimes complained that soldiers, black and white, assaulted and robbed them. In Houston freedmen became so dissatisfied with troop behavior that in January 1866 they organized a vigilance committee numbering thirty to forty men and swore vengeance on the soldiers. A local war seemed unavoidable until a bureau agent managed to conciliate the freedmen.[51]

Prejudice permeated command positions as well as the lower ranks. Most officers made it no secret that they did not accept full black equality.[52] Gen. William T. Sherman asserted that "the white men of this country will control it, and the Negroes, in mass, will occupy a subordinate place as a race."[53] Some commanders, of course, managed to overcome their prejudice, particularly those whose position necessitated frequent contact with freedmen. After gaining firsthand knowledge of the black plight, some officers changed their opinions of African Americans. They adopted attitudes which ranged from benevolent paternalism to outright sympathy.[54]

Even when prejudice did not limit the army, President Johnson's lenient Reconstruction plan did. Johnson, following his "easy" policy, did not envision a long occupation of Texas or the rest of the South. Nor did he foresee advancement of freedmen as one of the army's prime functions. To satisfy Johnson, former Confederate states had to acknowledge the end of slavery and accept federal law. The president intended to leave the black question to state authorities; he wanted rapid restoration and enjoined his military commanders from interfering with the organization and functioning of state governments.[55]

The impossibility of patrolling Texas with a limited force also hamstrung the army. Granger's original force of 1,800 men increased to 45,424 by September, partially because the Mexican Civil War made such a concentration necessary. But by January 1866 troop strength fell to 25,085. By February further reductions left approximately 5,000 soldiers in Texas. Furthermore, commanders were ordered to concentrate troops not along the coast or in the interior of the state but along the Rio Grande and in frontier outposts.[56] Thus undermanned in the areas of concentrated black population, the army could not provide the supervision needed to protect blacks or to adjudicate racial disputes.

The Freedmen's Bureau finally began to function in Texas during September 1865, when the first Assistant Commissioner for Texas, General E. M. Gregory, arrived in Galveston. Congress originally planned for the bureau to continue only one year after the end of the war. But when southern states passed the Black Codes and thus made known their determination to resist legal equality for African Americans, Congress renewed the bureau in 1866 over Johnson's veto and every year thereafter until 1870. As first conceived, the duties of the bureau varied. In Texas, because there were no abandoned lands to adjudicate, agents took legal jurisdiction over blacks if state courts appeared prejudicial and violated black rights and provided relief work if such aid seemed absolutely necessary. Bureau officials also encouraged blacks and their employers to honor labor contracts and sought to found and maintain bureau schools.[57]

In areas other than labor supervision, the early work of the bureau achieved only moderate success. In extending immediate relief and medical aid to distressed freedmen, efforts fell far short of what blacks needed. The bureau issued relief rations to only sixty-four African Americans in 1865. In view of widespread want and some cases of starvation and in view of the increased rationing of 1866, it became obvious to Gregory's replacement, Gen. J. B. Kiddoo, that the undermanned, underfinanced bureau reached only a small portion of the state's freedmen. The limited bureau established only one hospital, which never employed more than five doctors at any one time and was disbanded in September 1866.[58]

Likewise, in its educational endeavors, the bureau met with limited success. Edwin M. Wheelock, first superintendent of freedmen's schools in Texas, experienced difficulties in finding teachers and securing school supplies. He also found that the majority of white Texans opposed black education, which presented problems that would continue throughout the Reconstruction period. Nevertheless, Wheelock established the first black school in the state, with an initial enrollment of eighty pupils, at Galveston in September. With only limited income from tuition charges of $1.50 per month from each student, bureau schools reached few blacks in 1865. By October, Wheelock maintained five day, night, or Sabbath schools, with four teachers and an enrollment of 264. The bureau had increased the number to twelve, with nine teachers and 615 students by Christmas.[59]

To black Texans, the early absence of Freedmen's Bureau activity only mirrored similar developments which had occurred in the state in the first seven months after emancipation. Largely, African Americans found it possible to achieve their aspirations only in a most limited way. They hoped that freedom would bring economic and educational opportunity, religious autonomy, and family stability along with legal and political rights. True, they acquired more control over their family and social life and more freedom of movement and of expression, but only if they used their imagination could African Americans consider themselves free men. A majority of individual whites, the state government, the Johnson administration, and the army worked to limit black freedom. Whether they were city officials trying to force blacks out of urban areas, planters seeking to control black labor, or army officers wanting "order," Anglos discriminated against the new freedmen. Some whites who could not accept black emancipation committed barbarities on African Americans, including murder whenever they wanted to "thin out niggers a little." Blacks found little relief. Self-help associations slowly developed, and a few Unionists offered aid. The early months of emancipation revealed the tensions between black hopes and white fears which would influence efforts by freedmen as they sought to fulfill their aspirations in the decades to follow.

Notes

1. Ernest Wallace, *Texas in Turmoil* (Austin, 1965), 165.
2. *Galveston Tri-Weekly News*, June 30, 1865.
3. Statement of Will Adams, Federal Writers' Project, "A Folk History of Slavery in the United States from Interviews with Former Slaves" (Washington, 1941), Texas Narratives, XVI, pt. 1, 3, hereafter abbreviated as "Slave Narratives," Texas.
4. B. A. Botkin (ed.), *Lay My Burden Down: A Folk History of Slavery* (Chicago, 1945), 236–237.
5. Statement of William M. Adams, "Slave Narratives," Texas, XVI, pt. 1, 11; statement of Armstead Barrett, "Slave Narratives," Texas, XVI, pt. 1, 47–48; statement of Tom Holland, "Slave Narratives," Texas, XVI, pt. 2, 144–147; Walter Cotton, *History of Negroes of Limestone County* (Mexia, Texas, 1939), 11.
6. Statement of Sarah Ford, "Slave Narratives," Texas, XVI, pt. 2, 46.
7. Amelia Barr, *All the Days of My Life: An Autobiography* (New York, 1913), 251.
8. Allen W. Trelease, *White Terror: The Ku Klux Klan Conspiracy and Southern Reconstruction* (New York, 1971), xvii.
9. *New Orleans Tribune*, June 11, 17, 18 and August 5, 1865; F. Duggan to James Kirkman, August 1, 1867, Letters Sent, Sub-Assistant Commissioner, Columbia, Texas, Bureau of Refugees, Freedmen, and Abandoned

Land, Record Group 105, National Archives, Washington, D.C., hereafter abbreviated BRFAL, RG 105, NA.

10. *Houston Tri-Weekly Telegraph,* October 6, 1865; William F. Fleming, "San Antonio: The History of a Military City, 1865–1880" (unpublished Ph.D. dissertation, University of Pennsylvania, 1963), 29–30; Louis Constant to Andrew J. Hamilton, October 18, 1865, Andrew J. Hamilton Governor's Correspondence, Archives, Texas State Library, Austin, Texas.

11. Statement of Jacob Branch, "Slave Narratives," Texas, XVI, pt. 1, 142; statement of Sarah Allen, "Slave Narratives," Texas, XVI, pt. 1, 12–13; statement of Joe Barnes, "Slave Narratives," Texas, XVI, pt. 1, 46; Botkin (ed.), *Lay My Burden Down,* 229; William Ballinger Diary, July 11, 17, 1865, William Ballinger Papers, Archives, University of Texas Library, Austin, Texas; for a tabular analysis of black population trends in Texas from 1850 to 1930 see Mattie Bell, "The Growth and Distribution of the Texas Population" (unpublished M.A. thesis, Baylor University, 1935), 126–136.

12. Botkin (ed.), *Lay My Burden Down,* 223.

13. *Houston Tri-Weekly Telegraph,* June 30, July 12, October 6, 1865; *New York Times,* July 17, 1865; *San Antonio Herald,* October 14, December 29, 1865; Byron Porter to A. B. Coggeshall, October 15, 1866, Letters Sent, Sub-Assistant Commissioner, Austin, Texas, BRFAL, RG 105, NA.

14. Amelia Barr to Jennie, June 3, 1865, Amelia Barr Papers, Archives, University of Texas Library.

15. *Houston Tri-Weekly Telegraph,* July 10, 12, 1865; *Huntsville Item,* July 14, 1865.

16. *Flake's Daily Bulletin,* July 6, September 1, 1865.

17. Statement of Minerva Bendy, "Slave Narratives," Texas, XVI, pt. 1, 68–69; statement of Armstead Barrett, "Slave Narratives," Texas, XVI, pt. 1, 47; statement of Fred Brown, "Slave Narratives," Texas, XVI, pt. 1, 159; statement of Sarah Ford, "Slave Narratives," Texas, XVI, pt. 2, 46; statement of Eli Davison, "Slave Narratives," Texas, XVI, pt. 1, 295–296.

18. Botkin (ed.), *Lay My Burden Down,* 247.

19. Charles E. Culver to Charles Garretson, November 1, 1867, Letters Sent, Sub-Assistant Commissioner, Cotton Gin, Texas, BRFAL, RG 105, NA.

20. Statement of Lucy Thomas, "Slave Narratives," Texas, XVI, pt. 4, 90; statement of Ella Washington, "Slave Narratives," Texas, XVI, pt. 1, 133.

21. James McCleery to J. W. Alvord, September 7, 1869, Letters Sent, Superintendent of Education, Shreveport, Louisiana, BRFAL, RG 105, NA; *Harrison Flag* (Marshall), May 2, 1867; statement of John Love, "Slave Narratives," Texas, XVI, pt. 3, 26; Botkin (ed.), *Lay My Burden Down,* 76, 247.

22. Statement of Elige Davison, "Slave Narratives," Texas, XVI, pt. 1, 298.

23. *Houston Tri-Weekly Telegraph,* June 5, 28, 30, October 20, 1865; *Flake's Daily Bulletin,* June 8, July 10, 12, 1865.

24. Ballinger Diary, May 13, 1865, Ballinger Papers.

25. Barr to Jennie, October 25, 1866, Barr Papers.

26. *Flake's Weekly Bulletin,* November 19, 1865, February 7, 21, 1866; *San Antonio Weekly Herald,* August 31, 1865.

27. William L. Richter, "The Army in Texas During Reconstruction, 1865–1870" (unpublished Ph.D. dissertation, Louisiana State University, 1971), 203.

28. *San Antonio Daily Herald,* September 2, 1865.

29. *Galveston Tri-Weekly News,* October 13, August 25, 1865; Porter to Chancey Morse, February 1, 1866, Letters Sent, Sub-Assistant Commissioner, Houston, Texas, BRFAL, RG 105, NA.
30. Sallie M. Lentz, "Highlights of Early Harrison County," *Southwestern Historical Quarterly,* LXI (October 1957), 254; Fleming, "San Antonio: The History of a Military City, 1865–1880," 31.
31. *Galveston Tri-Weekly News,* October 13, 1865; *Flake's Daily Bulletin,* July 29, 1865.
32. Jacob DeGress to E. M. Gregory, October 24, 1865, Letters Sent, Provost Marshall of the District of East Texas, BRFAL, RG 105, NA; U.S., House of Representatives, *House Executive Documents,* 39th Cong., 2d Sess., 1866 (Serial 1292), Document No. 61, 1–4.
33. B. F. Barkley to Hamilton, October 30, 1865, D. B. Lucky to Hamilton, October 16, 1865, Hamilton Governor's Correspondence; *Houston Tri-Weekly Telegraph,* July 17, 1865.
34. Statement of Armstead Barrett, "Slave Narratives," Texas, XVI, pt. 1, 47; statement of Tom Holland, "Slave Narratives," Texas, XVI, pt. 2, 146.
35. Claude Elliott, "The Freedmen's Bureau in Texas," *Southwestern Historical Quarterly,* LVI (July 1952), 6.
36. See complaint books, 1865–1868, Sub-Assistant Commissioner, Houston, Texas, BRFAL, RG 105, NA; *Galveston Tri-Weekly News,* October 13, 1865; Lenard B. Groce Diary, December 18, 1866, January 15, 1867, Lenard B. Groce Papers, Archives, University of Texas Library.
37. U.S. House of Representatives, *House Reports,* 39th Cong., 1st Sess., 1866 (Serial 1273), Report No. 30, 46–47, 77.
38. Statement of John Bates, "Slave Narratives," Texas, XVI, pt. 1, 52; U.S. House of Representatives, *House Executive Documents,* 39th Cong., 1st Sess., 1866 (Serial 1256), Document No. 70, 146–147; *Harrison Flag,* May 2, 1867; DeGress to Provost Marshall, Millican, October 31, 1865, DeGress to Gregory, November 30, 1865, Letters Sent, Sub-Assistant Commissioner, Houston, Texas, BRFAL, RG 105, NA.
39. Statement of Anderson Edwards, "Slave Narratives," Texas, XVI, pt. 2, 8; statement of Josie Brown, "Slave Narratives," Texas, XVI, pt. 1, 164; Botkin (ed.), *Lay My Burden Down,* 233; Barkley to Hamilton, October 30, 1865, Hamilton Governor's Correspondence.
40. Porter to Albert Evans, December 28, 1866, Letters Sent, Sub-Assistant Commissioner, Austin, Texas, James Oakes to Kirkman, July 31, 1867, Sub-Assistant Commissioner, Austin, Texas, BRFAL, RG 105, NA; Botkin (ed.), *Lay My Burden Down,* 76.
41. *Flake's Daily Bulletin,* December 3, 1865.
42. DeGress to Gregory, October 19, November 30, 1865, Letters Sent, Sub-Assistant Commissioner, Houston, Texas, BRFAL, RG 105, NA.
43. Statement of Susan Merritt, "Slave Narratives," Texas, XVI, pt. 3, 78.
44. *Flake's Daily Bulletin,* August 2, 1865.
45. U.S. House of Representatives, *House Reports,* 39th Cong., 1st Sess., 1866 (Serial 1273), Report No. 30, 39; U.S. Senate, *Senate Executive Documents,* 39th Cong., 1st Sess., 1866 (Serial 1238), Document No. 27, 81–86, 147–150.
46. *New Orleans Tribune,* December 16, 1865; Constant to Hamilton, October 18, 1865, Hamilton Governor's Correspondence.

47. Charles F. Rand to Kirkman, April 30, 1867, Letters Sent, Sub-Assistant Commissioner, Marshall, Texas, BRFAL, RG 105, NA.
48. Wallace, *Texas in Turmoil,* 164–169; Hamilton's Proclamation to Freedmen, November 17, 1865, Hamilton Governor's Correspondence.
49. Hiram Christian to Hamilton, October 21, 1865, Hamilton Governor's Correspondence; U.S. House of Representatives, *House Executive Documents,* vol. III, pt. 1, 40th Cong., 3d Sess., 1868 (Serial 1367), Document No. 1, 1052; DeGress to Gregory, October 24, 1865, Letters Sent, Sub-Assistant Commissioner, Houston, Texas, BRFAL, RG 105, NA.
50. Robert W. Shook, "The Federal Military in Texas, 1865–1870," *Texas Military History,* VI (Spring 1967), 6; *New York Times,* July 17, 1865.
51. Bell I. Wiley, "Billy Yank and the Black Folk," *Journal of Negro History,* XXXVI (January 1951), 35–52; Porter to Gregory, January 13, 1866, Letters Sent, Sub-Assistant Commissioner, Houston, Texas, BRFAL, RG 105, NA.
52. James E. Sefton, *The United States Army and Reconstruction, 1865–1877* (Baton Rouge, 1967), 45.
53. William T. Sherman to John Sherman, February 23, 1866, in Rachel Sherman Thorndike (ed.), *The Sherman Letters* (New York, 1969), 263.
54. See Arlen L. Fowler, *The Black Infantry in the West, 1869–1891* (Westport, Connecticut, 1971), 139.
55. James D. Richardson (comp.), *Messages and Papers of the Presidents* (10 vols.; Washington, 1904), VI, 321–323.
56. Sefton, *The United States Army and Reconstruction, 1865–1877,* Appendix B, 261–262; Shook, "The Federal Military in Texas, 1865–1870," 18–19.
57. Elliott, "The Freedmen's Bureau in Texas," 4, 24; Shook, "The Federal Military in Texas, 1865–1870," 22.
58. U.S. Senate, *Senate Executive Documents,* 39th Cong., 2d Sess., 1867 (Serial 1276), Document No. 6, 151; U.S. House of Representatives, *House Executive Documents,* vol. III, 39th Cong., 2d Sess., 1867 (Serial 1285), Document No. 1, 721.
59. U.S. Senate, *Senate Executive Documents,* 39th Cong., 2d Sess., 1867 (Serial 1276), Document No. 6, 148–150; *New York Times,* February 19, 1866; C. S. Tambling to George Whipple, December 1, 1865, Texas Correspondence, American Missionary Association, Archives, Amistad Research Center, Dillard University, New Orleans, Louisiana.

The Evolution of Black Political Participation in Reconstruction Texas

MERLINE PITRE

HISTORIANS HAVE DEVOTED A GOOD DEAL OF ATtention in recent years to the question of Southern Reconstruction politics. The Republicans who initiated, shaped, and ultimately lost control of Reconstruction programs in the former Confederate states have been the focus of much historical controversy. While recognizing that Southern Republicans everywhere consisted of a coalition of newly enfranchised blacks, Northern carpetbaggers, and Southern white scalawags, scholars have disagreed and continue to disagree sharply over the origins, characters, and effectiveness of these political groups. Despite such disagreements, or perhaps in part because of them, an increasingly refined picture gradually has emerged on the identity, ideology, and political behavior of Southern Republicans, especially black Republicans.

True, recent historians have had little trouble dispelling the myth of Black Reconstruction, but they have been less successful in determining how blacks helped to shape Reconstruction in a state such as Texas which had the smallest number of blacks of any Confederate state. The purpose of this article is to shed light not only on the ideology and political behavior of blacks who served in the Reconstruction Convention of 1868–1869, but also on the role they played in helping to reconstruct their lives, their communities, and their state.

Historical and Biographical Background of Black Constitutional Delegates

The blacks of Texas, like those in many other Southern states, did not take an active part in politics until the passage of the Reconstruction Acts of 1867. These acts, which declared all previous actions of the state null and void and called for the drafting of new constitutions, made it possible for blacks to become actors rather than merely objects in politics. So, in keeping with their idea of making political rights a reality, Texas blacks went to the polls on February 10, 1868, and not only cast 35,952 votes in favor of a constitutional convention, but elected nine blacks to serve as constitutional delegates.

To many white natives, events in the Lone Star State in that winter month clashed sharply with fond remembrances of the old regime and the people they thought they knew best. The sudden politicalization of their ex-slaves was inexplicable. Unable to understand the activities of blacks, whites conjured up powerful and tenacious images about blacks in general and black delegates in particular. Created by the Democratic and conservative white Republican press, and nurtured by succeeding generations of historians and publicists, depictions of these black delegates as poor, ignorant ex-slaves ascending straight from the fields to the legislative halls were rife. These traditional images have been sustained to the present, largely by continued ignorance of who these delegates were and the roles they played in the constitutional convention.

To get a better understanding of the men who helped to draft the constitution of 1869, it is necessary to take a look at their backgrounds. The black who probably stood out most in the convention, by virtue of his training and background, was George T. Ruby. A free-born mulatto, Ruby was a native of New York. After acquiring a sound liberal arts education in Maine, Ruby journeyed to Haiti where he worked as a correspondent for the *Pine and Palm,* a New England newspaper edited by James Redpath. Ruby's job was to collect information about Haiti and send it to the United States to be read by black Americans who were searching for an alternative to slavery and discrimination.[1]

After the American Civil War, Ruby returned to the United States and settled in Louisiana where he was employed in 1866 as a schoolteacher. In September of that year Ruby left Louisiana and became an agent for the Texas Freedmen's Bureau in Galveston. One year later, he became President of the Loyal Union League of Texas. With a firm base in the urban setting, his acquaintance with leading Republicans of the state, and his support of blacks, Ruby at twenty-seven years of age was elected as a delegate to the Republican National Convention of 1868. In 1869, he was elected from a predominantly white district, which consisted of Galveston and Brazoria counties, to the Texas Senate. After failing in his bid for re-election to the Senate in 1874, Ruby returned to Louisiana.[2]

Another black elected to the legislature was James McWashington. He represented Montgomery County, where blacks outnumbered whites by 250 votes in 1868. McWashington was born a slave in Alabama but had lived in Texas sixteen years before his election to the convention. After serving as a delegate, he remained active in politics, attending many of the Republican Party's conventions. Siding with Andrew Hamilton in 1869, McWashington ran on the conservative ticket for a House seat, but met with defeat.[3]

From Harris County came Charles W. Bryant, a minister and a native of Kentucky. Born a slave, he became an agent for the Freedmen's Bureau of Texas before entering politics in 1869. Harris and Montgomery counties elected him as their delegate to the constitutional convention of 1868–1869. Though Bryant was a young man of thirty-eight years when elected to the convention, after his tenure in this body he did not become involved in politics again.[4]

Benjamin Franklin Williams was one of the most active black delegates at the Reconstruction Convention. He was born a slave in Brunswick County, Virginia, in 1819. As a slave, he was taken to South Carolina, then to Tennessee in 1830, before being brought to Colorado County, Texas, in 1859. After Emancipation, Williams became a traveling Methodist minister. He was the officiating minister when the Wesley Methodist Chapel in Austin was established in 1868, a church, according to the *Galveston Daily News,* which forbade blacks from attending if they were not Republicans. Combining religion with politics, Williams became a militant spokesman for his race. As early as 1868 he served as vice president of the Loyal Union League and as such kept the white Unionists abreast of what was happening in the black belt area. It was Williams' involvement in politics that won him a seat at the constitutional convention at the age of forty-eight.[5]

Apparently Williams made a good impression on his fellow blacks while serving in the convention because he was subsequently elected by Lavaca and Colorado counties to the 12th Legislature; by Waller, Fort Bend, and Wharton to the 16th; and by the counties of Waller and Fort Bend to the 19th. Likewise, Williams' popularity was manifested among his colleagues in the 12th Legislature when they nominated him for Speaker of the House; he lost by only three votes. It was Williams, the land speculator, mechanic, and engineer, along with other blacks, who was instrumental in the settlement and development of Kendleton, Texas.[6]

Two other delegates of note were Sheppard Mullins and Benjamin O. Watrous. Mullins was born a slave in Lawrence County, Alabama, in 1829. He was still a bondsman when he arrived in Texas in 1854. The skills of a blacksmith, which he acquired while in bondage, served him well in freedom. After the Civil War, he labored in his own behalf and acquired several lots as well as a block of land in Waco in McLennan County, Texas.[7] Mullins was elected to serve in the second session of the convention when McLennan County chose him as their delegate upon the death of the incumbent.

Mullins' colleague, Benjamin O. Watrous, was born a slave in Tennessee, where he was known as Ben Carter. After being set free he took the name of his last owner, John Watrous. A wheelwright and property owner, Watrous was also a minister. He had lived in Texas twelve years when Washington County chose him as their delegate to the convention.[8]

A dearth of biographical information exists on the other delegates: Mitchell Kendall, Ralph Long, Stephen Curtis, and Wiley Johnson. Kendall, a blacksmith from Georgia, represented Harris and Panola counties. He was fifty years of age when elected to the convention, but he probably was the wealthiest of the delegates. Despite his birth as a slave, while serving as a delegate his assets were valued at $2400.[9] His colleague, Ralph Long, was not as wealthy. Long, of Limestone County, was a Tennessean by birth and a farmer by occupation. At twenty-five years of age, Long was the youngest member of the convention. He had lived in Texas for only two of those twenty-five years before he became a delegate.[10]

In contrast to Long's youth, the oldest black man to serve in the constitutional convention was Stephen Curtis, who was sixty years of age. He was a carpenter by trade and was born a slave in Virginia. He became involved in politics almost from the organization of the Republican Party in Texas. He could be found at most, if not all, Republican gatherings held throughout the Reconstruction era.[11] Wiley Johnson, a man much younger than Curtis, represented Harris County in the convention and was a shoemaker by profession. His slave birth took place in Arkansas.[12]

Of the stereotypes drawn about these men, namely that they were a group of illiterate ex-slaves and penniless farmers, only one's *antebellum* status as a slave stands up to close scrutiny. As to occupations, there were two blacksmiths, three ministers, one carpenter, one teacher, and three farmers. Of the ten blacks who served in this convention, only three could not read or write. This does not mean that the other blacks were highly educated, but with the exception of Ruby, who was a teacher, all the others had acquired a rudimentary education or better.

As to the image of a penniless worker, at least three blacks had some form of property, real or personal, with the assets of one totaling $2400. Although the majority of these blacks did not own property and although the property held by the minority of them was minimal as compared to that of whites, these blacks cannot be classified as penniless farmers who were not interested in the fiscal policies and economic development of the state. In truth, these men were not drawn from a middle class because none existed in Texas at that time, but rather they came from a rank that was far below the ruling white class and a little above the black masses.

Blacks, Allies, and Adversaries at the Constitutional Convention

The process by which black delegates arrived at their political opinions generally involved a realistic appraisal of their vital self-interests. When the convention assembled in Austin on June 11, 1868, there were four major blocs—individuals with similar voting patterns. The first and largest bloc consisted of individuals who were loyal to Governor Elisha Pease and who probably best represented statewide Unionist opinions. This bloc supported the basic political and civil rights of blacks as defined in the Civil Rights Act of 1866, but was not willing to move beyond that point.

The second bloc represented the interests associated with the more populous part of the state—East Texas. These individuals were hostile to the interests of blacks, in large part because the majority of blacks resided in that section of the state. Fearing the potential of black power in that area, they rejected the civil rights of blacks as defined by the federal government and looked for ways to avoid its implementation.

The third bloc was sectional in that it consisted of individuals who resided in the Western counties that made up the Fourth Congressional District. This group held the broadest view of the rights of blacks among whites in the convention. Moreover, they made more concessions in the areas of office-holding and education to blacks than did any other group. It goes without saying, then, that they became the blacks' strongest ally.

Unlike the first three blocs that typified political divisions that existed prior to the Civil War, the fourth group consisted of the black delegates, who operated in a manner designed to achieve the interests of blacks. Among other things, the blacks desired political and civil rights and worked for free public education.[13] In keeping with their interests, blacks took an active part in the *ab initio* controversy, the first major issue to appear before the convention.

The *ab initio* controversy began when Andrew J. Evans of McLennan County introduced a resolution which stated that since the United States government was constituted by the people and their representatives in Washington, rather than by the states, "the constitutional convention of Texas should not recognize or sanction the Ordinance of Secession on March, 1861, or any bills, laws, ordinances, acts, resolutions, or rules that were passed, made or enacted since the passage of the Ordinance."[14] In other words, Evans' proposal called for the nullification of the civil government which existed in Texas during the period of 1861–1866.

Since rejection or approval of the *ab initio* would determine which direction the constitutional convention would take, the delegates took a long time discussing it and were mixed in their reactions toward *ab initio*. Some sided with Evans because they wanted the nullification of laws which granted lucrative railroad charters to a group of former Confederates; others wanted to invalidate land seizures made during the war; still others (blacks) joined Evans because the school fund was attached to *ab initio* and they believed that restoration of the school fund would hasten the organization of public schools. Conversely, many Democrats opposed *ab initio* on principle.

Because of the diverse interests represented at the convention, it soon became apparent to the Republicans that Evans' bill would not pass unless it was altered. Thus, a number of substitute bills were introduced to keep the ideas of *ab initio* alive. After a lengthy discussion, the convention adopted an amendment which stated that the Texas constitution would make valid all legislative enactments and decisions since secession, insofar as they did not interfere with existing federal laws, aid rebellion, or "operate to bring harm to any class of citizens."

That blacks were not satisfied with the amendment became evident when six out of nine—Ruby, Williams, Long, Johnson, Bryant, and Watrous—voted in a losing cause to defeat this measure. Not willing to accept defeat, Ralph Long offered a resolution similar to Evans' one week later, that would declare invalid all obligations incurred by the purchase of slaves or debt payments made with Confederate money and asking to set the statute of limitation ahead to include the war years. This motion was defeated by almost two to one.[15]

After the *ab initio* issue was settled, blacks and other delegates turned their attention to other matters. Because blacks had supported West Texans on *ab initio,* the West Texans came to the aid of blacks in trying to get civil rights clauses inserted into the constitution. When B. F. Williams introduced a resolution to ensure that blacks would have equal access to public accommodations, his bill was referred to the committee on General Provisions, a committee which was controlled by a westerner, Morgan Hamilton. Hamilton knew that on its merits Williams' bill would not pass; therefore, he tried to attach it to Section Four of the proposed Bill of Rights of the constitution, which was being drafted and discussed. Section Four, if adopted as originally proposed, would have gone beyond equal protection before the law to equal treatment in the areas of the private sector.

Section Four provoked outrage among most white delegates—Democrats, Conservatives, and Republicans alike—because they viewed this section as an attempt to accord blacks social equality. Thus, barring some form of compromise, this bill was doomed to failure. Because Edmund Davis, a westerner who controlled that bloc, realized that this section would never pass as written, he offered a substitute bill which outlawed racial discrimination but authorized the owners whose facilities were in question to prescribe rules and regulations necessary to secure "comfort, good order, and decency."

In a word, this bill committed the state to civil rights on paper, but not in practice; and at the same time the state took a laissez-faire attitude toward the owners. Still, the majority of the delegates refused to pass even this modified proposal. They substituted their own bill which only recognized the "equality of all persons before the law."[16] But all was not lost for blacks; while they failed to get Williams' resolution incorporated into the constitution, they nevertheless secured a political ally in West Texas.

Bills, Resolutions, and Declarations Initiated by Blacks

Contrary to the opinion of Ferdinand Flake, editor of the *Flake's Daily Bulletin,* who asserted that black delegates did not add one constructive idea to the work of the convention, blacks did offer some resolutions, declarations, and bills which showed not only merit and thought, but also their concerns for the people they represented. Thus, early in the first session, and then again in the second session, George T. Ruby offered a declaration that "no one should prevent any qualified elector of the state from free exercise of the elective franchise by violence or bribery, or by threat of violence."[17]

When Ruby moved to suspend the rules to take up discussion on the declaration, his motion was defeated by a vote of eighteen to forty-four. It is interesting to note that only the so-called black radicals—Long, Ruby, Williams, Watrous, and Bryant—voted for this motion. The other blacks, for some unknown reasons, did not feel it necessary to suspend the rules at this time. As a result, this declaration never reached the floor; instead it got lost in the legislative shuffle.

Concomitant with their efforts to achieve suffrage, blacks were also concerned with the right to hold office. Hence, Watrous presented a resolution to the convention urging that the right to hold office be extended to all men without regard to race, color, or creed. This act was referred to the Committee on Bills of Rights, reported back favorably, and incorporated in Article I, Section 2, of the Constitution.[18]

Blacks were not only concerned with the problems of blacks, but also with promoting the general welfare of the state. This idea became evident in resolutions they presented to regulate the practice of medicine and law. For example, B. F. Williams proposed that "no one should be allowed to practice medicine in the state without having first attained a diploma from some medical college or otherwise a certificate from some regular medical board." Williams' resolution called for a penalty of $500 or five years in jail if one were found in violation of the law.[19]

Wiley Johnson drafted a similar resolution with regard to lawyers: "That no person shall be eligible to the office of judge of the Supreme Court, or Criminal Court without being admitted to the bar of Counselor-of-law at the Supreme Court of the state."[20]

Discussion of marriage laws and reform was also crucial to black delegates. McWashington and Bryant championed the cause in this regard. McWashington first offered a resolution that "all marriages solemnized among free people of color during slavery should be declared legal and binding and that all the children born to that marriage should be declared legitimate."[21] After no action was taken on this resolution, Bryant of Harris County offered one of his own. His resolution called for making illegitimate black children, or children of slave parents, legitimate with all the legal rights of inheritance upon the marriage of their parents.[22] Unlike McWashington's resolution, Bryant's was adopted and was incorporated in Article XII, Section 27, of the constitution. McWashington would not be too easily silenced nor discouraged on marriage reform. He later proposed that the personal property of a lady, acquired either before or after marriage, should not come under jurisdiction of her husband.[23]

Activities of Blacks in the Second Session of the Convention

It should be noted that the convention delegates were extremely dilatory in drafting a constitution. It was not until after one session of dealing with *ab initio,* listening to resolutions and declarations, and another of discussing the issue of division that the delegates got down to work on drafting the constitution on January 27, 1869. After that date, the convention moved rapidly with each section and each article because various acts and provisions of the constitution had been worked over in committee.

Only the question of suffrage provoked any real discussion. Radicals and black delegates supported a provision that established a system of registration and disfranchisement that would exclude all federal and state officers, ministers, and newspapermen who had favored and openly supported rebellion. But the Conservatives, who managed to get moderate Republicans on their side, offered a substitute motion that allowed all men to vote except those disqualified by the United States Constitution.[24] Rather than accept defeat on this issue, Edmund J. Davis and the Radicals attempted to adjourn the convention instead of finishing its work.

When the convention completed its work on February 6,

1869, only forty-five delegates willingly signed the constitution. Edmund Davis, president of the convention, signed only upon the orders of General E. R. Canby. Other than Davis, there were only two white Radicals, W. Frank Carter and William R. Tyle, and five blacks, Stephen Curtis, Mitchell Kendall, Wiley Johnson, Benjamin O. Watrous, and James McWashington. Other individuals who signed included four conservatives and thirty-four white Republicans who can be classified as moderates.[25]

The blacks who did not sign objected to the constitution on the grounds that enfranchising ex-rebels might cause them to become strong enough to regain political control of the state, to violate the will of Congress, and to suppress the rights of blacks. Thus, Ruby and Wiley Johnson signed a protest letter saying that "not only the rights of loyal blacks and whites are imperiled by this constitution, but that the expressed will of Congress has been ignored."[26] In the same vein, B. F. Williams wrote, "I was under the impression that I voted for a substitute that would include the future, not the past; I protest against the past."[27] Ralph Long joined in written protest with Edmund Davis, stating that he was opposed to the constitution "except only that part which charges deception and intimidation on the part of its members."[28]

Unhappy with the constitution largely because it did not disfranchise all ex-rebels, Ruby joined forces with Edmund Davis and Morgan Hamilton of the Radical group in sending a commission to Washington to lobby against acceptance of the document. When Congress turned a deaf ear to their plea, this dissident faction accepted the constitution as a *fait accompli,* and fielded a slate of candidates to be elected at the same time as the constitutional referendum.

Despite the fact the Texas constitution was the least radical of the constitutions drawn up at that time, the delegates to the 1868–1869 convention established a workable structure of government which many authorities regard as the "best constitution" the state has ever had. As for blacks, this document recognized the quality of all persons before the law; proposed that office holding and jury service be open to blacks; and that equal educational opportunities and general civil rights be accorded to the freedmen. The education article provided for the opening of state-supported schools on an equal basis, regardless of color or previous condition of servitude. Despite the convention's leniency on the suffrage section, it granted the right to vote to "every male citizen of the United States of age twenty-one and upward." More importantly, the delegates were able to accomplish their primary goal—to draft a constitution which was ratified by the electorate on November 9, 1869, and which was accepted by Congress.[29]

After helping to write a constitution which would serve as the organic law of Texas for six years, the black delegates returned to their organizational work in the hinterlands, towns, and cities. They helped prepare the way for themselves as well as for scores of others who were elected to state and local offices under both Republican and Democratic regimes. This constitutional convention not only gave black delegates experience in politics, but the biographical and political profiles of these delegates also provide one with some indication of the makeup of black leadership as well.

If one were to judge future leaders based on the backgrounds of these constitutional delegates, it would be safe to say that the leadership cadre would come from the ranks of the ex-slaves; that the average age would be somewhere in the mid-thirties; and that the majority would not be native-born Texans. Indeed, this seems to have been the norm in Reconstruction and post-Reconstruction legislatures in Texas. Out of a total of forty-one black lawmakers who sat in the legislature between 1868 and 1898, all except five had been slaves, seventeen were mulattoes, and only five were native Texans. Moreover, the majority of them served for only one term in the legislature. The same analogy holds true for the majority of these black delegates. The larger percentage of them did not run for the legislature in 1869. As a matter of fact, most of them did not seek public office after they left the convention. However, it was their hope that the constitution that they helped to draft would be implemented with the help of black lawmakers in the Reconstruction Legislature.

Notes

1. Randall Woods, "George T. Ruby: A Black Militant in the White Business Community," *Red River Valley Historical Review*, I (1974), 269–280; Barry Crouch, "Self Determination and Local Black Leaders in Texas," *Phylon*, XXXIX (December, 1978), 344–355; J. Mason Brewer, *Negro Legislators of Texas and Their Descendants* (Dallas, 1935), 20, 27, 47–48, 115, 125.
2. G. T. Ruby to Charles Garretson (Acting Adjutant General), September 14, October 17, 1867, Bureau of Refugees, Freedmen, and Abandoned Lands, Record Group 105 (National Archives, Washington, D.C.); *Austin Daily State Journal*, October 13, 1870; *Austin Weekly Republican*,

August 29, 1868, July 18, 1869; James M. Smallwood, *Time of Hope, Time of Despair: Black Texans During Reconstruction* (Port Washington, New York, 1981), 71, 91, 108, 138–141, 146–148.

3. Carl H. Moneyhon, *Republicanism in Reconstruction Texas* (Austin, 1980), 242; *Austin Weekly Republican,* April 24, July 18, 1868; Harrell T. Budd, "The Negro in Politics in Texas, 1867–1898" (M.A. Thesis, University of Texas at Austin, 1925), 18.

4. Brewer, *Negro Legislators of Texas,* 20, 23–24, 28, 115, 125; *Houston Telegraph,* February 16, 17, 18, 1866; *Flake's Daily Bulletin,* February 16, 17, 18, 1868; U.S. Congress, Senate Document, 40th Congress, 2nd Sess., No. 53 (Serial 1317); Moneyhon, *Republicanism in Reconstruction Texas,* 79.

5. Brewer, *Negro Legislators of Texas,* 20, 24, 47, 49, 53; *Houston Union,* July 6, 1870; *Austin Daily State Journal,* August 17, October 13, 1870; Clarence Wharton, *History of Fort Bend County* (San Antonio: Naylor Co., 1939), 187. See also B. F. Williams, "Circular of the Union League," James Newcomb Papers, Eugene Barker History Center, University of Texas at Austin; B. F. Williams to J. P. Newcomb, July 17, August 28, 1869, July 24, 1870, Newcomb Papers.

6. Texas Legislature, *House Journal of the 12th Legislature,* 1st Sess. (Austin, 1870), 1482.

7. *New National Era* (Washington, D.C.), June 16, 1870; Central Texas Genealogical Society, McLennan County, Texas, Cemetery Records, I (2 vols.; Waco, 1865), 87; Betty J. Sandlin, "The Texas Reconstruction Convention, 1865–1869" (Ph.D. Dissertation, Texas Tech University, 1970), 51.

8. Budd, "The Negro in Politics in Texas," 18; *The Austin Weekly Republican,* April 29, July 18, 1868; Moneyhon, *Republicanism in Reconstruction Texas,* 246.

9. Sandlin, "The Texas Reconstruction Convention," 231; Moneyhon, *Republicanism in Texas,* 241; *Austin Weekly Republican,* April 24, July 16, 1868.

10. Ray A. Walter, *History of Limestone County* (Austin, 1959), 56–58; Sandlin, "The Texas Reconstruction Convention," 278; Moneyhon, *Republicanism in Texas,* 242; *Grosbeck New Era,* July 29, 1876.

11. Budd, "The Negro in Politics in Texas," 19; Moneyhon, *Republicanism in Texas,* 238; *Austin Weekly Republican,* April 29, June 18, 1868.

12. Budd, "The Negro in Politics in Texas," 19; Brewer, *Negro Legislators of Texas,* 24, 125; Sandlin, "The Texas Reconstruction Convention," 213; Moneyhon, *Republicanism in Texas,* 242.

13. *Journal of the Reconstruction Convention of 1868–1869,* I (2 vols.; Austin, 1870), 12–17, 235, 696–697; *Galveston Daily News,* April 26, September 8, December 21, 1867; June 16, August 22, 1868; *Flake's Evening Bulletin,* April 22, May 6, 14, July 5, December 22, 1867; *Weekly Freeman's Press,* July 20, 1868, clipping in the E. J. Davis biographical file, Barker History Center.

14. *Journal of Reconstruction Convention,* I, 28, 275; Moneyhon, *Republicanism in Texas,* 86–87.

15. *Journal of Reconstruction Convention,* I, 794, 797, 921–922.

16. *Journal of Reconstruction Convention,* I, 235, 696–698; see also Article XII, Section 21 of the *Constitution of 1869.*

17. *Journal of Reconstruction Convention,* II, 510–511.

18. *Journal of Reconstruction Convention,* II, 308, 488; *Constitution of 1869,* Article I, Section 2.
19. *Journal of Reconstruction Convention,* II, 90.
20. *Journal of Reconstruction Convention,* II, 247; see also Article XII, Section 3 of *Constitution of 1869.*
21. *Journal of Reconstruction Convention,* I, 267.
22. *Journal of Reconstruction Convention,* I, 416; see also Article XII, Section 27, *Constitution of 1869.*
23. *Journal of Reconstruction Convention,* I, 456; see also Article XII, Section 14, *Constitution of 1869.*
24. *Journal of Reconstruction Convention,* II, 518–59, 527–529; *Galveston Daily News,* February 14, 1869; *Austin Weekly Republican,* January 23, 1869.
25. Sandlin, "Texas Reconstruction Convention," 213. Bryant did not cast a vote on the constitution because he had been expelled. However, given his record, it is logical to assume that had he remained in the convention, he would have sided with the "Radicals." Mullins, for some unknown reason, abstained from voting.
26. *Journal of Reconstruction Convention,* II, 520.
27. *Journal of Reconstruction Convention,* II, 520.
28. *Journal of Reconstruction Convention,* II, 520.
29. See *Constitution of 1869.*

The Violent Possibility
The Tenth Cavalry at Texarkana

GARNA L. CHRISTIAN

On a wintry afternoon in 1899 an animated group of East Texans crowded the Texarkana station platform and eagerly pushed toward the troop trains waiting to transport the Tenth Cavalry to garrisons across the state. From a distance the scene might have appeared a festive reunion or a farewell celebration. It was neither. The civilians angrily denounced the escape from arrest, with the aid of fellow enlisted men, of a member of the regiment that was returning triumphantly from the Spanish-American War. And from the train windows gleamed the barrels of government-issued rifles, mutely poised at the vocal throng. Already in motion was the chain of events that would ignite civilian-black military outbursts of violence in Texas communities at the turn of the century and foreshadow the nationwide urban riots of later decades.[1]

Recent acts of heroism in Cuba had garnered the black units governmental citations, public attention, and a curious mixture of admiration and suspicion, but that heralded tour of duty merely climaxed decades of little-noted danger and drudgery on the western frontier. While blacks had served in every American war since national independence, Congress delayed the formation of regular army organizations open to them until after the Civil War. Between 1866 and 1869 four black regiments were created, the Ninth and Tenth Cavalry and the Twenty-fourth and Twenty-fifth Infantry.[2]

Each unit served some time in Texas over the next fifteen years, then moved on to more remote areas of the West with the completion of the railroads and the final defeat of the Plains Indians. The duty included the laborious tasks of constructing and repairing roads, telegraph lines, and their own forts, while protecting railroads and often uncaring or antagonistic civilians from all manner of lawless elements.[3]

The black soldiers received little gratitude from the citizenry for these efforts. Indeed, part of the decision to station them in the sparsely populated West stemmed from their rejection by Eastern communities, both North and South. Until 1898 only one company of black troops was garrisoned at a post east of the Mississippi. Accordingly, "the Buffalo Soldiers," as the Indians dubbed them, served the nation in outbacks of Kansas, Oklahoma, Wyoming, Montana, and West and South Texas.[4]

Conditions of service ranged from barely tolerable to horrendous. Rations, equipment, and shelter usually failed to match even the meager standards accorded white soldiers. White officers, commanding blacks thought to be unfit to provide their own leadership, took pride in reputations as strict disciplinarians. Yet the limited opportunities for advancement, together with even bleaker possibilities in civilian life, contributed to a lower desertion rate among black troops than for their white counterparts.[5]

Racial prejudice often denied blacks the traditional military safety valve of carousing during off-duty hours in tolerant garrison towns. While the sight of fighting, stumbling white soldiers seldom drew excessive disapprobation from prospering merchants and secure citizens, raucous conduct on the part of African Americans reinforced negative racial stereotypes. When the political and business leaders of a town recognized the advantages of garrisoning troops near them, a spirit of cooperation between the civilians and military establishments acted to reduce the inevitable racial tensions. Otherwise, careless comments by community spokesmen or hostile press reporting signaled invitations to bored or vengeance-seeking sheepherders, cowboys, and even peace officers to victimize the black soldiers.[6]

Occasionally a particularly odious action on the part of civilians stirred the military to action. In 1881 Tenth Cavalry troops from Fort Concho shot up neighboring San Angelo, without casualties, after a string of racial incidents culminated in the murder of a comrade. In its fury the attack grimly predicted the "retaliatory violence" of the twentieth century, but the assault stood virtually alone, failing to spark the "contagion phenomenon" of later years. More typical was the tragedy at Fort McKavett, Texas, in 1870. There, without incident, a jury freed a white man who had killed three black soldiers, two of whom acted under orders to apprehend him.[7]

Racial clashes, as opposed to white harassment and violence, intensified with the Spanish-American War, partly because of black resistance. All four black regiments, and several African American volunteer units, served with distinction in the brief war of 1898. Heroism at El Caney, Las Guasimas, San Juan Hill, and elsewhere brought plaudits from the government and much of the white press and public. Newly confident of his worth and potential, the black Spanish-American War veteran, like his counterparts of the twentieth century, expected the democratic rhetoric of the war to translate into constitutional guarantees for black Americans.[8]

The rising expectations of the servicemen collided with the intensification of a national trend toward further segregation and discrimination. Racial ideologies, the strains of industrialization and immigration, and political threats to white supremacy converged with emasculating court decisions to push blacks farther into the lower reaches of society. While the complexity of the far ranging forces obscured their full impact and direction, perceptive blacks and whites recognized the immediate signs of decline in the former's fragile status.[9]

The black soldier suffered relatively less than most members of his race. As a representative of the national government, usually serving hundreds or thousands of miles from home, he enjoyed a measure of immunity from local and familial pressures. His uniform, military bearing, and record of achievement cast him inexorably as a role model for the African American community. While many whites felt uncomfortable with any challenge to the existing racial order, some, particularly in the traditional South, perceived the black soldier as a distinct threat to their way of life and resolved to humble him.[10]

With the Spanish forces in disarray, black regiments were ordered to West and South Texas after an absence of almost two decades. Contrary to the experience of the 1870s, violence erupted at a number of sites following the appearance of the troops. Members of the Twenty-fifth Infantry assaulted a peace officer at Laredo in October, 1899, following complaints of police brutality, and they killed a lawman at El Paso in February, 1900, while attempting to release a comrade from custody. Ninth Cavalry troopers turned a Gatling gun on Rio Grande City in November, 1899, to counter a suspected civilian onslaught on Fort Ringgold. These relatively obscure incidents preceded the widely publicized Brownsville Raid of August, 1906, in which unidentified soldiers of the Twenty-fifth Infantry allegedly invaded the South Texas town, killing one civilian and wounding another. In turn sixteen Houstonians lost their lives eleven years later when armed members of the Twenty-fourth Infantry sought revenge on the police.[11]

The return of the Tenth Cavalry to Texas in early 1899 offers an insight into the accumulative effects of racial tension and the selective perception of participants and onlookers. When twenty rail cars delivered the regiment from Huntsville, Alabama, to Texarkana, Texas, on January 31, local whites and black soldiers had not encountered each other in years. Yet neither group came unencumbered to the other. Whites sought to block any encroachments on East Texas mores. The soldiers carried with them recent psychological scars from Alabama and Mississippi.[12]

Huntsville had proven an unwelcome community for the Tenth Cavalry, not only from the standpoint of the white citizenry but also from an unexpected military source, the provost guard. Several troopers celebrated their arrival in October, 1898, by seeking out the restricted zone, an area reserved for the pleasure of white customers only. An altercation ensued and the military police arrested one of the sojourners. At that point armed comrades of the apprehended man interfered, and in a confusing exchange of fire, they mortally wounded two guards. Three of the soldiers sustained wounds, while the others disappeared into the crowd. In a military investigation, witnesses failed to identify the fugitives.[13]

Although the tragedy involved only a few men of the Tenth Cavalry, animosity between the regiment and the white Sixteenth Infantry guards continued. Captain S. L. Woodward accused the latter of singling out members of his unit for weapons searches at a circus performance in Huntsville. "There need be no fear," the officer assured a superior, "that the Tenth Cavalry will behave more disorderly or require more watching than other organizations . . . [or] appear in the streets . . . mounted, drunk, falling from horses, and vomiting over themselves as was the case yesterday . . . with men of another regiment."[14]

Controversy and peril had dogged the black regiment into Texas. As the troops passed through Meridian, Mississippi, from Huntsville, Alabama, on January 30, 1899, unknown assailants fired upon the trains. Lieutenant H. B. Dixon, commanding one of the sections, reported that a dozen bullets smashed windows and doors of a coach, miraculously striking no one. The darkness of night, accentuated by rain and the motion of the cars, concealed the culprits. While Dixon believed the shooting deliberate, railroad employees suspected "reckless men [acting] for no other reason than mere sport."[15]

Such was the preamble to the unit's brief but stormy passage through Texarkana. Ironically, the incident duplicated almost identically the clash at Huntsville, though with civil authorities and no fatalities. Unidentified Tenth Cavalrymen utilized a rest stop to patronize the Belmont House in the red light district. A frightened, partially clothed resident managed to escape the intruders and rushed to the courthouse to relate the occurrence in emotional terms. A peace officer, accompanied by several local officials, overtook a soldier proceeding from the site of the disturbance to the depot. As Constable J. F. Rochelle attempted to arrest the man, a group of cavalrymen crowded around the pair, jostling the prisoner free. The soldier concealed himself on a crowded train while a number of his regimental fellows intimidated the officials and townspeople by pointing rifles from the coaches' windows.[16]

At the request of civil authorities, military officers delayed the departure of the trains for several hours in order to effect a search. Although several witnesses had promised to identify the wanted man and his rescuers, a prolonged inspection proved fruitless. When the locomotives finally steamed out of the station, the relatively minor incident had not yet run its course, however. Still to come were provocative news reports, strained exchanges between state and military administrators, and an accumulation of mutual ill-feeling that would burden civilian-military relations even before the troops reached their assigned garrisons at San Antonio and along the Mexican border.[17]

Newspapers across the state carried the report, datelined Little Rock, below such compelling headlines as "The Tenth Cavalry Made a Rough House Out of Texarkana" and "Drunken Soldiers at Texarkana." "When they arrived here they were a drunken mob," asserted the writer, "and an effort was made by them to tear up the town." After sketching the main points of the story, the unnamed reporter stated that at the point of the soldiers' arrest, "Every car window held a drunken negro [*sic*] with a cocked rifle. . . ." Irate Texarkanans, equipped with dynamite, surrounded the trains, "ready to send the entire horde to destruction." The scribe concluded that "every negro would have been dynamited out of existence" had not cooler heads prevailed.[18]

Although some embellishments of the facts faded under closer scrutiny, enough of the story remained to attract the intervention of Governor Joseph D. Sayers, a Confederate veteran just beginning his term of office. The interest of the state's chief executive stemmed from a communication dispatched by Horace W. Vaughan, county attorney. As he divulged to the press the contents of his letter, Vaughan denied that there had been any threat of dynamite.[19]

In other particulars the local official negated the tone of the original news release. He delayed four days before informing Sayers of the situation, though he admonished himself mildly for not having acted sooner. Vaughan acknowledged that the soldiers had attracted "no particular attention" during the hour-and-a-half which they passed in the town before the disturbance and cited no abuse of alcohol on their part.[20]

The county attorney, nevertheless, corroborated the essential elements of the news story. He stated that he had been present in the courthouse with Constable Rochelle, Justice of the Peace G. Henry, and Deputy Sheriff L. C. Lynch when the distraught prostitute burst in. He confirmed the reported chase, the foiled arrest, and the display of weapons by members of the regiment. Fortunately, "a tall yellow officer" positioned himself between the armed soldiers and the gathering crowd, ordering the troops to hold their fire. "While this was transpiring," attested Vaughan, "the soldiers were guilty of conduct that almost precipitated a riot here. They used language that was calculated to fire up the blood of any white man on earth and were very insulting in their conduct." The local official requested of Sayers "to demand of the proper authority in the proper way, an investigation" that would facilitate prosecution by the state.[21]

The communication stirred the Governor to action. He assured Vaughan, "I will do everything within my power to carry out what you desire" and fired off identical telegrams to Secretary of War Russell A. Alger and United States Senators Roger Q. Mills and Horace Chilton of Texas:

> Soldiers of the Tenth U.S. Cavalry in passing through Texarkana acted in a most outrageous manner violating the law, insulting citizens and putting their lives in jeopardy.

> Please see President at once and obtain from him an order directing a trustworthy officer to proceed immediately to Texarkana and inquire into the matter, first conferring with Honorable Horace W. Vaughan . . . Please answer.[22]

Meanwhile, the press exposed differences of opinion between some military officers and civil authorities, tending to place the latter in a better light. A statement by Capt. Guy Carleton of the Tenth Cavalry denying the reported outburst drew the derisive comment of being "regarded as a huge bluff by the people of Texarkana." The item stated that Representative J. L. Sheppard of East Texas had placed the matter before Secretary of War Alger, while repeating accusations of African American drunkenness and lack of cooperation by army officers.[23]

The news release revived other emotional, if questionable, issues. The discredited dynamite episode resurfaced, with townspeople purportedly purchasing ninety pounds of explosives from local hardware stores to protect themselves from rampaging blacks. Expanding on the theme of African American destruction, the writer alleged, "Every railroad station from Little Rock to Texarkana shows signs of the soldiers' depredations. The sign board on every depot designating the colored waiting rooms was demolished." Interestingly, in this offhand and accusative reference to firing from trains, the press came as close as it ever would to reporting the shooting incidents of which the military complained at Meridian and, subsequently, near Houston.[24]

Happily, an encounter at Houston between a reporter and an army officer ended on a more amicable note, despite early misgivings on the part of the interviewee. On the day following the Texarkana incident, a contingent of the Tenth Cavalry that had bypassed the East Texas town and had drawn fire at Meridian stopped in Houston en route to Fort Clark. When a reporter posed a question to Col. T. A. Baldwin on the destination of the troops, the agitated officer turned him back with the reply: "I have absolutely nothing to say. You would print whatever you wished, any statement of mine to the contrary notwithstanding." On reflection Baldwin attributed his bad humor to the reporting of the Texarkana controversy rather than any action of the local newspaper. An accompanying junior officer voiced the sentiments of his superior and, doubtless, other army officers who had commanded black troops. "They fought like tigers before Santiago," exclaimed the lieutenant, who had suffered a stomach wound in the campaign, "and I cannot bring myself to believe that they could commit such acts of lawlessness as have been ascribed to them."[25]

The journalist displayed more sympathy for the black soldiers than was the case with many of his colleagues. "The men were given their liberty all during the time they were here [approximately three hours]," he stated, "and it can be said to their credit that they conducted themselves in a manner which elicited nothing but commendation from those who saw them." Extolling their war record, the writer described the troops as "a fine, lusty looking set of fellows" and accepted an invitation from Colonel Baldwin to visit the headquarters at Fort Clark.[26]

The optimistic mood established at Houston dissipated in the adjoining countryside before a hail of bullets as the troop movement resumed in the evening. When the train bearing Troops C and D steamed passed Harlem, shots rang out from the darkness. In what must have seemed a recurring nightmare, Lieutenant Dixon heard reports from a .44 or .45 caliber single action pistol at ten o'clock, while most of the men slept in dimly lit or darkened coaches. "A badly executed volley" of both rifle and pistol shots quickly followed from both sides of the track, striking the cars in front of him and breaking glass in a dozen windows. Some of the soldiers returned fire, the crack of their .30 caliber carbines "plainly distinguishable" from the sounds of the other weapons. After ordering his command to cease fire, Dixon discovered no serious injuries but treated a number of cuts and scratches about the face and hands. It appeared to Dixon that only the reclining position of the soldiers, asleep in their berths at the time of attack, prevented tragic casualties.[27]

Although the attack occurred only a few miles from Houston, it went unnoted in the local press except for a terse item and an angry letter to the editor. An entry datelined Richmond, Texas, described "outrageous conduct" on the part of soldiers whose alleged target practice from trains left "houses all along the line filled with bullets." Under the heading, "Bad Conduct of Negro Soldiers," a resident of Harlem complained of troops firing "indiscriminately in every direction" from their coaches on the night of the attack. The writer protested that shells struck several houses, narrowly averting mortalities, and ended on a sardonic note: "If such conduct can't be stopped, as I live very near the railroad, I would thank anybody who would let me know that they are coming, so we can escape with our lives, and will leave them our house and furniture and consider ourselves lucky."[28]

Unknown to the general public, apprised only of accusations against the soldiers, the military filed complaints of its own. Upon receipt of Lieutenant Dixon's report, Colonel Baldwin forwarded the account to the adjutant general at Washington with the comment: "I would respectfully state that I make this report to show how the colored troops have been treated while changing station and request that some steps be taken to enable them to pass through country which they are sworn to protect without danger from hidden assassins." Secretary of War Alger dispatched copies to the governors of Texas and Mississippi and requested the United States Attorney General "to ferret out the perpetrators of these outrages and to prevent their reoccurrence."[29]

The exchange between Washington and Austin officials conformed to diplomatic correctness, masking any sentiments that may have accompanied the communications. Secretary Alger begged of Governor Sayers "such consideration and action, with a view to discovering the parties engaged in the outrage, as may seem to you to meet the ends of justice." The state executive responded that he had "taken the necessary steps to secure a thorough investigation of the affair" and promised to advise the cabinet officer "fully" of the results.[30]

In compliance with Special Orders No. 36 Capt. B. H. Byrne, Sixth Infantry, drew the assignment to investigate the Texarkana affray. He departed Fort Sam Houston, San Antonio, on February 9 and arrived in the East Texas town the following day. There he contacted county attorney Vaughan for "a detailed account of the alleged misdeeds" of the troopers, only to be presented with a duplicate of the letter which the local official had sent to the Governor. Vaughan insisted that the communication contained the entire story. Captain Byrne then asked that Vaughan and Constable Rochelle, also present, produce participants or eye witnesses.[31]

The attendants of the Belmont House described the abrupt arrival of six or seven soldiers, prominent among them a tall mulatto and a short dark man. One woman recalled that the former placed his foot in the door when she attempted to prevent their entrance and shouted, "Open that door and open it damned quick you God Damned whores, bring your white bitches or we will tear the house to pieces." The other tenants and a black porter corroborated the narrative, the latter distracting the soldiers sufficiently for one of the prostitutes to escape. The porter reproved the intruders, "You are in the wrong country to do any thing like that," prompting two of the men to threaten to "blow [him] . . . to hell." The mulatto intervened, according to the custodian, exclaiming: "He is a colored gentleman like ourselves, don't hurt him, it is the white sons of bitches we are after."[32]

Other witnesses described the attempted apprehension of the soldier and his escape, with some confusion on detail. Some disagreement arose on the point of contact between the arresting officer, Rochelle, and the wanted man. There was also a lack of consensus on whether Rochelle had spotted the soldier or was directed to him by an accuser. Witnesses presented the investigating officer a rather wide range of numbers of soldiers involved in freeing the fugitive.[33]

Constable Rochelle, unquestionably the most reliable witness, depicted his role essentially as reported in the press. He stated that about three in the afternoon on the day in question "one of the inmates of Lottie Stewart's house of ill fame came running to the Justice of the Peace office very much excited, asking for an officer [and] saying that there was a crowd of Negroes in her house tearing it up." Rochelle, Vaughan, and Lynch, the deputy sheriff, rushed to the site and saw the men proceeding toward Union Station. The constable overtook "a tall yellow Negro" and placed him under arrest, only to lose the prisoner to "about forty or fifty [soldiers] . . . each with a gun." Immediately, "about two hundred Negroes . . . some of them loading their guns," poured out of the coaches, prompting the three civil officials to seek shelter, though an army sergeant commanded the troops not to fire. "We had no chance against these men," judged Rochelle. "They could have cleaned the town out."[34]

From the standpoint of the inquiry, all roads from Lottie Stewart's house reached a dead end. Although a number of witnesses had believed themselves capable of identifying the wanted soldiers, none was able to do so during the lengthy inspection following the incident. Nor could bystanders sought out by Captain Byrne clarify the confusion. Indeed, the civil officials at

Texarkana doubted that any additional useful information could be gleaned from the populace. Still undetermined was the company or companies to which the disorderly men belonged and the units to which they escaped.[35]

The inspecting officer hoped that an internal military investigation might yet disclose the wanted information. The testimony suggested that the second section of three troop trains carried the disruptive soldiers. Accordingly, Captain Byrne shifted the focus of his inquiry to the command of the Tenth Cavalry. He soon discovered a striking contrast to the civilians' statements in the level of emotion and certitude.[36]

On the essential matters of identification and responsibility, the officers commanding the troop movement contributed negligibly. Major J. L. Fowler, in charge of the second section, learned of the incident only after noticing a crowd gathering on the platform. He disciplined a train guard who apparently had been drinking, although the soldier comported himself well and employed courtesy and restraint to the angry townspeople. The major quoted the civil authorities as satisfied with the military cooperation and doubted that members of his command had participated in the misdeed.[37]

The regimental commander, Colonel S. M. Whitside, also acknowledged no first hand knowledge of the matter. Traveling aboard the third section, he noted "nothing to attract attention" at his arrival and took lunch at the depot dining room. While the colonel ate, "the sheriff," probably Constable Rochelle, entered the restaurant and approached the table. The peace officer appeared so little agitated that he insisted upon waiting for Whitside to complete the meal before telling him of the disturbance. The colonel immediately appointed Capt. L. P. Hunt to assist the civil officers in a search of the trains. The regimental commander saw no evidence of intoxication on the part of any soldier during the entire journey from Alabama.[38]

Captain Hunt, who assisted in the search, first learned of the trouble by asking some soldiers the cause of a gathering crowd. They replied that "two citizens had disarmed a soldier and . . . some of the latter had resisted and threatened to shoot." He accompanied Vaughan through the coaches on two separate occasions, the second time with a witness who had claimed that he could recognize "the yellow man." Although Hunt required each soldier to directly face the front, the wanted man remained at large.[39]

Capt. Charles G. Ayers, leader of the first section, discounted the surmise of some officials that the fugitive fled on an early departing train. Like the other officers, he denied direct knowledge of the incident that prompted the delay and search and asserted that no mention of trouble arose until the other sections arrived at the depot. "Men under my orders and control have yet in my career to make a disturbance as is herein described," Ayers attested, not commenting on the possibility that a soldier from another section had stolen away in his train's departure.[40]

There the matter lay. A subsequent army report concluded: "From the tone of the accompanying endorsements it would seem that no special effort has been made to ascertain the identity of the men who made the visit to the house of ill fame and who were responsible for the consequent conditions although such inquiry may have been made." Indeed, the tenor of each officer's response seemed primarily designed to release that commander and his unit from any share of culpability. No such frank appraisal accompanied the unrecorded efforts of the governors of Mississippi and Texas to locate the attackers of the troop train at Meridian and Harlem. Given the circumstances, one may doubt that the undertaking manifested much zeal.[41]

Curiously, the relationship between Texas Governor Sayers and the Tenth Cavalry thawed momentarily as the investigations floundered. Fear of a smallpox epidemic moved Sayers, at the behest of the state health officer, to dispatch Texas Rangers to Laredo in order to vaccinate an unwilling Hispanic population. When an irate mob defied the fabled lawmen, the Governor called upon the assistance of the black garrison at Fort McIntosh to pacify the populace and thwart the spread of the feared disease.[42]

Within a few months, however, the conditions reverted to their ominous beginnings. Racial clashes at Rio Grande City and Laredo raised a public outcry, echoed by Sayers, for the withdrawal of the Tenth Cavalry from Texan soil.[43]

By the measurements of later civilian-military clashes, the incidents at Texarkana and Harlem pale in comparison. Although both sides brandished arms, and in the latter instance one group resorted to their use, no serious physical injuries and only limited property destruction resulted. The spectacle of a half-dozen enlisted men scurrying from depot to bawdyhouse during a rest stop hardly merited mention, nor the attempt by a hunted soldier, with the aid of friends, to avoid arrest. Neither was the practice of firing at trains "for sport" as unusual as rail employees would have liked. The racial factor turned obnoxious, if recurring, actions into potentially devastating events. The sharply etched memory of a white mob demanding a black soldier and the recollection of armed black troops leveling rifles at civilians, whether or not in self-defense, overpowered subsequent gestures at comity between garrisons and communities. In that stark moment at the Texarkana depot, the approaching violence at Rio Grande City, Laredo, El Paso, Brownsville, and Houston became possible.

After the incident at Texarkana army and state governmental reports on military-civilian clashes in Texas would no longer enjoy the luxury of indifferent inquiry.

Notes

1. Civilian-black military conflicts at the turn of the century and the early 1900s are depicted in Robert V. Haynes, *A Night of Violence: The Houston Riot of 1917* (Baton Rouge, 1976); Ann J. Lane, *The Brownsville Affair: National Crisis and Black Reaction* (Port Washington, 1971); John D. Weaver, *The Brownsville Raid* (New York, 1970); Jack D. Foner, *Blacks and the Military in American History* (New York, 1974), 82–83, 95–97, 113–115. Urban riots of the period of World War I and later are described in Elliott M. Rudwick, *Race Riot at East St. Louis, July 2, 1917* (Carbondale, 1964); William M. Tuttle, *Race Riot: Chicago in the Red Summer of 1919* (New York, 1970); Hugh David Graham and Ted Robert Gurr, eds., *The History of Violence in America* (New York, 1969); Allen D. Grimshaw, ed., *Racial Violence in the United States* (Chicago, 1969).
2. John M. Carroll, ed., *The Black Military Experience in the American West* (New York, 1971), 65, 77, 91, 95; Robert Ewell Greene, *Black Defenders of America, 1775–1973* (Chicago, 1974), 51.
3. Arlen L. Fowler, *The Black Infantry in the West* (New York, 1974), 18–36; Foner, *Blacks and the Military*, 52–67; William H. Leckie, *The Buffalo Soldiers: A Narrative of the Negro Cavalry in the West* (Norman, 1967), 98.
4. Jack D. Foner, *The United States Soldier Between Two Wars: Army Life and Reforms, 1865–1898* (New York, 1970), 133, 147.
5. Foner, *Blacks and the Military*, 56; Leckie, *Buffalo Soldiers*, 98.
6. Foner, *Blacks and the Military*, 57; Frank N. Schubert, "Black Soldiers on the White Frontier: Some Factors Influencing Race Relations," *Phylon*, XXXII, no. 4 (Winter 1971), 415; Marvin E. Fletcher, *The Black Soldier and Officer in the United States Army, 1891–1917* (Columbia, 1974), 25.

7. J. Evetts Haley, "Racial Troubles on the Conchos," Carroll, ed., *The Black Military Experience,* 451–456; J. Evetts Haley, *Fort Concho and the Texas Frontier* (San Angelo, 1952), 235–237; Leckie, *Buffalo Soldiers,* 99.
8. Foner, *Blacks and the Military,* 77–79. Other examples of racial tension produced by an underprivileged class entering the military are shown in L. Kennett, "Camp Wadsworth Affair," *South Atlantic Quarterly,* LXXIV (Spring, 1975), 210–211.
9. C. Vann Woodward, *The Strange Career of Jim Crow* (New York, 1966), 67–109.
10. Foner, *Blacks and the Military,* 79; Kennett, "Camp Wadsworth Affair," 210; William B. Gatewood, Jr., "Negro Troops in Florida, 1898," *Florida Historical Quarterly,* XIX (July 1970), 8.
11. *Galveston Daily News,* October 20, 1899, November 20, 1899; *El Paso Herald,* February 17, 1900; Garna L. Christian, "The Twenty-fifth Regiment at Fort McIntosh: Precursor to Retaliatory Racial Violence," *West Texas Historical Association Year Book,* LV (1979), 149–161; Garna L. Christian, "Rio Grande City: Prelude to the Brownsville Raid," *West Texas Historical Association Year Book,* LVII (1981), 118–132; Garna L. Christian, "The El Paso Racial Crisis of 1900," *Red River Valley Historical Review,* VI, no. 2 (Spring 1981), 28–41; Foner, *Blacks and the Military,* 82–83, 95–97, 113–115.
12. Foner, *Blacks and the Military,* 74–75.
13. S. W. Dunning, Captain, 16th Infantry, to the Adjutant General, 4th Army Corps, Huntsville, Alabama, October 17, 1898, AGO file 2046322, RG 94, National Archives.
14. S. L. Woodward, Captain, 10th Cavalry, to Lieutenant Colonel T. A. Baldwin, 10th Cavalry, Huntsville, Alabama, October 28, 1898, AGO file 2046322, RG 94, N.A.
15. H. B. Dixon, 2d Lieutenant, 10th Cavalry, to Baldwin, Fort Clark, Texas, January (*sic*) 7, 1899, AGO 184450, RG 94, N.A.
16. B. H. Byrne, Captain, 6th Infantry, to the Adjutant, Fort Sam Houston, Texas, February 13, 1899, AGO 184450, RG 94, N.A.
17. Mattingly, "Resume," n.p., March 30, 1899, AGO 184450, RG 94, N.A.
18. *Houston Daily Post,* February 1, 1899; *Galveston Daily News,* February 1, 1899.
19. *Galveston Daily News,* February 5, 1899; Horace W. Vaughan, County Attorney of Bowie County, Texas, to Honorable Joseph D. Sayers, Governor, Texarkana, Texas, February 3, 1899, AGO 184450, RG 94, N.A.
20. *Galveston Daily News,* February 5, 1899; Vaughan to Sayers, February 3, 1899, AGO 184450, RG 94, N.A.
21. *Galveston Daily News,* February 5, 1899; Vaughan to Sayers, February 3, 1899, AGO 184450, RG 94, N.A.
22. Sayers to Vaughan, Austin, Texas, February 4, 1899, Governors' Papers: Joseph D. Sayers Letter Press Books 2–11/420, vol. I, no. 197, Archives, Texas State Library, Austin; Assistant Adjutant General to Commanding General, Department Gulf, Washington, D.C., February 8, 1899, AGO 200526, RG 94, N.A.
23. *Houston Daily Post,* February 3, 1899.
24. *Houston Daily Post,* February 3, 1899.
25. *Houston Daily Post,* February 2, 1899.
26. *Houston Daily Post,* February 2, 1899.

27. Dixon to Baldwin, January 7, 1899, AGO 184450, RG 94, N.A.; Baldwin to the Adjutant General, Fort Clark, Texas, February 7, 1899, AGO 184450, RG 94, N.A.
28. *Houston Daily Post,* February 3, 1899, February 4, 1899.
29. Baldwin to Adjutant General, February 7, 1899, AGO 184450, RG 94, N.A.
30. Secretary of War R. A. Alger to His Excellency, the Governor of Texas, Washington, D.C., March 4, 1899, Joseph D. Sayers Correspondence 2–11/378, Austin; Sayers to Alger, Austin, Texas, March 11, 1899, AGO 184450, RG 94, N.A.
31. Byrne to Adjutant, February 13, 1899, AGO 184450, RG 94, N.A.
32. Byrne to Adjutant, February 13, 1899, AGO 184450, RG 94, N.A.
33. Byrne to Adjutant, February 13, 1899, AGO 184450, RG 94, N.A.
34. Byrne to Adjutant, February 13, 1899, AGO 184450, RG 94, N.A.
35. Byrne to Adjutant, February 13, 1899, AGO 184450, RG 94, N.A.
36. Byrne to Adjutant, February 13, 1899, AGO 184450, RG 94, N.A.
37. J. L. Fowler, Major, 10th Cavalry, to Regimental Adjutant, 10th U.S. Cavalry, Fort Sam Houston, Texas, February 28, 1899, AGO 184450, RG 94, N.A.
38. 3rd Endorsement, Fort Sam Houston, Texas, February 20, 1899, AGO 184450, RG 94, N.A.
39. 5th Endorsement, Fort Sam Houston, Texas, February 24, 1899, AGO 184450, RG 94, N.A.
40. 9th Endorsement, Fort McIntosh, March 13, 1899, AGO 184450, RG 94, N.A.
41. Mattingly, March 30, 1899, AGO 184450, RG 94, N.A.
42. W. F. Blum, M.D., State Health Officer, to Sayers, Austin, Texas, March 9, 1899, Correspondence 2–11/378, Austin.
43. *Galveston Daily News,* November 23, 1899.

Child or Beast?

White Texas' View of Blacks, 1900–10

BRUCE A. GLASRUD

IT WAS JUST, IT WAS RIGHT, IT WAS IMPERATIVE HE should die," proclaimed a white Texas writer in the aftermath of a 1905 lynching of a black Texan.[1] This comment echoed the thoughts of many whites in the state during the first decade of the twentieth scentury. Blacks frequently faced white displeasure and wrath; whether white contempt and fear assumed violent or nonviolent forms, blacks were reminded often of white racism. Whites were haunted by fear of racial amalgamation, a fear expressed in their apprehension about sexual relations between black males and white females. They worried also that blacks might arm themselves for retaliation against brutal treatment.

The overwhelming white domination attained during this decade fashioned two basic attitudes—that blacks were either childlike or beastlike. Few whites supported the concept of racial equality. For some whites, paternalistic concern, rooted in an assumption that blacks were inferior beings who required white help and guidance, superseded fear and contempt for the black race. Others saw blacks as beasts subject to rigid control, whipping, and, too often, lynching. The best indications of white public opinion can be found in utterances of public officials, in newspaper editorializing and treatment of African American news, and in the general white acceptance of the violence and intimidation that were a part of the pattern of race relations in the Lone Star state.

Senators Charles Culberson and Joseph Bailey voiced the dominant opposing racial attitudes of the first decade. A paternalist, Senator Culberson emphasized that demands for equality menaced whites, and that

> aside from its impossibility, social equality would lead imperceptively to more intimate personal relations, to lower standards and ideals of ultimately, if fully attained, to

> marriage and partial or complete amalgamation, with the consequent debasement, degradation or destruction of the white race.

However, Culberson advocated providing black Texans with "education, forbearance, moral training, just treatment, [and] opportunities for labor"; he did not endorse destructive tactics.[2] Although a paternalist, Culberson's fear of racial amalgamation engendered lynching and other forms of violence as surely as the contempt articulated by his colleague in the Senate, Joseph Bailey.

Senator Bailey, the nearest approximation to a demagogue the state has produced, illustrated the other side of racial beliefs. Bailey frequently brought the issue of race into his campaigns and speeches and criticized both Democrats and Republicans for being too friendly toward blacks. In 1904, after condemning Pres. Theodore Roosevelt's association with Booker T. Washington, Bailey asserted, "I believe more in the purity of the Anglo-Saxon race than in the principles of democracy."[3] In a speech at Fort Worth the Senator emphasized that blacks should not live side by side with educated whites; since blacks were trained for servitude "nothing in the world could be more supremely foolish than to spend the people's money in trying to educate a race of menials." However, Bailey reminded his audience, "lest I be misunderstood, I have no prejudice against the negro in his place, but I think his place is the white man's kitchen and not the white man's dining room." According to Bailey, blacks must remain in their place: "I want to treat the negro justly and generously as long as he behaves himself, and when he doesn't I want to drive him out of this country."[4]

Other politicians[5] expressed views similar to those of either Bailey or Culberson. After Theodore Roosevelt invited Booker T. Washington to the White House in 1901, Texas Congressman Albert Sidney Burleson denounced the President and refused to attend social functions at the White House for the remainder of Roosevelt's administration. Gov. Joseph Sayers reminded the Texas legislature in 1901 that "the negro is . . . the weaker race and in matters of legislation, he is altogether dependent upon the white man." Gov. S. W. T. Lanham, although willing to use troops to protect individual blacks, warned African American Baptists in 1904 to keep "out of partisan politics" and to "respect the social limitations between the races. If these are transcended there will be trouble."[6] Four years later, M. J. Denman, who opposed John Nance Garner for the Democratic nomination to Congress, advocated sending all blacks to the Philippines in order to alleviate racial tension. The next year a member of the Texas legislature introduced a resolution opposing any appropriations to the black school at Prairie View on the grounds "that the cotton field is the proper place for the negro."[7] The essential difference between these politicians and Senator Bailey was that Bailey emphasized the question of race and probably profited politically from it.

Not only did white politicians voice their racial views, they also acted by restricting blacks from participation in politics. Neither the Democratic nor the Republican parties sought black members during this decade. In fact, the Democrats in the state legislature established a poll tax as a prerequisite for voting in Texas elections with the result that the size of the black electorate was substantially reduced.[8] And, when the legislature enacted the Terrell Election Law establishing a direct primary system, the Democratic state executive committee allowed local committees to bar blacks from the Democratic primary. The Republicans, who in the nineteenth century became a viable political force by attracting the black voter, turned to a "lily white" strategy in the twentieth. The Republicans refused to contest local and state elections where victory was dependent upon black votes, and distributed patronage to whites only.[9]

Disfranchisement and political ostracism[10] were not the only indications of hostility to blacks; Texas politicians also perfected an elaborate segregation code. Both *de facto* and *de jure* Jim Crow existed in Texas from before the Civil War, but during the first decade of the twentieth century the most rapid expansion of legal segregation took place. Legislation of the period 1900–1910 decreed segregation on all forms of public transportation, in railroad depots, and in eleemosynary and penal institutions. In 1907, any place of public amusement or recreation was permitted by law to segregate blacks or to bar their admission. The same legislature stipulated that no white couple could adopt a black child, and that no black couple could adopt a white child.[11]

Even when the law made no differentiation on the basis of race, the legal system operated against blacks. Those convicted of a crime usually received longer and harsher sentences than whites convicted of a similar offense. For example, a white charged with attempted assault of a black girl received a sentence of two years, but a black man charged with assaulting a white girl was punished with thirty-eight years in prison.[12] Since the presence of blacks on juries was virtually non-existent, white juries had little sympathy for the black defendant. Texas courts frequently ruled that the lack of blacks on a jury was not sufficient evidence of discrimination. The presence of an African American on a jury was sufficiently unusual that newspapers reported the incident. In 1908, when Washington Williams was a juror, *The San Antonio Daily Express* commented, "it is very seldom that a negro is taken on a jury."[13]

The white sentiments which led to violence or disfranchisement or segregation were faithfully reflected in Texas newspapers: the newspapers helped to mold them as well. News coverage accorded blacks in the white press consisted of three types: crime reports, humorous incidents, and news of lynching or other forms of white violence directed against blacks. Accounts of African American criminal acts were scattered throughout Texas papers. For example, the December 26, 1901, issue of the *Houston Daily Post* carried brief stories from around the state on the deaths of three blacks, the wounding of three others, and the shooting and stabbing of whites by blacks. No other information concerning blacks was in the paper. Humorous stories depicting the black Texan as childish and unlearned were common. *The Dallas Morning News* carried a cartoon in the Sunday edition entitled "Sambo," which displayed the childlike qualities supposedly inherent in blacks.[14] Social, economic, and political reports of interest to blacks were suppressed. The inevitable result of such reportorial bias was a picture of blacks as simple or sinister; one or the other view fitted the preconceptions of most whites.

Editors became increasingly sensitive to the image of the state in reporting clashes between white and black. At the turn of the century, newspapers reserved page one and bold headlines for news of lynching. But, early in the twentieth century, accounts of lynching were frequently remanded to inside pages and received less sensational coverage. National publicity, Senate criticism, and the frequency of the violence were responsible for the diminished reports. Often, stories of lynching were not carried in the press; some papers reported a given lynching while others did not. Yet, the suppression on lynching news was less frequent than the suppression of other news about blacks in the state. At least one paper could be counted on to provide lynch news; little mention was made of the accomplishments or life style of black Texans.

The press not only ignored African American accomplishments and activities, but the terminology used in accounts of race violence was indicative of the prejudices of the era. Newspapers often referred to the black "beast," the black "fiend," or the black "brute." Other African Americans were described as "insolent," "idle," or "trifling."[15] The editor of the *Lubbock Morning Avalanche* characterized blacks as "kinky headed coons." A short time later, he opposed the entrance of blacks into Lubbock since "negroes are like Johnson grass when it comes to taking root and increasing in a town."[16] Press approval of lynching was implicit in the terms used to describe the victim. Guilt was assumed; he was a murderer, a rapist, or a trespasser, and the lynching was probably needed. Referring to a lynching at Whitesboro in 1901, *The Dallas Morning News* headlined, "Negro murderer is burned."[17]

Some newspapers approved burning and hanging as punishment and warned blacks of an armed white repression. A Nacogdoches paper declared in 1903 that "you can say what you please, but the negro will never rise in respectability or even be classed as a human being, until he ceases his damnable outrages on women. He has either got to stop it, leave the U.S., or be exterminated." The same year a Carthage paper expressed similar views; according to *The Panola Watchman,* "the negro can stop lynching tomorrow. Let him let white girls alone." A newspaper editorial from Longview argued that:

> almost every day some negro brute assaults a white woman in this state, and often one to a half-dozen murders are committed in an effort to hide the crime. . . . If rape and murder by brutish negroes are to become common, the negro must expect extermination. . . . Burning or hanging the culprit does not seem to check it and if nothing else will do, the people will rise in their might and put an end to it.

The same year, 1905, some white Houstonians asked Gov. S. W. T. Lanham to allow mobs to punish blacks guilty of assaults upon white women. They asserted that these assaults must be stopped "even if it is necessary to wipe out the race."[18]

Other papers seldom expressed themselves as openly, but

their failure to condemn the mobs and their recitals of extenuating circumstances for lynching implied approval. In 1910, for example, after a mob estimated at well over 5,000 persons took Allen Brooks, a black man under indictment for assault, from the courthouse at Dallas during a recess in the trial and hanged him from a pole, *The Dallas Morning News* refused to condemn the lynching. Instead, the *News* asserted that:

> something may be said, in certain instances, not in justification, but in extenuation of the conduct of those who resort to lynching. . . . Many of them are moved by their contempt for the delays, reversals, and failures of courts.[19]

The inconsistencies of white attitudes were also reflected by the press. The white paternalists' capacity for holding contradictory views could be observed in newspaper editorials inveighing against race prejudice while supporting separation of white and black. According to the editor of *The San Antonio Daily Express*, "there is and must always be race distinction, but there is no excuse for race prejudice." A writer for the *Houston Chronicle* noted that "the negro is inferior not because he is black nor is he black because he is inferior, but he is inferior because he belongs to an inferior race."[20]

An extreme example of race prejudice took place in 1910 with white Texans' response to a boxing match between the world heavyweight champion, Jack Johnson, a Galveston black, and Jim Jeffries, the "white hope." Johnson defeated Jeffries to the delight of blacks and the consternation of whites. Minor disturbances arose, and whites demanded that films of the bout be prohibited. The belief prevailed that if blacks watched their champion defeat a white in a boxing match, full-scale outbreaks would occur.[21] Texas Governor Thomas M. Campbell was widely applauded after he asked the state legislature to bar showing of the film. Although the legislature responded by enacting a law banning movies of prizefights, some members of the legislature attempted unsuccessfully to ban only those fight pictures in which blacks were participants.[22]

The Johnson-Jeffries fight and its aftermath epitomized the racial dogmas which produced this period in Texas history. The irrational belief in white supremacy and the concomitant emphasis on forcing blacks into a subordinate and separate caste permeated all classes of white society; few raised voices of opposition. Perceiving blacks as childlike and/or beastlike led to treating blacks with paternalistic concern, or to dominating their lives. Yet, definite improvements in race relations in the Lone Star state eventually took place; violence continued to occur, but the year 1910 marked the end of an era when it was used with impunity against black Texans. Blacks struggled successfully to acquire a more equitable status in Texas society, and more and more whites made genuine efforts to extend the rights of full citizenship to all Texans.

Notes

1. *Waco Weekly Tribune,* August 12, 1905.
2. *The Dallas Morning News,* November 21, 1901. For additional information on Culberson see James William Madden, *Charles Allen Culberson* (Austin, 1929). White paternalism can also be noticed in a book written by a white Texas minister, James Jefferson Pipkin, *The Story of a Rising Race: The Negro in Revelation, in History, and in Citizenship* (New York, 1902). Pipkin claimed that "what the Negro needs is encouragement in every line of lawful endeavor, all the aid that can be extended to him by generous whites without inducing idleness, an open recognition of whatever manhood he evinces in the inevitable struggle of the poor and lowly, and the arousing of renewed determination to do his part in the uplifting of his people" (v).
3. Sam Hanna Acheson, *Joe Bailey, The Last Democrat* (New York, 1932), 171; *Houston Daily Post,* September 7, 1904; *The City Times* (Galveston), September 24, 1904; *The Dallas Morning News,* October 23, 1904. The former Democratic Governor, James S. Hogg, disagreed with Bailey and declared that "I don't want the young men of this country to understand that they are to make any attack upon any human being unless it is by due process of law." Hogg received national publicity and a letter of thanks from G. W. Jackson, black president of the Central Texas Negro Fair Association of Corsicana for his response to Bailey. Robert C. Cotner, *James Stephen Hogg: A Biography* (Austin, 1959), 562–563; *The Dallas Morning News,* October 13, 1904. Also see Bob Charles Holcomb, "Senator Joe Bailey: Two Decades of Controversy" (Unpublished Ph.D. dissertation, Texas Tech University, 1968), on Bailey's checkered career.
4. *The Dallas Morning News,* March 22, 1907. Politicians were not the only ones to express such views. William Hayne Levell, minister for the largest Presbyterian Church in Houston, asserted that lynching was a needed punishment for the rape of white women by black men. It was also needed to keep blacks from "getting the upper hand." William Hayne Levell, "On Lynching in the South," *Outlook,* LXIX (November 16, 1901), 731–733.
5. Politics and politicians of the period have been studied in a number of different ways. See, for example, Alwyn Barr, *Reconstruction to Reform: Texas Politics, 1876–1906* (Austin, 1971); Maurice Henry Sochia, "The Progressive Movement in Texas, 1900–1914" (Unpublished Master's thesis, Southwest Texas State Teachers College, 1959); and James A.

Tinsley, "The Progressive Movement in Texas" (Unpublished Ph.D. dissertation, University of Wisconsin, 1953).

6. Adrian Norris Anderson, "Albert Sidney Burleson: A Southern Politician in the Progressive Era" (Unpublished Ph.D. dissertation, Texas Tech University, 1967), 81; *The Dallas Morning News,* January 11, 1901, September 15, 1904. On Sayers, see James Leighton Tenney, "The Public Services of Joseph Draper Sayers" (Unpublished Master's thesis, University of Texas, 1933); and on Lanham see Martha Lanham, "Governor S. W. T. Lanham" (Unpublished Master's thesis, Baylor University, 1930), and Ruby Lee Martin, "The Administration of Governor S. W. T. Lanham, 1903–1907" (Unpublished Master's thesis, University of Texas, 1937).

7. *The Galveston Daily News,* June 22, 1908; *The San Antonio Daily Express,* May 1, 1909.

8. On the poll tax in Texas see Dick Smith, "Texas and the Poll Tax," *Southwestern Social Science Quarterly,* XXIV (1964), 167–173; Donald S. Strong, "The Poll Tax: The Case of Texas," *American Political Science Review,* XXXVII (1944), 693–709; Laura Snow, "The Poll Tax in Texas: Its Historical, Legal, and Fiscal Aspects" (Unpublished Master's thesis, University of Texas, 1936); Judith Kidd Rudoff, "The Poll Tax in Texas: Political Panacea" (Unpublished Master's thesis, East Texas State University, 1968); Edwin Larry Dickens, "The Poll Tax in Texas" (Unpublished Master's thesis, Texas College of Arts and Industries, 1963). However, the most accurate treatment of the poll tax and its background in Texas is found in Lawrence Rice, *The Negro in Texas* (Baton Rouge, 1971), 22–25, 132–139.

9. *General Laws of the State of Texas,* regular session, 1903, chapter CI, section 93; first called session, 1905, chapter II; *The Dallas Morning News,* March 30, 1903, April 19, 1904; Paul Casdorph, *A History of the Republican Party in Texas, 1865–1965* (Austin, 1965), 7–97. The position of the two parties during this period can also be seen in Ernest William Winkler (ed.), *Platforms of Political Parties in Texas* (Austin, University of Texas Bulletin No. 53, 1916), 411–519, and Barr, *Reconstruction to Reform,* 188–208.

10. Systematically denied political participation by the Republicans and Democrats by the end of the decade, some blacks turned their attention to the prohibition crusade which culminated in an important election in 1911. Some whites asserted that blacks needed to be on the prohibition side because blacks were "about to exchange the slavery of the white man for the slavery of drunkenness." Thomas S. Henderson to L. L. Campbell, May 1911, Thomas S. Henderson Papers, University of Texas Archives. Additional information concerning blacks and prohibition can be found in Anti-Saloon League, *The Brewers and Texas Politics,* 2 volumes (San Antonio, 1917).

11. *General Laws of the State of Texas,* regular session, 1907, chapters XIV, section 1, XXXVI, XLVII, section 1; regular session, 1909, chapter LVI, article 2949; second called session, 1909, chapter XIII, section 1; first called session, 1910, chapter X, section 36; third called session, 1910, chapter III; *The Dallas Morning News,* July 12, 30, 1907. Secondary stud-

ies of Jim Crow and its background in Texas include Bruce A. Glasrud, "Jim Crow's Emergence in Texas," *American Studies,* XV (1974), 47–60; Leonard Brewster Murphy, "A History of Negro Segregation Practices in Texas, 1865–1958" (Unpublished Master's thesis, Southern Methodist University, 1958); Barry A. Crouch and L. J. Schultz, "Crisis in Color: Racial Separation in Texas During Reconstruction," *Civil War History,* XVI (1970), 37–49; George E. Hopkins, "The Origins of Jim Crow Laws in Texas" (Unpublished paper delivered at annual meeting, Texas State Historical Association, 1966); Artis Hill, "'Jim Crow-ism' in Several Areas of Twentieth Century Life Relative to the Negro: Transportation, Eating and Lodging Places, Public Parks, and Movie Theaters" (Unpublished Master's thesis, Abilene Christian College, 1969).

12. *The Dallas Morning News,* August 30, 1904, October 18, 1905; *The Galveston Daily News,* February 2, 1910.
13. *Smith v. State,* 69 SW 151 (1902); *Thomas v. State,* 95 SW 1069 (1906); *Hanna v. State,* 105 SW 793 (1907); *Thompson v. State,* 74 SW 914 (1903); *The San Antonio Daily Express,* February 29, 1908. Without legal protections, black Texans reverted to other means for protecting their rights and resisting the implementation of segregation codes; see August Meier and Elliott Rudwick, "The Boycott Movement Against Jim Crow Streetcars in the South, 1900–1906," *Journal of American History,* LV (1969), 756–775.
14. *Houston Daily Post,* December 26, 1901; *The Dallas Morning News,* March 22, June 21, 1908.
15. *The Dallas Morning News,* May 26, 1902, April 1, 1905, November 26, 1906; *Semi-Weekly Courier-Times* (Tyler), March 5, 1910; *The Times-Clarion* (Longview), October 5, 1905; *Houston Daily Post,* November 16, 1900, November 23, 1902, September 8, 1905; *The San Antonio Daily Express,* July 15, 1908.
16. *Lubbock Morning Avalanche,* November 18, December 4, 1909.
17. *The Dallas Morning News,* August 21, 1901.
18. *Nacogdoches Weekly Sentinel,* 1903, cited in David W. Livingston, "The Lynching of Negroes in Texas, 1900–1925" (Unpublished Master's thesis, East Texas State University, 1972), 110; *The Panola Watchman* (Carthage), August 26, 1903; *The Times-Clarion* (Longview), October 5, 1905; *New York Times,* October 7, 1905.
19. *The Dallas Morning News,* March 4, 1910.
20. *The San Antonio Daily Express,* May 1, 1909; *Houston Chronicle,* October 22, 1902.
21. Richard Bardolph, *The Negro Vanguard* (New York, 1961), 268–269; David G. McComb, *Houston: The Bayou City* (Austin, 1969), 161; *The Dallas Morning News,* July 7, 8, 1910. Studies of Johnson's life include Jack Johnson, *Jack Johnson in the Ring and Out* (Chicago, 1927); Denzil Batchelor, *Jack Johnson and His Times* (London, 1956); Finis Farr, *Black Champion: The Life and Times of Jack Johnson* (New York, 1964); and Al-Tony Gilmore, *Bad Nigger! The National Impact of Jack Johnson* (New York, 1975). Johnson has also been the subject of a play by Howard O. Sackler, *The Great White Hope* (New York, 1968). Part of the reason for the white south-

ern antipathy toward Johnson was because he associated with white women. See Al-Tony Gilmore, "Jack Johnson and White Women: The National Impact," *Journal of Negro History,* LVIII (1973), 18–38.

22. *The Dallas Morning News,* July 7, 8,1910; *General Laws of the State of Texas,* third called session, 1910, chapter VIII.

Constructing Good Success

The Church of God in Christ and Social Uplift in East Texas, 1910–35

KAREN KOSSIE-CHERNYSHEV

> I was deprived of a schoolroom education. . . . However, I was undaunted in my quest for literary training. I studied hard at home by the scant light of the old pine knot fire. Laboring under untoward circumstances, i.e., meager resources, poor facilities, hard labor, with approximately nine months in the school room, exemplifies the object lesson of this booklet that God can make a man. Not a self-made man but a God-made man.

E. M. PAGE, THE FIRST BISHOP OF THE CHURCH of God in Christ (COGIC) in Texas, wrote the above passage in his autobiography.[1] Like many blacks whose lives were marked by the rise of Jim Crow, peonage systems of labor, and political disenfranchisement, Page determined to educate himself against all odds, an earnest quest for progress that many early observers of black Pentecostals overlooked. Either enthralled or appalled by the exoticism of Pentecostal worship, onlookers tended to focus on calisthenics: women and men dancing down the aisles of the church, children playing tambourines and clapping their hands in polyrhythmic abandon, and people possessed by the spirit either collapsing under the power or taking victory laps around a wood-framed church. In all the clamor, the unique story of black Pentecostals' progressive ideals was muted.

Zora Neale Hurston, in her anthropological study *The Sanctified Church* (1935) described the African American Pentecostal Church as a "protest against highbrow tendency in Negro Protestant congregations as Negroes gain[ed] education and wealth" and "a revitalizing element in Negro music and religion."[2]

Hurston's description conversely suggested that black Pentecostals were anti-educational and that they accommodated poverty. Subsequent scholarly studies investigated Hurston's take but generally presupposed that education and progress were the antitheses of being black and Pentecostal.

Few studies have examined Black Pentecostals in Texas apart from Ada Moorhead Holland's and Reverend C. C. White's *No Quittin' Sense* (1969),[3] an in-depth biographical study of White's life and ministry, and Alwyn Barr's *Black Texans: A History of Negroes in Texas: 1528–1971* (1973).[4] Even fewer studies focus on the Church of God in Christ's commitment to the social uplift efforts that absorbed the creative energies of many Southern blacks at the turn of the century.[5] Drawing on the self-published works of members, newspapers, eulogies, city directories, deed records, and in-house COGIC publications, this essay aims to clarify an otherwise obscure story that unfolded in East Texas early in the twentieth century. The early Texas COGIC leader E. M. Page countered claims of "otherworldliness" by embracing the ideals of the Progressive era, particularly its emphasis on social uplift through civic involvement and education.

E. M. Page's foresight and example made him the perfect champion for COGIC in Texas.[6] He was born on the Marlin Stubblefield farm in Yazoo County, Mississippi, May 9, 1871. The eldest son of Richard and Pollie Ann Page, his firsthand knowledge of the rigors of rural life helped him develop the leadership and organizational skills needed to guide the early COGIC church in Texas.

Despite prevalent claims to the contrary, the same held true for members of the Church of God in Christ, spiritual newcomers to a region dominated by Baptists and Methodists. The same decade of his birth, black migrants from Central Texas established "The Little Flock Church" in Hearne, Texas, worshipping in an edifice that had once served as a hospital for railway workmen.[7] The staying power of this group provided the foundation for later families who filled the rolls of the voluntary associations, schools, and churches that rose to address the social needs of a community in transition.

Although "separate but equal" policies guaranteed these men and women limited support from public and private funding sources, they and other blacks in East Texas were just as interested in educational progress as were their white contemporaries. In separate contracts dated February 15 and March 7, 1918, the William M. Rice Institute for the Advancement of Literature, Science, and Art sold four blocks and two lots to Robertson County residents for $400 and $115 in separate transactions.[8] On March 18 of the same year, "patrons of the Colored School District No. 16" purchased a one half acre lot near Zion Hill Baptist Colored Church from the Mumford School District, No. 16, Precinct 7 for $125. The deed stipulated that the plot be used for "School purposes, exclusively."[9] Several months later, on June 18, Baylor University sought to clarify ownership of "several pieces of land" in the area.[10] In short, for blacks and whites, secular and sacred, education was serious business. "Black" and "Pentecostal" and stereotyped as poor, ignorant, and otherworldly, they had to struggle for acceptance and against marginality. E. M. Page noted that "it hurt him so bad"[11] to think of moving to Dallas, Texas, where the second COGIC church of Texas was officially organized in 1910 "amid great turmoil and religious intolerance."[12] Because many black Dallasites "viewed" COGIC newcomers "with a sense of alarm," D. J. Young, the first representative appointed to the region, "met . . . the combined opposition of a unified community of homes, other churches and schools." Before his Texas appointment, Young ministered in Pine Bluff, Arkansas, for seven years and established a church in Beaumont, where membership grew from fifty to 250. Success in Beaumont notwithstanding, life for blacks in Dallas was different. The level of "persecution" was "so widespread" "in certain quarters that it flared into outbursts of violence, vandalism and sabotage against the members and property of their church."[13]

Frequent reports reached the public that attempts had been made, not only against the church, "but [also] on the life of the pastor himself." Protesters of COGIC presence allegedly doused the tent where the early church met with kerosene and "set it afire" in a futile effort to destroy "the very symbol" of the COGIC.[14] Petitions were circulated to have the church declared a public nuisance because "services tended to disturb the tranquility of the neighborhood." It "became increasingly difficult for the church to purchase property and expand its efforts," one writer noted, "[a]s if the Church of God [in Christ] were something loathful [*sic*], people everywhere seemed to resent its very presence."[15] Given the "bitter opposition" facing the COGIC, it seemed that the organization's efforts in Dallas were "doomed." But in January 1914, Bishop C. H. Mason, after "carefully" assessing the situation, "sent the young, energetic and astute Elder E. M. Page to take charge of the church." Page arrived in Texas from Memphis on January 27, 1914, and the church received him "gladly."[16] The same reporter wrote: "On that bleak January day, when a small group of oppressed and greatly discouraged members gathered about him with their stories of woe, [Page] issued this reassuring statement: 'If God is for you He is more than a whole world against you. The church will carry on!'" And so it did, thanks to Page's decisive leadership. More diplomatic than his predecessor, Page won "almost universal praise and respect" from the community. As opposition decreased, the membership of the church grew to more than 100 members from January to May 1914. As a "reward for Page's outstanding contribution to the Dallas church," Bishop C. H. Mason appointed him overseer of Texas at the state convocation held in Houston in July 1914. Houston was a fitting place for the convocation as the "Mother" COGIC church of Texas, Center Street COGIC, now "First COGIC," was founded in the Bayou City in 1909. Page Temple in Dallas, named in honor of E. M. Page, and an unnamed church in Hillsboro vie for second place.

From 1914 on, the organization's efforts were defined by establishing churches and encouraging education. The COGIC Educational Board first considered founding a "holiness" school in Texas at a "Ministers' and Workers Meeting" in 1917, ten years after Bishop C. H. Mason founded the denomination and only two years after E. M. Page assumed his position as overseer of COGIC efforts in Texas. Also in 1917, the General Council of the predominantly white Assemblies of God, many of whose early leaders were ordained by C. H. Mason,[17] encouraged holy-spirit filled young people to enroll in "some properly and scripturally accredited Bible training school."[18] Page Normal Industrial and Bible Institute was one of three COGIC schools established in the United States South.[19] Saints Industrial and Literacy School, located in Lexington, Mississippi,[20] though conceived the same year, was the first, and the Bible College, in Little Rock, Arkansas, the second. In 1918 the Texas COGIC Educational Board purchased 268 acres in Hearne on Henry Prairie Rd.,[21] where the administration building and the girls' dormitory for the Page

Normal Industrial and Bible Institute were the first two edifices constructed.[22]

Although Page asserted that organizers began the school "on a small scale," with only $1000 "in the bank for school purposes,"[23] the Page Normal School attempted to combine the approaches of both its COGIC predecessors.[24] Course proceedings of the Bible Institute fill pages of the *Texas Bulletin,* a monthly magazine of the Texas COGIC Jurisdiction printed in San Antonio and published "in the interest of Christian religion and Christian education."[25] Highlights from a homiletics class appeared for the benefit of aspiring ministers throughout the state. Less visible to the newspapers, the "Page Industrial and Literary School" trained students in the principles of holiness and the fundamentals of education through activities on and off campus.[26]

Historian Grant Wacker in his recent work *Heaven Below* (2001) noted that the general Pentecostal interpretation of the "social gospel" outlined in William Gladden's *Tools of Men* (1893) focused on the immediate moral behavior of individuals rather than on larger social ills such as poverty and the unequal distribution of wealth.[27] Black Pentecostals in Texas, however, showed a dual commitment to spiritual and intellectual growth; in their view "holiness" was the spiritual foundation for success. By becoming upstanding members of the community, students were better positioned to address social problems.

The declaration of principles set forth by the organization encouraged supporting the church financially, entertaining and contributing to home and foreign missions, and providing COGIC youth with a religious education. It forbade drinking, going to the movies and other places of amusement, dancing, card playing, furnishing intoxicating drinks to guests on any occasion, and participating in secret, oath-bound societies.[28] Anything perceived to be a "stumbling block in the way of the unconverted, and a grief to brethren whom we should not willingly offend" was to be avoided.[29]

In "Following His Steps," O. T. Jones, Overseer of Pennsylvania and National President of the Young People Willing Workers, reiterated the churches' moral charge to COGIC youth, stating that "[t]he great need of the young people of this present age is a deeper consecration when we realize that the multitude still follow[s] the broad way of ease and pleasure, which only lead[s] to shame and degradation."[30] Outlining the COGIC moral prescription for success, Jones argued that "[t]he epicurean philosophy, 'Let us eat and drink, for tomorrow we die,' is the general creed of the vast majority. But no great achievement, no good influence, no real success ever comes from that source." Emphasizing the importance of building character, Jones also noted:

> We may be sure there was a life of consecration and obedience at the foundation of the achievement. The earnest praying, studious person is often shunned by the thoughtless, frivolous crowd. But when his earnest praying and consecrated efforts have bourn their first fruit in character and achievement, the crowd will look on him with envy and regret, that they did not follow the course that led to some worthwhile end.[31] Young people, in striving to build for ourselves a strong character, we must, however, be careful not to confound reputation with character. A good or malicious character is not inherited like riches; man is his own tutor for his character. It is true that life itself is given of God, but it is also true that the character of each life is determined by his possessor. Let me urge you then as young people to build your character on [a] Christian foundation.[32]

In addition to offering students lessons in character building, Jones demonstrated his commitment to educating COGIC youth during the Eighteenth Annual Convention of the COGIC in 1926, when he donated fifty of the total $339 dollars pledged for "Educational Work." Only Charles Harrison Mason, bishop and founder of the COGIC organization, matched Jones's contribution.[33] In fact, the philanthropic disposition that Jones demonstrated was evident in COGIC donations to the poor, imprisoned, and "a blind girl," for whom $128, $100, and $23.64 were collected respectively.[34] Students affiliated with Y.P.W.W. and other departments within the organization also learned to raise funds, a skill that COGIC members from Texas had practiced to near perfection. For that year, under the direction of State Mother Hannah Chandler, Texas raised $3489.90 to support COGIC operations. The "Women's Work" faction of Oklahoma, also under Page's jurisdiction, reported $3503, and Arkansas, $5046.[35]

Students also gleaned from the self-help philosophy that organization advanced by encouraging members to join the National Burial Association. Page's assistant overseer, J. Houston Galloway of Austin, TX, was president of the association. By 1926, Galloway had been "instrumental in legislating for the success of the Benevolent Burial Association" for eight years, and as a result of his involvement, the association "obtain[ed] membership in several states."[36] Those affiliated with the Dallas church learned the importance of political activism via the church's involvement with the campaign efforts of the local NAACP. On May 31, 1919, the COGIC was listed among the twenty-five area churches that were to host NAACP campaign speakers Sunday, June 1, 1919. Although the COGIC congregation's reaction is unknown, the pastor's invitation affirmed his desire to have a politically informed flock.

Students could also look forward to applying their knowledge and demonstrating their talents at state and national Convocations. Those who attended "Educational Night" on the thirteenth day of the Eighteenth Annual COGIC Convocation were no doubt inspired by the "beautiful program" that students from the Geridge School in Arkansas had organized. The recording secretary noted: "Jesus was magnified in every song, in every speech and in every action. How the power did fall, all the saints going up in a shout."[37]

On the Page campus, civic and moral lessons were reinforced by classes in reading, writing, and mathematics, thanks to the leadership of Principal Emma F. Bradley Barron. Born to Professor Sam Henry and Mrs. Rosie Bradley in 1894,[38] she earned her high school diploma in Tyler and pursued an undergraduate degree at Prairie View A&M University. Under the tutelage of faculty members eager to introduce students to Booker T. Washington's pragmatic philosophy, Emma acquired the knowledge and confidence to become a leader, activist, fundraiser, nurturer, and educator. After graduating in 1915, she followed in her father's footsteps and taught in the Hillsboro school system. When COGIC leaders in Texas decided to establish an academic, industrial, and bible training institute for the COGIC and other children, they called on Emma Bradley Barron to serve as the first principal of the school, a position which put her many skills to immediate use.

For fifteen years, the Page Normal Institute made "rapid progress," thanks to the "jurisdictional system" implemented to raise funds for the institute;[39] moreover, it received an important stamp of approval when the COGIC founder, Bishop C. H. Mason, sent his son to study there.[40] Progress at Page Normal led COGIC leaders in Texas to expand their efforts. In 1922, the Educational Board and trustees of the COGIC bought an additional seventy acres of land in Robertson County from Martine Altimore for $225.[41] Page also made a concerted effort to increase the organization's property holdings and presence in the state. More churches meant more members, and more members ultimately meant more funds to enhance school activities.

In this enthusiastic atmosphere of growth and expansion, "several" students were graduated from the Page Normal and Industrial Institute with "high honors" and were "sent out to take their places in the world."[42] Emma Frances Searcy Crouch, a Morris County native, was among the stellar students graduated from Page Normal. Having graduated salutatorian from Booker T. Washington High School in May 1932, Emma entered Page Normal to prepare for a life of service to the church. After earning her diploma in 1934, she studied cosmetology at the C. J. Walker School of Beauty and Culture, and enrolled in Bishop College later in the 1950s.[43] Little did she or Principal Barron know at the time that young Emma would one day rise to the highest position a woman can hold within the COGIC organization, that of International Supervisor of the Women's Department, the financial powerhouse of the COGIC. Based on Emma Crouch's eventual success, Page Normal had trained her well.

Despite the school's positive example, operations were eventually suspended so that priority could be given to the senior schools in Lexington, Mississippi, and Geridge, Arkansas.[44] By 1920, the Lexington school had become so prominent that "the idea of making it a national institution" was introduced at the National Convocation in Memphis, Tennessee. "After some deliberation . . . the [Lexington] school was accepted as a national institution on the endorsement of Bishop Mason."[45] After fire devastated the Page complex in 1932,[46] the institute was never rebuilt. However, the "jurisdictional system" that emerged from its development remains the aegis of national COGIC administration, and the progressive spirit inculcated in Page graduates such as Emma Crouch continues to make Texas a premier state within the COGIC organization. Her dedication to the church along with Emma Bradley Barron's and E. M. Page's contributions to the COGIC organization and the communities it served collectively affirm that education and social uplift were indeed on the minds of the COGIC in East Texas. Territory that had once absorbed sweat from the furrowed brows of their enslaved ancestors had now become a perfect place to plan a better future and construct a better world.

Notes

1. Cited in Charles H. Pleas, *Fifty Years of Achievement—From 1906–1956: A Period in History of the Church of God in Christ,* Reprint, 1991, 39. See also *The History and Life Work of Bishop C. H. Mason,* compiled in 1924, reprinted in 1987, 103–105.
2. Zora Neale Hurston, *The Sanctified Church* (Tustin, California, 1989), 103–105.
3. Ada Moorhead Holland and Reverend C. C. White, *No Quittin' Sense* (Austin, 1969).
4. Alwyn Barr, *Black Texans: A History of Negroes in Texas: 1528–1971* (1973; Austin, 1988).
5. Bobby Dean, *This is the Church of God in Christ* (Atlanta, Georgia, 2001).
6. *Year Book of the Church of God in Christ for the Year 1926,* 73–74.
7. J. W. Baker, *History of Robertson County, Texas,* fourth edition (Waco, Texas, 1988), 282.
8. Deed Records, Robertson County, Vol. 68, 202–203, 287–288.
9. Deed Records, Robertson County, Vol. 68, 217–218.
10. Deed Records, Robertson County, Vol. 68, 387–388.
11. *Year Book of the Church of God in Christ for the Year 1926,* 67.
12. *Dallas, TX, Negro City Directory 1941–42,* LXIII.
13. *Dallas, TX, Negro City Directory 1941–42,* LXIII.
14. *Dallas, TX, Negro City Directory 1941–42,* LXIII.
15. *Dallas, TX, Negro City Directory 1941–42,* LXIII.
16. *Year Book of the Church of God in Christ for the Year 1926,* 67.
17. Vinson Synan, *The Holiness-Pentecostal Tradition: Charismatic Movements in the Twentieth Century* (Grand Rapids, Michigan, 1997), 171, 172; Dean, *This is the Church of God in Christ,* 57–59.
18. Cited in Grant Wacker, *Heaven Below: Early Pentecostals and American Culture* (Cambridge, Massachusetts, 2001), 152.
19. Dean, *This is the Church of God in Christ,* 55.
20. Pleas, *Fifty Years of Achievement,* 47.
21. Norman Lowell McCarver, Sr. & Norman Lowell McCarver Jr. *Hearne on the Brazos* (San Antonio, 1958), 104.
22. Pleas, *Fifty Years of Achievement,* 41.
23. *The History and Life Work of Bishop C. H. Mason,* 99.
24. Pleas, *Fifty Years of Achievement,* 41.
25. *Texas Bulletin: A Monthly Magazine of the Church of God in Christ, Texas Jurisdiction* (July 1938).
26. Glenda Williams Goodson, *I Commend Unto You Phebe: Female Leader-Activists in the Missionary Societies and Ministries of the African American Church 1900–1925* (Rev. ed.; Lancaster, 2001).
27. Synan, *The Holiness-Pentecostal Tradition,* 47.

28. Synan, *The Holiness-Pentecostal Tradition,* 78.
29. Synan, *The Holiness-Pentecostal Tradition,* 78.
30. *Year Book of the Church of God in Christ for the Year 1926,* 69.
31. *Year Book of the Church of God in Christ for the Year 1926,* 69.
32. *Year Book of the Church of God in Christ for the Year 1926,* 69.
33. *Year Book of the Church of God in Christ for the Year 1926,* 81–82.
34. *Year Book of the Church of God in Christ for the Year 1926,* 82.
35. *Year Book of the Church of God in Christ for the Year 1926,* 58.
36. *Year Book of the Church of God in Christ for the Year 1926,* 64.
37. *Year Book of the Church of God in Christ for the Year 1926,* 57.
38. Funeral Program, Mother Emma Bradley (1894–1996), Saintsville COGIC, Dallas, TX.
39. Glenda Williams Goodson, E-mail to Karen Kossie-Chernyshev, Tuesday, March 26, 2002.
40. Glenda Williams Goodson, E-mail to Karen Kossie-Chernyshev, Tuesday, March 26, 2002.
41. Deed Records, Robertson County, Vol. 80, 276.
42. Pleas, *Fifty Years of Achievement,* 78.
43. Dean, *This is the Church of God in Christ,* 165.
44. Dean, *This is the Church of God in Christ,* 41.
45. Pleas, *Fifty Years of Achievement,* 48.
46. McCarver, *Hearne on the Brazos,* 104.

Melvin B. Tolson
Texas Radical

GAIL K BEIL

MELVIN TOLSON WAS A POET, PLAYWRIGHT, NOVelist, professor, popular lecturer, journalist, and debate coach during his long career in historically black Southern colleges. Particularly at Wiley College in Marshall, Texas, he was more than that. He was also identified as a campus radical by colleagues and students, a Christian socialist, and Democrat when most African Americans called themselves "Lincoln Republicans." During his long teaching career he molded the lives of a number of the courageous leaders of the modern civil rights movement.

He described himself once in a poem that became his epitaph.

Bootblack and Poet
Dishwasher and Teacher
Cook and Philosopher
Waiter and Lecturer
Meatpacker and Mayor
Humorist and Humanist
Coach of football and drama, boxing and debate
Fighter for Freedom—Lover of Man.[1]

This was an accurate description of Tolson's life, but his role as teacher and fighter for freedom is being forgotten as his reputation as a poet and playwright grows.

Tolson began his teaching career in 1924 in Marshall where he remained until 1947. At Wiley, a small Methodist-related institution founded by the Freedman's Aid Society of the Methodist Episcopal Church North in 1873, he inspired one of his students to become a leading civil rights leader in the 1960s, another who successfully sued to integrate the University of Texas School of Law, and others who changed the segregated face of the nation in quieter ways.

Born in Missouri in 1898, Melvin Tolson was a Methodist preacher's son. He was educated at Lincoln University in Pennsylvania, the nation's first historically black college. He found his first job at Wiley College in 1924, after receiving his bachelor's degree in English.

Tolson's son and namesake, Dr. Melvin B. Tolson Jr., said his father chose to come to Wiley College for two reasons. "I've been told that at the time he finished Lincoln, his father, who was a Methodist Episcopal minister, knew of the fine reputation of Dr. M. W. Dogan and Wiley College. I don't know if he knew Dogan [president of Wiley College from 1895 to 1942] personally, but the whole black Methodist Episcopal Church was one—all the leaders knew each other—that's the reason he got the appointment."

Dr. Tolson also said that Wiley College was among the best of historically black colleges, "the Fisk University West of the Mississippi. It was known as a place where the faculty enjoyed academic freedom." That freedom was a luxury not available on many historically black campuses where even personal habits of the faculty were matters of censure by college presidents. Dogan might be uncomfortable with the statements, writings, and actions of some of his faculty, but he stewed in private. Once, after Tolson made a heated speech to the board of trustees gathered on the steps of the Carnegie Library, Dogan stepped to the podium and said quietly that Tolson did not always speak for the administration.[2]

That freedom, as well as Dogan's encouragement for faculty and students to have meaningful dialogue outside the classroom, offered Tolson an important additional forum, under a tree on the campus or in his own living room at night, to educate and influence his students. "Students would see Tolson coming across the campus, sometimes barefooted, and they would flock around him," said Mildred Lewis Mason, who studied under him in the early 1930s. "He loved to argue—he would argue with a tree."

Miss Lewis, who graduated from Central High School in Marshall, was a high school classmate of Tolson's wife, Ruth Southall Tolson. Mrs. Tolson had not graduated from high school when Tolson married her in 1922, so even though she was the mother of four children, Ruth Tolson determined to graduate from high school and then from Wiley College.

"She decided her children were not going to get ahead of her," Dr. Tolson said. Not only was she older—and the subject of teasing from some of her younger classmates—she suffered from a handicap. "My mother came from a family where every second child was hard of hearing. She was number four." She graduated with her eldest son, Melvin Jr., from Wiley College in 1939.[3]

In 1933, the first African American in Texas with a Ph.D., Dr. J. Leonard Farmer, who first taught at Wiley College in 1920, returned to the East Texas college. His precocious son, James Farmer Jr., enrolled at Wiley the following year at the age of fourteen. Dr. Farmer was admired by Tolson for his intellectualism and his preaching ability. The son soon became one of Tolson's top debaters and an actor in many of the plays Tolson directed. The boy later founded the Congress of Racial Equality, and by so doing joined Martin Luther King Jr., of the Southern Christian Leadership Conference, Whitney Young of the National Urban League, and Roy Wilkins of the National Association for the Advancement of Colored People to change the way the nation viewed the Negro race. Dubbed by the media "The Big Four," they became the most important leaders of the modern civil rights movement. "The banquet of my Wiley years was the tutelage of Tolson," Farmer said.

Farmer's description of Tolson, found in his autobiography, *Lay Bare the Heart,* captured the essence of his teacher.

> A scholar without credentials (he had only a bachelor's degree), a poet and dramatist who had not yet published, Tolson taught English. But that was the least of the things he taught. He stretched the minds of all whose minds would be stretched.
>
> When he read to us of Harlem, he came fully alive. New York was Mecca to him and every summer he went to kneel at its altar. In that off season he worked on his master's at Columbia. Breathing the air of Langston Hughes and Countee Cullen and others of the Harlem Renaissance, he recharged his batteries. He engaged in argument those thinkers who could teach him as he taught us. He also peddled his poems to publishers and his folk operas to producers. Only 34 at the time, he spoke of New York in hushed tones, as of the promised land.[4]

Farmer's words reflect not only Tolson's influence on his own political beliefs but his way with words, both spoken and written, an eloquence he attributed to Tolson.

Harlem Renaissance poet Langston Hughes, who visited Wiley College at least three times, returned Tolson's admiration. Hughes' column, "Here to Yonder," published in the *Chicago Defender* in 1945, provides a cogent impression of the Texas poet and firestarter:

> That Texas is some state! I've been down there once or twice myself. And I've found some pretty amazing things—including Melvin Tolson.
>
> Melvin Tolson is the most famous Negro professor in the Southwest. Students from all over the world speak of him, revere him, remember him, and love him. He is a character. He once turned out a debate team that beat Oxford, England. He is a great talker himself. He teaches English at Wiley College, in Marshall, Texas, but he is known far and wide. He is a poet of no mean ability, and his book of poems, "Rendezvous With America," is a recent fine contribution to American literature.
>
> But Melvin Tolson is no highbrow. Kids from the cottonfields like him. Cowpunchers understand him. He is a great teacher of the kind of which any college might be proud. . . . And the likes of him is found no where else but in the great State of Texas—because there is only one Tolson![5]

If Dr. Farmer was the campus intellectual, Tolson was the firebrand. During Farmer's sojourn at Wiley, Tolson was threatened with lynching if he did not leave town. It took Dogan's intervention to save Tolson. Dogan called the town's most influential banker, Hobart Key, to help save his outspoken professor and the college's English department. The banker, doubtless aware of the financial contribution the college made to Marshall's economy, did so. Precisely why Tolson was threatened in Marshall is the subject of speculation. Farmer thought it might be because Tolson organized a boycott of local stores. Melvin Tolson Jr. didn't think so. His father was a great speaker and much in demand for high school commencements, fraternities and churches, but except for his union organization work among sharecroppers in Arkansas later in the 1920s, he was not an organizer of protest, according to his son. He provided instead its inspiration.

The saga of Tolson's debate program is an example of academic life on the Wiley College campus in the 1930s and 1940s. Debate was among the most popular extracurricular activities.

Contests between the teams of two colleges, black or white, usually were staged in the home college's largest auditorium. "Debate was so popular, you could charge admission and get a full house," remembered Melvin Tolson Jr. "At Wiley, when you had debates, whatever team was coming it was a prize occasion. People piled in."[6] Each year a nation-wide debate topic was chosen; it was timely, controversial, and required debaters to do considerable research and to hone arguments on both sides of topics as broad ranging as self-government for the Philippines, free trade, or federal support for education. Each debater on a two-man team was allowed a ten-minute speech and a five-minute rebuttal; winners were determined by how well one team met and defeated the arguments of the other.[7]

In a rattletrap Ford whose eccentricities once saved their lives—it stalled just before crossing a railroad track in a thick fog in Arkansas one night, some ten feet from a train traveling sixty-nine miles per hour—Wiley's legendary teams toured the country.[8] They broke new ground in 1930 with their first interracial debate, held in Oklahoma City at Oklahoma City University. Later, they debated Texas Christian University, the University of Kansas, and Kansas State University. Proceeds from ticket sales to the debates enabled Tolson to support his team and its travels.

The most spectacular encounter Wiley debaters had may have been with a team from England's Oxford College that was on a good-will trip across the United States in 1933. But the crowning moment for the team of fifteen-year-old James Farmer, Hobart Jarrett, and Henry Heights came in 1935 in Los Angeles when they debated the national champions of that year, the University of Southern California. This trip was made in Dr. Farmer's Dodge, a much more dependable vehicle than Tolson's old Ford. The business managers of both teams were particularly pleased, since more than 1,200 tickets had been sold for the event even before Tolson's three-man team arrived in Southern California. The audience grew to 2,300 on the night of the debate.[9] Fearing that his debaters would be overwhelmed by their University of Southern California opponents since the Trojan speech department was larger than all of Wiley College, Tolson refused to let them tour the Southern California campus. Before a packed house in Bovard Auditorium, Wiley beat Southern California. Hobart Jarrett wrote an article about the adventure in the

NAACP's publication, *The Crisis*. "Interracial debates are a real adventure for both Negro youth and white youth," Jarrett wrote. "For centuries the Caucasian has believed that his superiority lies in his brain power. . . . There was a time when white colleges thought that debating against a Negro institution was mental dissipation, but that view has passed forever. Negro teams have shown they are as capable as their white opponents despite the library handicaps which limit research."[10]

Tolson's experience in Los Angeles included a visit with movie star Mae West, who read about the debates and sent a request to meet the fabled coach. Her autographed photograph, now in the Library of Congress with Tolson's papers, was one of his prized possessions. Although black college debaters were not allowed to join Pi Kappa Delta, the honorary debate fraternity, Tolson was asked to contribute an article to its journal, *The Forensic*.

"From the time Floyd C. Covington, who presided, opened the program until its close the vast audience was held in rapt attention by the scholarly presentations of both teams. All through the debate warm applause cheered the speakers as they scored strong points or relieved the tenseness of their appeals with clever and witty thrusts," wrote Tolson in the *Forensic*.[11]

Debates held in Marshall often included a few whites in the audience. The elaborate effort to preserve segregation while enjoying the challenging atmosphere at Wiley was described by a white Marshall school administrator, Emma Mae Brotze, and her English teacher sister, Selma. As young women they often attended Tolson's debates with their Presbyterian minister. "They would seat us right down front," Miss Emma Mae Brotze said. "Then they would leave a row of empty seats, then the Negro audience would be seated."[12]

James Farmer's debating skills, honed by Tolson, stood him in good stead when he hammered out the argument for the founding of the Congress of Racial Equality in 1941, as he defended his actions and those of CORE before two presidents, and most certainly when he agreed to debate Malcolm X three times during 1961, debates that both men agree Farmer won.[13]

Tolson's reputation as a writer, educator, and debate coach led Texas Governor James Allred to authorize him to represent Texas at the August 4, 1935, "National Negro Day Celebration" held during the International Exhibition in San Diego, California. "We are glad to have a man of your standing represent Texas, and are quite proud of the name Wiley College has made for itself through its debating team, with you as coach," Allred wrote.[14]

Debating was not the only intellectual experience Tolson offered Wiley students. He read his own poetry and plays to his classes for their critique and comment. In 1938 he organized the Southern Association of Dramatic and Speech Arts, had three of his students write one-act plays for its first contest, and invited V. F. Calverton, drama critic, writer, editor of *Modern Monthly,* and columnist for *Current History,* to judge them. Calverton, who was white and was well known to Harlem Renaissance writers and poets, was particularly fond of Tolson. "Mr. Tolson is a bright, vivid writer who attains his best effects by understatement," Calverton wrote. "The Negroes he describes in his poems come to life, candidly, unforgettably."[15]

Calverton's visit to Wiley was quite an experience for the students, the faculty, and particularly for President Dogan. Calverton, at young Farmer's invitation, but with Tolson's encouragement, agreed to spend a week at Wiley for the small sum of $100, providing Tolson could arrange other Texas appearances. He arrived in a convertible with a woman not his wife, and refused to stay in the segregated Hotel Marshall—"how barbaric," he wrote Farmer Jr. So his hosts arranged for accommodations in the home of one of Wiley's music teachers.[16]

Calverton put Dogan's teeth on edge by smoking a huge stogie in the auditorium, which also served as the chapel. "Dogan saw him with the cigar and was very disapproving," said Farmer. "But Dogan wasn't about to say anything because he hoped Calverton's visit would lead to more funds for Wiley."[17]

Calverton found two of the three plays presented by Wiley College "positively lousy—too lousy to say much about." The third, however, was "the best amateur play I've ever seen." One of Wiley's actors, Virgil Richardson, was singled out as outstanding, and Calverton was able to get Richardson a part in a professional play in New York. Farmer's acting talents did not fare so well. Calverton said that Farmer never quit being Farmer, and was better off sticking with the critical thinking required of a debater.[18]

In his "Cultural Barometer" column in May 1938, Calverton wrote of his Wiley College experience:

> This month at Wiley College, Marshall, Texas, a Play Festival was organized by the Southern Association of Dramatic and Speech Arts, which is a Negro cultural organization of great influence in the South. Attending the festival were dramatic groups from the following Negro universities: Dillard University, New Orleans; LaMoyne College, Memphis; Texas College, Tyler; Houston College for Negroes, Houston; Langston State College, Langston, Oklahoma; and Bishop College. Among the plays produced the most interesting were three one-act plays: *A Southern Tragedy* by Orange Clemens, a sharecropper's drama laid in Arkansas; *The Road to Damascus* by Jimmy Lilly and Inaree Miller, the tragic story of an outcast octoroon and an old Negro man, and *Dawn,* [by Jimmy Lilly] a play built around the unconventional love life of a Negro professor in a Negro medical school. All these plays were written by students at Wiley College under the direction of M. B. Tolson.[19]

Calverton also described dramatized reviews of books by T. S. Eliot, Carl Sandburg, and Robert Briffalt, performed in a crowded auditorium, which "have increased the sale of books in the community, and have made books the most vital form of conversation on the campus."[20]

When Calverton died unexpectedly in 1940, Jim Crow laws kept Tolson from flying to New York, the only way he could have attended the funeral. In despair, Tolson wrote a tribute to his friend and mentor in the memorial issue of *Modern Quarterly* dedicated to Calverton.[21]

Seventeen-year-old Farmer and another of Tolson's student debaters, Benjamin Bell, inspired by their English professor's nightly bull sessions and his own commitment to the NAACP, decided the time had come to organize a chapter on the Wiley campus. Bishop College, across town, had had a chapter for a year, and the town itself had one as early as 1919, although it folded as a result of the Longview race riots. Another was organized in 1927.[22] The Wiley students did not face an easy task, for Dogan, who had spent forty years as Wiley's president, was not anxious to create controversy in a town whose African American population exceeded its Caucasian. Roscoe Dunjee, editor of Oklahoma City's *Black Dispatch* newspaper, sent a telegram to Wiley College requesting Dogan's assistance for Juanita Jackson, field secretary for the NAACP, in her efforts to organize a youth chapter at Wiley College. Dogan replied:

> We will do all we can to make the coming of Miss Jackson comfortable. As stated in my wire, we will talk over with her the advisability of organizing an NAACP chapter here. You understand, I am sure, that racial antagonism can more easily develop in sections where Negroes constitute a large part of the population, as is the case in Marshall. I support the NAACP financially because I feel it is a fine organization, but up to this time, it has not been thought best by some of us here in Marshall to form a chapter here.[23]

When Farmer Jr. wrote a two-page letter to Jackson three months later, he told her, "You have no idea what a battle we have had to wage here at Wiley against powerful opposition. We have met rebuffs at every hand where opportunities could have meant much to our cause." Farmer promised a "dynamic membership campaign" and, ever conscious of the rivalry between Wiley and Bishop, promised that by the following year Wiley would make Jackson proud. "You have a number of hustling chapters . . . but remember reserve number one place for the Wiley College chapter. WE WILL EARN IT! [The emphasis was Farmer's]. Farmer expected to have at least seventy-five members by 1938, and if Marshall or Wiley College was afraid of dynamic Negro speakers, "We will have able speakers, even if we find it necessary to bring white citizens or men from other cities here."[24]

Farmer's bravado in 1938 grew into the courage to found CORE, and lead the nation's first restaurant sit-ins in Chicago in 1942, the bloody Freedom Rides in 1961, and the deadly Mississippi Freedom Summer voter-registration drives in 1964, events that contributed to the passage of the Civil Rights Act of 1964 and the Voting Rights Act of 1965.

Farmer was not the only civil rights pioneer who drew inspiration from Tolson. Another was Heman Sweatt, plaintiff in the successful lawsuit to integrate the University of Texas School of Law, filed in Austin in 1946 and finally decided by the United States Supreme Court in 1952. Sweatt graduated from Wiley College in 1934 and told an interviewer that in addition to his father, the man with the most influence on his life was Tolson. "When directed against racial discrimination, Tolson's eloquence was devastating, Whether speaking to black students in his classes or to white students at the University of Texas, the gentle genius captivated his audiences with his satirical wit, his imagery and his piercing analysis," wrote Michael Gillette in *Black Leaders: Texans for Their Times.*[25]

Probably at the invitation of J. Frank Dobie, on March 11, 1946, Tolson spoke to the organization Common Sense which met at the Community Congregational Church located near the University of Texas campus. Sweatt's unsuccessful attempt to enroll in the School of Law had made statewide newspapers. Homer Rainey, demoted from the presidency of the University to academic dean in 1944, had just been fired from that position for his liberal views. Tolson, speaking to a packed house, mentioned both and urged the students to sign the petitions available in the hall for Sweatt's admission to the U.T. School of Law. As he had done for years with his speeches to all-black audiences, Tolson made it clear that in his view racism had economic roots. "That is why the Negro wanted a mule and forty acres of land after the Civil War, for without economic independence he couldn't hope to have political freedom."[26]

One Wiley student became President Lyndon Johnson's icon for the need to pass a meaningful civil rights bill in 1963 and 1964. She was Zephyr Wright, the Johnson family cook. When Michael Gillette, then oral historian for the LBJ Library, interviewed Wright on September 4, 1980, she told him, "The one person that helped me most was Dr. Tolson, because he would help me in the evenings. He helped me with diction and things like that, and he was very, very good."[27]

In 1948, another of Tolson's students and a classmate of Farmer, Fred Lewis, filed suit through the NAACP against the Harrison County Citizens' Party, an all-white political party that had chosen every candidate for city and county office since its founding in 1874. The NAACP won the suit in 1950, and Lewis attributed the courage to take on the white establishment in his home town to Tolson's teachings.[28]

Tolson began writing a regular column for the *Washington Tribune,* an African American weekly, in 1937. He called it "Caviar and Cabbage," an expression students said he often used in class to demonstrate the randomness of the subjects he would cover. For the next seven years, Tolson wrote about his experiences at Wiley College, his favorable view of Franklin D. Roosevelt and the New Deal, and his disgust about the situation in which Negroes found themselves in the United States. Although he heard the siren song of communism and felt that capitalism was the great force pulling his people down, he never joined the Communist Party and remained loyal to the social gospel of the Methodist Episcopal Church. He could best be defined as a Christian socialist. He saw the value of defending the common man, and had little use for "mouth Christians" no matter their race.[29]

In a column on the death of lawyer Clarence Darrow, Tolson wrote:

> The case of Clarence Darrow points a lesson. Black folks are too easily deluded by superficial facts. Call a man an infidel or a radical and you can hoodwink us to death. Why should a black man fear a radical? The abolitionists were radicals in their day. At one time it was radical in America to say, "I believe the black man has a soul; I believe a black man can be educated." If it had not been for the radicals, every black man would be in a cotton patch with a white man standing over him with a forty-four and a horsewhip three yards long.
>
> And whenever you hear anybody denounce radicals, remember this: persecuted races get their rights only through the agitation of radicals. The man who denies the truth of this is as dumb as Balaam's jackass. Amen![30]

Tolson also addressed the heart of his own concept of Christianity in his account of a Mother's Day sermon delivered at Wiley College by Dr. Farmer, who brought his own brand of radical theology learned at Boston University School of Theology to the pulpit:

> Said Dr. Farmer: "Jesus was teaching contrary to the social and religious traditions of his people. . . . Yes, the Big Boys were against Jesus, and if He should return today the Big Boys would be against Him. They would call Him an infidel, an atheist, a radical, a red."
>
> In one clean sentence, Dr. Farmer pointed out the dilemma of a man like Jesus—a man who wants to help the people: "The more popular He became with the masses, the more hostile these leaders became toward him, and the more determined to destroy them."
>
> Parents say, "Take the world as it comes and make the best of it." Christian youth says, according to Dr. Farmer, "Change the world and make it what it ought to be. I'll take

> my stand with American youth and Dr. Farmer and Jesus, the young radical.[31]

Tolson left Wiley College for Langston University in the Oklahoma city of the same name. Dogan had retired in 1942, and soon Wiley was in chaos. A student strike paralyzed the college in 1947, but that alone was not the reason for Tolson's departure. Mrs. Tolson believed her husband to be unappreciated by the faculty and the alumni of the schools, both of whom had made many promises to their outstanding English professor. One of the unfulfilled pledges was a new building, to be called the Log Cabin Theater, to house Tolson's dramatic productions. By 1947 Hobart Jarrett was chairman of the English Department at Langston University in Oklahoma, and he invited his old mentor to join him. Tolson really did not want to leave his East Texas college. But instead of asking him to stay, Wiley College President I. W. McCloud told Tolson to do whatever he himself wanted. Ruth Tolson resented such indifferent treatment on the part of the administration.[32]

There were economic considerations as well. Wiley College did not offer retirement benefits, but state-supported Langston did. Tolson's sons also believe that Tolson's desire to write had a good deal to do with the decision. He had published his first book of poetry, *Rendezvous With America,* in 1944, but was too busy with other pursuits to complete other works, including plays, a novel, and a three-volume book of poetry he called *A Gallery of Harlem Portraits.* Wiley's loss was the literary world's gain, for Tolson, not so involved with debate or other pursuits, completed works begun earlier, published more poetry in contemporary magazines, and finished the first—and only—volume of *A Gallery.* Another occurrence made leaving easier. Debate was no longer as exciting as it once was. After World War II other entertainments killed it as a spectator activity.[33]

While he was living in Langston, Tolson chose to enter the political arena. In 1954, he was elected mayor of the historically black town. He served eight years, facing the difficulties one might expect in an economically deprived community and adding grist for his writer's mill. When his service was over, he wrote in his journal: "I wouldn't take anything as a writer for having lived in an All-Negro town: I now know what is human, what is American and what is Negro."[34]

In 1964 Tolson, who was a heavy smoker most of his adult life, was diagnosed with cancer. His first surgery resulting from the disease was in April 1964. By December the doctors told him he had six months to live. They missed their prediction by about a year, and Tolson lived the last eighteen months of his life as vigorously as he had the previous sixty-six years.

In those months he received many awards for his poetry and plays. In 1966, he returned to the days of his Texas radicalism and inspiration to his students. He reviewed James Farmer's *Freedom When?* for the *New York Herald Tribune* on February 20, 1966. In it he called his former student, retiring as executive director of CORE, the Negro's greatest spokesman. He was a "mystery guest," surprising Farmer when the latter was honored by dignitaries including Sammy Davis Jr., Harry Belafonte, and Duke Ellington at New York's Philharmonic Hall on March 6.

In the years since his death on August 29, 1966, in a hospital in Dallas, Tolson's fame as a writer, poet, and playwright has grown. But history largely has failed to record the inspiration he provided his students. This may have been his greatest contribution.

Notes

1. This poem appeared in the obituary of Tolson, September 3, 1966. Tolson was buried in Guthrie. Oklahoma. A copy of the program is among Tolson's papers at the Library of Congress.
2. Description of former student Mildred Lewis Mason. Interview with author, April 9, 1999.
3. Author's telephone interview with Melvin Tolson Jr., August 9, 2000.
4. James Farmer, *Lay Bare the Heart* (Fort Worth, 1983), 116–117.
5. *Chicago Defender*, December 15, 1945.
6. Tony Scherman, "The Great Debaters," *American Legacy*, Spring 1997, 40.
7. The author was a Spring Branch (Houston) High School and Oklahoma State University debater from 1950 to 1960. Debates at that time were conducted in the same manner as they were in the 1930s and 1940s, although they did not draw the crowds in the 1950s they had before World War II.
8. Tolson, "Caviar and Cabbage" column, "I Get the Jitters," in the *Washington Tribune*, April 16, 1938.
9. Although a team consisted of only two debaters, three men went to Los Angeles. Having three debaters, Farmer said, allowed Tolson to vary the team according to their strengths and whether they were on the negative or affirmative side in each round. The author, a friend of Farmer for more than fifteen years, talked often with him about his years at Wiley.
10. Hobart Jarrett, "Adventures in Interracial Debates," *Crisis*, August 1935, 240.

11. Melvin Beaunorus Tolson, "Interracial Debates," *Forensic,* July 1935, 16–19.
12. Author's interview with Emma Mae and Selma Brotze in Marshall, February 12, 1984.
13. Farmer, *Lay Bare,* 224–227.
14. Governor James Allred to Melvin B. Tolson, June 17, 1935, Tolson papers, Correspondence, file C, Library of Congress.
15. V. F. Calverton, "The Cultural Barometer," *Current History,* February 1938, 15.
16. Farmer remembered that Calverton took over the apartment of a bachelor professor who agreed to move out. Tolson remembered that it was an English teacher's home. Farmer, *Lay Bare,* 138; Robert Farnsworth, *Melvin B. Tolson: Plain Talk and Poetic Prophecy* (Columbia, Missouri, 1983), 105.
17. Calverton's visit is recorded in Farmer, *Lay Bare,* 143–147, as well as recounted in the author's interview with Farmer, March 13, 1999. Tolson's experiences with Calverton are found often in his "Caviar and Cabbage" columns.
18. Farmer, *Lay Bare,* 145.
19. V. F. Calverton, "Cultural Barometer," *Current History,* May 1938, 18.
20. V. F. Calverton, "Cultural Barometer," *Current History,* May 1938, 46–47.
21. Farnsworth, *Melvin B. Tolson,* 60, 64.
22. NAACP Branch files, Library of Congress, "Marshall," "Bishop," and "Wiley" folders. Bell may have had a role in the forming of the Bishop chapter. A postcard identical to the one he wrote Juanita Jackson from Wiley was written to her with a "Bishop College" return address. Bishop organized its NAACP chapter the year before Wiley College, according to NAACP records.
23. Dogan to Dungee, March 12, 1937, NAACP Branch files, Library of Congress. Dogan actually misspelled Dunjee's name with a "g" where there should have been a "j."
24. Farmer Jr. to Jackson, June 4, 1937, NAACP Branch files, "Wiley College," Library of Congress.
25. Alwyn Barr and Robert A. Calvert, eds., *Black Leaders: Texans for Their Times* (Austin, 1981), 163.
26. Helen Campbell, "'Problem is Economic, not Racial,' Negro says," the *Daily Texan,* March 12, 1946, 1.
27. Gillette's interview with Wright, Lyndon B. Johnson Presidential Library.
28. Author's interview with Fred Lewis, Jan. 3, 2000. Lewis placed all his correspondence with Maceo Smith, then president of the Texas NAACP, and all the legal documents relating to the case in the Marshall Public Library.
29. Robert Farnsworth, ed., *Caviar and Cabbage: Selected Columns by Melvin B. Tolson from the* Washington Tribune, *1937–1944* (Columbia, Missouri, 1982). All column quotations are from Farnsworth's book.
30. Tolson, "The Death of an Infidel," *Washington Tribune,* April 2, 1938.
31. Tolson, "Portrait of Jesus, the Young Radical," *Washington Tribune,* June 4, 1938.
32. Author's interview with Melvin B. Tolson Jr., August 9, 2000.
33. Author's interview with Melvin B. Tolson Jr., March 14, 1998.
34. Farnsworth, *Melvin B. Tolson,* 210–212.

Women in the Civil Rights Movement
Juanita Craft versus the Dallas Elite

STEFANIE DECKER

UNTIL VERY RECENTLY, HISTORIANS HAVE NEglected the contributions women made to the civil rights crusade. Many remember Rosa Parks of Montgomery, Alabama, and Daisy Bates of Little Rock, Arkansas, but few recall local or regional leaders such as Juanita Craft of Dallas, who helped desegregate one of the largest cities in Dixie.

Some people overlook the civil rights movement in Dallas because it appeared to lack the deep segregation of other Southern cities. A *Texas Monthly* article in 1991 claimed that the movement bypassed Dallas.[1] But blacks in Dallas experienced the same discrimination as African Americans in other parts of the South. Even after all the civil rights advances of the 1950s and 1960s, in 1970 Dallas ranked fourth on a list of the twenty most segregated cities in the nation. Before the *Brown* decision of 1954, Jim Crow maintained a strong foothold in Texas in segregated state parks, education, and transportation, and a Texas statute outlawed miscegenation.[2] Although there were only five Jim Crow laws, Juanita Craft recalls that "they had the strength of a thousand. And they were doubly enforced by tradition."[3]

In the 1950s and 1960s, while other Southern cities reluctantly integrated public facilities, Dallas lagged behind. Blacks in Dallas lived in conditions similar to those at the end of the Civil War, and most African Americans worked as janitors or domestics, for lower wages than whites. Women's jobs were relegated overwhelmingly to the service sector. As in most Jim Crow cities, whites barred African Americans from eating in restaurants, trying on clothes in department stores, or using public restrooms and drinking fountains. Housing was also segregated; blacks mostly lived in the South Dallas area of Oak Cliff.

Dallas had a small percentage of blacks compared to other Southern cities, but that percentage was growing. In 1960, African Americans constituted approximately nineteen percent of the total population in Dallas. By 1970, although they only made up 24.8 percent of the population, they ranked the highest of any group, 44.5 percent, in the Dallas Independent School District.[4]

When the Supreme Court announced its decision in *Brown vs. Topeka* in 1954, Dallas whites recognized that desegregation was inevitable but did not take voluntary action to accelerate it. After the violence that erupted in Little Rock, Arkansas, Birmingham and Selma, Alabama, and Jackson, Mississippi, Dallas' elite decided to begin the process of integration and control it before others launched the local civil rights movement on a path they did not wish to trod. In the 1960s, a small group of white businessmen and clergy ran the city's government. Known as the "Dallas Way," these men governed the social, economic, and political structure of the city. Hand-picking African Americans, they sought an integrated council that would peacefully oversee local desegregation. The white business leaders had one primary goal—preventing violence in order to promote business.[5]

With the tragic assassination of President John F. Kennedy in Dallas, citizens realized they must make changes to restore the city's image. Earlier, Dallasites had assaulted Ambassador to the United Nations Adlai Stevenson when he tried to give a speech there. Shortly after Stevenson was mobbed, Vice President Lyndon B. Johnson and Mrs. Johnson were attacked in downtown Dallas by reactionaries dubbed the "mink coat mob" because many were wealthy. They struck Mrs. Johnson several times. Indeed, Dallas had a bad image. While local leaders continued to allow militant whites free rein, the Dallas Way decided to reform the city's image through censorship of local affairs. The leading newspapers, including the African American owned *Dallas Express,* agreed to practice self-censorship by refusing to report activities or demonstrations that might lead to violence on the part of blacks.[6] Dallas businessmen were willing to undertake any task to maintain a good image for their city that would foster prosperous business relations. Thus, when the civil rights movement started to gain strength in Dallas, a strong, intelligent, and dedicated leader was willing to fight the white business structure to end segregation. Juanita Craft proved to be the perfect choice.

Juanita Jewel Craft was born in 1902 in Round Rock, Texas. The granddaughter of slaves, she graduated from Prairie View Normal and Industrial School in 1921 with a certificate in dressmaking. After a failed marriage, she moved to Dallas in 1925 and became a bellmaid at the Adolphus Hotel, twice attending Eleanor Roosevelt. After watching her mother die after white physicians refused her entrance to an all-white hospital, Craft became involved in the struggle for black equality.[7]

In 1935, Craft joined the National Association for the Advancement of Colored People (NAACP). The Texas NAACP had two primary goals in the 1930s—ending discrimination in the Texas Democratic primary election and expanding educational opportunities for blacks. In 1945, Craft led a massive NAACP membership campaign in Dallas, expanding its rolls to 7,000 in 1946. The NAACP also appointed Craft state organizer in 1946, an unpaid position that she held for eleven years.[8] Traveling from town to town, Craft held meetings, solicited contributions, and organized new chapters—she was "like a blood transfusion to a very weak patient."[9] By 1958, Craft had organized 182 new branches in Texas. She also was involved in voter registration drives and was the first black woman deputized to sell poll taxes and the first black woman to vote in Dallas County. She traveled throughout the state, convincing African Americans it was worth paying the $1.50 poll tax to vote.[10] She recalled, "You had to put on your best argument to convince a lot of people that it was worth it."[11]

With the aid of A. Maceo Smith, the NAACP's Executive Secretary, Craft sought to strengthen the NAACP in Dallas and promote it statewide. Thus, the Dallas chapter of the NAACP became the center from which flowed the efforts to integrate the University of Texas, overturn the Democratic primary, and equalize teachers' salaries. Although Craft organized numerous branches and held a number of important positions, she never became president of the Texas NAACP. Only in recent years has the NAACP and the city of Dallas recognized her contribution.[12]

The most important position Craft held in the NAACP was that of youth advisor. Through the NAACP, Craft's goal was to end *de facto* segregation in Dallas and give African American youths equal opportunity in education, in jobs, and in social situations. Although the NAACP Youth Councils served primarily as social organizations, Craft tried to make them educational instruments as well. She viewed the Councils as training programs for the youths, teaching them about the NAACP and the many doors the organization opened for blacks. The children also served an important role for the NAACP.[13] The youths were more than future NAACP members; they were "vitally needed as plaintiffs in school cases as well as discrimination suits involving employment and recreation facilities."[14] Only through training of the young people could the NAACP succeed, and education was the key to preparing the youths for school integration and to reduce prejudice.

Besides organizing new local and collegiate chapters, Craft encouraged young people to attend the NAACP national conferences. She held youth meetings in her backyard and taught children about the responsibilities and privileges of citizenship. Occasionally, as many as one hundred youths gathered in her yard to socialize; in time, they became members of the NAACP and active in the civil rights movement.[15] From strategy planned in some of these backyard meetings came perhaps the most memorable event of Craft's term as Dallas youth director—the desegregation of the State Fair of Texas, held annually in Dallas.

The Youth Council, in 1955, threatened to demonstrate against the Negro Achievement Day at the State Fair. Negro Achievement Day, usually the last day of the fair, was set aside for blacks to enjoy the State Fair and promote their school organizations apart from whites. By peacefully demonstrating against Negro Day, the young people hoped to make whites recognize the "burden and humiliation of a one day restriction."[16] Although blacks were allowed to attend the State Fair on any given day, local white hostility and local tradition forced all but the most daring to wait for "their" day despite the obvious discrimination—a problem the State Fair's board of directors claimed had not existed since 1953. James H. Stewart, general manager of the Fair, admitted in 1955 that two rides remained closed to blacks because they entailed physical contact with whites. Some eating establishments did not serve African Americans, and those that did forced them to eat standing or perched on stools.[17] Stewart justified these actions as maintaining "harmony and good operations," to prevent a racial crisis that "would lead to violence."[18] Ironically, Stewart concluded by stating that the State Fair "belongs to everyone and is open to all people at all times regardless of race, creed or color."[19]

In 1955, the Youth Council decided to investigate the validity of Stewart's statement. The members agreed that if they found no discrimination, they would not picket Negro Achievement Day. The investigation proved Stewart's pronouncements false. The Fair's employees allowed some of the black children to ride, eat, and drink, while refusing others. Pepsi Cola consistently refused to serve blacks, and all were denied access to the two rides that put them in direct contact with whites. The youths also discovered that Stewart had issued a letter the day before their investigation, warning all concessions to "be nice to them."[20] Concluding that the State Fair practiced inconsistent, but obvious, discrimination, the young people decided to set up a picket line at the State Fair on Negro Achievement Day. The youngsters peacefully marched throughout the day, carrying signs that read, "This is Negro Achievement Day at the Fair—Keep Out," "Racial Segregation is Un-Clean, Un-American, and Un-Moral—Stay Out," and "Don't Sell Your Pride for a Segregated Ride—Stay Out."[21]

The Youth Council also sent warnings throughout the state to African Americans who planned to attend Negro Achievement Day. The *Parrott*, the NAACP Youth Council's newsletter, cried, "Up to date Negroes have been too dumb and stupid to see through the whole scheme of the Negro Achievement Day."[22] Stating that even one incident of segregation was too much, the paper discouraged blacks from crossing the picket line.[23] The *Dallas Express* warned blacks that their attendance would "encourage the officials of the Fair to further insult every intelligent Negro in the state of Texas, and will do irreparable injury to our children."[24] The larger grievance, however, claimed that a day set aside for African Americans was "segregation within itself, aside from the fact of discrimination."[25] Although many high school bands turned away from the picketed gates, several blacks continued to participate in Negro Achievement Day.[26]

Craft knew that most white Texans would not approve of the demonstration, but she was surprised that some African Americans did not agree on the issue of picketing. The Texas Citizens Council, a lily white organization, condemned the NAACP's tactics, as was expected. Stewart claimed he did not understand the picketing, stating the State Fair "has been a pioneer in making available to Negroes . . . facilities that are not open to them anywhere in the state."[27] Even more discouraging, African Americans did not overwhelmingly support the boycott. The Dallas Negro Chamber of Commerce first denounced the picket, then supported it, and many blacks crossed the picket line. The *Dallas Express* and the *Dallas Morning News* debated whether the demonstration actually discouraged attendance. Three days after the event, the *Morning News* claimed that a larger crowd attended Negro Achievement Day in 1955 than the previous year, rendering the boycott unsuccessful. In rebuttal, the *Express* stated that the participants noticed far fewer people than the previous year, and many who attended did not know about the picket or they would have stayed at home. The *Dallas Express* concluded that the issue of picketing the State Fair split blacks throughout the state.[28]

Regardless of its success, the picket demonstrated the discontent of African Americans with the segregation and discrimination at the State Fair; but, it did not change the Fair's policies. So, the next year, Craft encouraged another statewide boycott. Urging members of the Youth Council to meet with people in their churches, organizations, and homes to discourage attendance, Craft offered a prize to the person who brought the most people to help picket. But because of problems within the state NAACP organization, the Youth Council canceled the demonstration in 1956. The young people continued their campaign the following year, mailing out letters discouraging attendance and sponsoring a dance to compete with Negro Achievement Day. When the Fair finally desegregated in 1963, adults had taken over the picketing, but they remembered it was the Youth Council who had initiated the fight. Craft and her kids had made local history. Theirs was the first picket line organized in Dallas for the purpose of direct action against segregation.[29]

Craft also worked with the NAACP to desegregate the University of Texas and North Texas State University. In 1946, Heman Marion Sweatt, encouraged and supported by the NAACP, applied for the University of Texas Law School. When he was denied, the NAACP took direct action, demonstrating and picketing while also bringing suit in court.[30] Craft assumed the jobs of organizing the youth for demonstrations and helping raise funds for Sweatt's suit—a case he triumphantly won in 1950, four years before the *Brown* decision.[31] It was a time Craft remembered as "the most traumatic period" of her NAACP activity.[32] Craft, through the NAACP, also desegregated North Texas State University in 1955. In July, she took an African American student to the university to enroll. When he was denied, Craft got the administration to admit they would not enroll him because of his race. The NAACP and Craft filed suit against the university, and in December a federal judge ordered the university to integrate. Although Craft never participated directly in the public school desegregation cases in Dallas, she attended many of the NAACP meetings and listened to the deliberations, the majority of which led to successful litigation.[33] As a strong proponent of school desegregation, she hoped to "get young Negroes to see the importance of a first-class education."[34]

Juanita Craft and the Youth Council turned their attention in 1961 to the desegregation of lunch counters. The young people developed a simple tactic. The NAACP lawyers told them that they could not be denied service unless the owners displayed a sign stating "No Negroes Allowed." The majority of stores in Dallas did not display such signs. Therefore, the youths visited such stores, purchased items, then walked to the lunch counter and asked for Cokes. When the waitress refused, they questioned why they could buy items at any counter except that one. While they asked to speak to the manager, two more waited outside to repeat the process. In the meantime, others called, inquiring about the store's lunch counter policy. The young peoples' goal was not only to draw attention to discrimination, but also to frustrate the employees and slow business. Adults decided that the desegregation of restaurants should be their jobs, so they took over the sit-in movement by summer. To prevent the further disruption of business, stores agreed to serve African Americans. By July, thirty-six restaurants and lunch counters peacefully desegregated, including the "up-scale" Zodiac Room at the Neiman Marcus department store.[35] Although African Americans claimed a few Dallas lunch counters still practiced segregation, it was the Youth Council who initiated the sit-ins, prompting Dallas "on its way to integration."[36]

Soon after the Youth Council began the lunch counter sit-ins, members also started their attack on the downtown Majestic and Palace theaters with "stand-ins" and freedom walks. As with the sit-ins, the Council had a system. Every Sunday, the black youths got in line to purchase movie tickets. When the ticket clerk refused to sell tickets to them, they put their money back in their pockets and went to the end of the line. They continued this throughout the day, causing one clerk to cry in frustration, "I cannot take this any longer." Highly effective, these "stand-ins" caused business to slow. The youths also staged a freedom walk at Ferris Plaza. They peacefully walked in a circle, clapping hands, singing, and praying for "Freedom—NOW!" As the young people demonstrated, some of them wearing holes in their shoes, Craft tried to hustle food for them.[37] During one walk, the *Dallas Express* noted "traffic cruised to a near halt as they watched the peaceful but effective demonstration."[38] The protests gave the Dallas elite yet another message that integration could no longer be delayed. When asked the meaning of the stand-ins and freedom walks, Juanita Craft offered, "these kids are tired of not enjoying the full rights of democracy and want their Freedom—Now."[39] By the mid-1960s, most public facilities in Dallas desegregated, in part because of the efforts of Craft and her Youth Council.

Craft focused her attention on educating her community and getting citizens to vote after 1963. She also continued to put her energy primarily into educating the youth.[40] In one of the many speeches she made to high schools, she frankly told the children, "no matter how many doors are open you can't go in them unless you have some money, and you're not going to have the money if you don't have the education."[41] Part of Craft's educational activities with the Youth Council was taking the members on summer trips. She took them to observe the various businesses in Dallas, and she traveled with them across the country to NAACP national conferences. She took more than one thousand black youngsters coast to coast during the 1960s, on trips funded by donations made by local businesses.[42] In 1968, she sponsored the first integrated bus trip to Atlantic City, stopping in Washington, D.C., to attend a Coke party in Senator Ralph Yarborough's office in their honor. Craft hoped the kids might "know the people that are governing them. Let them see their Congress in action."[43] She gave many African American children an opportunity to see the United States and to be exposed to their government.

Craft also organized a number of programs for the Youth Council. She understood the difficulty of teaching African American children—who had been denied an equal education—to come forward and accept the responsibilities of full citizenship and freedom. Thus, she did everything possible to prepare the children. In 1967, the Youth Council sponsored a "Stay in School" program. Members plastered bumper stickers reading "Stay in School" and "Learn and Earn; Stay in School" around town. They also went to the public pools, parks, and playgrounds wearing sandwich signs stating "I'm Going Back to School. What About You?" In 1968, the group sponsored a program that honored thirteen African Americans—the first black postman, the first black policeman, first black to attend class at the University of Texas, and others who had made contributions to the civil rights struggle. Craft also worked hard to find clothes for needy children in her community, and she got scholarships and jobs for many blacks.[44] Having no children of her own, she dedicated herself to those in her community. She considered them her family. In 1975, she told an interviewer, "I don't have any children of my own. They're all mine. I'm in better shape than the old lady who lived in the shoe."[45]

Many observers and later historians noted that the civil rights movement in Dallas was peaceful. The efforts of Craft are at least partially responsible for controlling militant youths. She was actively preaching non-violence when the *New York Times* reported that curbing militancy was perhaps one of the major contributions of African Americans in Dallas during the desegregation process. Yet, the all-white Citizens Council still feared violent protests in 1964 and was concerned that a visit by the NAACP executive secretary, Roy Wilkins, might spark violence. To forestall such a development, the Dallas businessmen decided to establish the bi-racial Committee of 14. When whites picked African Americans for the committee, they selected Craft primarily because of her close contact with youth and her aversion to violence. Although the Committee played an instrumental role in helping desegregate Dallas, its primary function was to prevent riots. Craft feared that if the Committee of 14 had not been successful, the same violence that swept the country from 1965 to 1968 might have reached Dallas.[46]

As riots swept major cities throughout the country in 1967, Craft and other African American leaders found effective ways to prevent violence in Dallas. She decided to take a busload of teenagers to Watts in 1966 so they could see what happened when violence got out of control. She told them, "Remember that when you are burning down houses, you are burning down your houses."[47] Craft felt that young people's charges of white domination did not justify violence. She spoke frankly to the youngsters and told them that they were not old enough to know of white domination; she stated, "if your mind cannot be dominated, then you can't be dominated. Now, this is up to you whether or not you're going to let somebody tell you that you're inferior."[48] Her most successful effort to curb violence was an

"Anti-Riot" program in the summer of 1968. The Youth Council and Craft distributed approximately 20,000 bumper stickers and placards reading, "Keep It Cool. Don't Be A Fool," "Think Before You Act," and one that just said "Don't." Craft also tried to quell rumors. She told the kids to talk to their parents or to her if they heard rumors of violence. Although she never considered herself a follower of Martin Luther King Jr., she preached that violence and riots proved detrimental to the gains and goals of the NAACP.[49] Craft told the youths that the NAACP's "slow but steady" legal route resulted in the major civil rights legislation. She also reminded them that it was the NAACP that "bailed CORE freedom riders out of jail."[50] Craft strongly believed that the "glamour of dissent [violence] is not the way to reach equality."[51] She never felt that African Americans should not fight for their freedom—only that they should do it within the legal framework. She once said about herself, "I'm violent only with words. I work within the system and play by its rules."[52] The *New York Times* repeatedly applauded the success of African Americans in Dallas in their attempt to "curb militancy."[53]

Juanita Craft's work did not go unrecognized. In 1956, Roy Wilkins presented two awards to her for her distinguished achievements in NAACP youth activities; the awards recognized her "valiant fight" against segregation. Craft also received four White House invitations—two from Kennedy, one from Johnson, and one from Nixon—to attend conferences that dealt with the growing problems and concerns among the nation's youth.[54] When Kennedy took his fateful trip to Dallas in November 1963, Craft was among those invited to a luncheon to honor the President and Mrs. Kennedy. Amid Craft's honors, the most notable was the Linz Award, Dallas's oldest civic honor, for her 1968 campaign exposing fraudulent trade schools. These schools lured young people to Dallas, promising luxurious housing, food, and jobs; the reality was poor housing, no food, and no jobs. As Craft sheltered, fed, and found employment for the youths who were misled by the trade schools, she provided authorities with information to close the schools. Her work resulted in the passage of state, local, and federal legislation that regulated trade schools.[55] The following year, she received the Linz for her success.

Craft's work with young African Americans not only gained her recognition, but also led to her participation in wider civic activities. In the late 1960s and early 1970s, Dallas mayor Erik

Jonsson held a number of conferences entitled "Goals for Dallas," to which he invited Craft. Jonsson and the conferences drew up goals for Dallas in the areas of city government, health, safety, education, and economy. Craft felt honored by the invitation, telling Jonsson that it was the first time she ever felt like an American citizen.[56] She also kept busy traveling throughout Dallas, speaking to white churches of all denominations. Her purpose was to get through "to some of the people that otherwise would not have paid any attention to a Negro."[57] In the process, Craft gained the respect of many Dallas citizens who, in 1975, urged her to run for city council. Her campaign issues included the revitalization of the inner city and the development of low-interest home improvement loans for South Dallas.[58] Although her age seemed an issue for some, Craft responded with, "Stupidity. I've never heard anyone criticize Eleanor Roosevelt because of her age. . . . Old wine is the best wine."[59] Winning at age seventy-five, she became, at that time, one of four African Americans ever to sit on the Dallas City Counci1.[60] After three more successful elections, she decided that the civil rights "struggle isn't over yet" and retired from the Council in 1980 to resume her activities and trips with the youth.[61]

Craft accumulated a number of awards and honors throughout her life, becoming one of Dallas's most respected and admired citizens. The NAACP readily acknowledged Craft's contributions. In 1978, the organization honored her with the Golden Heritage Life Membership Award, and in 1985 she served as a special delegate to the NAACP national convention where attendees honored her for fifty years of service and leadership.[62] She also received the Eleanor Roosevelt Humanitarian Award for "public service which best exemplifies the civic example of Mrs. Roosevelt." When Mrs. Craft died in 1985, at the age of eighty-three, Dallas mourned the loss of a great lady. Among those who spoke at her funeral were Governor Mark White, State Treasurer Ann Richards, State Attorney General Jim Mattox, and United States Senator Ralph Yarborough.[63]

Juanita Craft actively pushed for African Americans' civil rights throughout her lifetime. She courageously took on the Dallas elite and won more battles than she lost on the civil rights front. More importantly, she always put the needs and education of children first. She fulfilled the role of informal educator, encouraging children to become responsible citizens and to recognize the importance of education. Although she worked primarily with the NAACP Youth Council, she reached out to all young people in her community. For many children she became a second mother. Before her death, she expressed the importance of working with children: "Everything comes down to the child . . . the child acquires the world, [s]he carries on what we have left, what we have prepared. If we want to know who we are, what we have accomplished, then just look at the children."[64]

Notes

1. Dana Rubin, "The Ghosts of the Freedmen," *Texas Monthly* 19 (July, 1991), 146.
2. Alwyn Barr, *Black Texans: A History of Negroes in Texas, 1528–1971* (Austin, 1973), 220; Bruce A. Glasrud, "Jim Crow's Emergence in Texas," *American Studies* 15 (1974), 47–60.
3. Juanita Craft, interview by David Stricklin and Gail Tomlinson, March 29, 1979, Dallas Public Library, Texas/Dallas History and Archives Division, Dallas.
4. *Dallas Morning News*, September 14, 1980, 20; Steve Kenney, "The Struggle for Power," *D Magazine* (June 1981), 101, 136; Leonard B. Murphy, "Negro Segregation Practices" (MA thesis, Southern Methodist University, 1958), 47; Juanita Craft, interview by Stricklin and Tomlinson, January 23, 1979, 13–14; J. W. Rice Correspondence, 1954, Dallas Negro Chamber of Commerce, Texas/Dallas History Archives Division, Dallas Public Library, Dallas, Box 2; *Dallas Express*, July 25, 1953, 1; Department of Commerce, Bureau of the Census, *United States Census Population: 1960*, Vol. I, *Characteristics of the Population*, Part 45, Texas (Washington, D.C., 1963), 118; Bureau of the Census, *United States Census Population: 1970*, Vol. I, *Characteristics of the Population*, Part 45, Texas (Washington, D.C., 1973), 1277; *Tasby v. DISD*, 1976, Juanita Craft Collection, Box 19.
5. For more information on the white power structure in Dallas and its attempts at desegregation, see William J. Brophy, "Active Acceptance, Active Containment: The Dallas Story," in *Southern Businessmen and Desegregation*, edited by Elizabeth Jacoway and David R. Colburn (Baton Rouge, 1982); Lewis W. Jones and Herman H. Long, *The Negotiation of Desegregation in Ten Southern Cities* (Nashville, 1965); Jim Schutze, *The Accommodation: The Politics of Race in an American City* (Secaucus, NJ, 1986); Richard Austin Smith, "How Business Failed Dallas," *Fortune* 70 (July 1964), 157–163, 211–216; Carol Estes Thometz, *The Decision-Makers: The Power Structure of Dallas* (Dallas, 1963).
6. *Dallas Morning News*, September 14, 1980; Patricia Evridge Hill, *Dallas: The Making of a Modern City* (Austin, 1996), 165; Juanita Craft, interview by John Egerton, June 10, 1968, Juanita Craft Collection, Dallas Public Library, Texas/Dallas History and Archives Division, Dallas.
7. *Dallas Weekly*, February 15–22, 1995, 9.
8. Martin Herman Kuhlman, "Civil Rights Movement in Texas: Desegregation of Public Accommodations, 1950–1964" (Ph.D. diss., Texas Tech University, 1994), 68; Michael Lowery Gillette, "The NAACP in Texas,

1937–1957" (Ph.D. diss., University of Texas at Austin, 1984), 28–29; Juanita Craft, interview by Stricklin and Tomlinson, February 5, 1979.

9. Gillette, "NAACP," 29.
10. Juanita Craft, interview by Stricklin and Tomlinson, February 5, 1979.
11. *Dallas Morning News,* August 30, 1970, 14.
12. Juanita Craft, interview by Stricklin and Tomlinson, February 20, 1979; *Dallas Morning News,* August 30, 1970, 14; Juanita Craft, interview by Stricklin and Tomlinson, February 20, 1979; W. Marvin Dulaney, "Whatever Happened to the Civil Rights Movement in Dallas?" in *Essays on the American Civil Rights Movement,* edited by W. Marvin Dulaney and Kathleen Underwood (College Station, 1993), 70, 73; *Dallas Weekly,* February 15–22, 1995, 9.
13. Gillette, "NAACP," 145, 142; Juanita Craft, interview by Stricklin and Tomlinson, January 23, 1979.
14. Gillette, "NAACP," 142.
15. Gillette, "NAACP," 12; Juanita Craft, interview by Stricklin and Tomlinson, January 23, 1979; Juanita Craft, interview by Egerton, June 10, 1968.
16. *Dallas Express,* January 12, 1952, 10.
17. *Dallas Morning News,* October 14, 1955, 3; *Dallas Morning News,* October 16, 1955, 1, 15.
18. *Dallas Morning News,* October 17, 1955, 2.
19. *Dallas Morning News,* October 16, 1955, 15.
20. *Dallas Express,* October 15, 1955, 10.
21. *Dallas Express,* October 15, 1955, 10; *Dallas Morning News,* October 18, 1955, 1.
22. *Parrott,* October 15, 1955, Juanita Craft Collection, Box 23.
23. *Parrott,* October 15, 1955, Juanita Craft Collection, Box 23.
24. *Dallas Express,* October 15, 1955, 10.
25. *Dallas Express,* October 22, 1955, 17.
26. *Dallas Morning News,* October 18, 1955, 1–2.
27. *Dallas Morning News,* October 18, 1955, 1.
28. *Dallas Morning News,* October 16, 1955, 1; *Dallas Morning News,* October 18, 1955, 1; *Dallas Express,* October 29, 1955, 1; *Dallas Express,* October 22, 1955, 1.
29. *Dallas Morning News,* August 18, 1955, 16; NAACP Youth Council minutes, October 10, 1956, Juanita Craft Collection, Box 23; Kuhlman, "Civil Rights Movement in Texas," 107; *Dallas Express,* October 22, 1960, 1, 8; Juanita Craft, interview by Egerton, June 10, 1968.
30. Juanita Craft, *A Child, the Earth, and a Tree of Many Seasons: The Voice of Juanita Craft,* edited by Chandler Vaughan (Dallas, 1982), 17.
31. For more information on *Sweatt v. Painter,* see Patricia Lefforage Davis, "*Sweatt v. Painter:* Integration in Texas Higher Education" (M.A. thesis, University of Texas at Austin, 1971).
32. Juanita Craft, interview by Stricklin and Tomlinson, January 23, 1979.
33. Juanita Craft, interview by Stricklin and Tomlinson, April 24, 1979.
34. Juanita Craft, interview by Egerton, June 10, 1968.
35. Craft, *A Child,* 19–20; Robert Weisbrot, *Freedom Bound: A History of America's Civil Rights Movement* (New York, 1990), 39–40; "Dining in Dallas," *Time* 78 (August 4, 1961), 15; *New York Times,* July 28, 1961, 1.
36. *Dallas Express,* August 5, 1961, 8.
37. Juanita Craft, interview by Stricklin and Tomlinson, January 23, 1979.

38. *Dallas Express,* February 25, 1961, 1.
39. *Dallas Express,* February 25, 1961, 6.
40. Peyton Davis, "Sunday Q & A," *Dallas Times Herald Sunday Magazine* (November 21, 1976), 17.
41. Speech notes, Juanita Craft Collection, Box 1.
42. Juanita Craft, interview with Egerton, June 10, 1968; Juanita Craft, interview with Stricklin and Tomlinson, January 23, 1979; various letters to Juanita Craft, Juanita Craft Collection, Box 9.
43. Juanita Craft, interview with Egerton, June 10, 1968.
44. Juanita Craft, interview with Egerton, June 10, 1968.
45. *Dallas Morning News,* December 24, 1975.
46. Dulaney, "Whatever Happened?" 79; Steve Kenney, "The Struggle for Power," *D Magazine* (June 1981), 139; Juanita Craft, interview with Stricklin and Tomlinson, February 20, 1979; Juanita Craft, interview with Stricklin and Tomlinson, March, 20, 1979.
47. Juanita Craft, interview with Egerton, June 10, 1968.
48. Juanita Craft, interview with Egerton, June 10, 1968.
49. Juanita Craft, interview with Egerton, June 10, 1968.
50. *Dallas Morning News,* October 1, 1967, 11.
51. *Dallas Times Herald,* February 9, 1972.
52. "This is Their South," *Southern Living* 7 (June 1972), 76.
53. *New York Times,* July 30, 1961, 1.
54. Craft attended two conferences under Kennedy's administration that dealt with integration and the prevention of school dropouts. She was also one of the participants in Johnson's "To Secure These Rights" program which sought to promote the civil rights movement and the passage of the Voting Rights Act. Nixon invited Craft to attend his White House Conference on Children, a program intended to encourage youths to achieve their maximum potential.
55. Ike Smalls Award pamphlet, 1956, Juanita Craft Collection, Box 52; Juanita Craft, interview with Stricklin and Tomlinson, January 23, 1979; Kennedy invitation, November 22, 1963, Juanita Craft Collection, Box 9; *Dallas Times Herald,* February 20, 1969, 1; "Their South," 76; *Dallas Times Herald,* February 20, 1969, 1.
56. Erik Jonsson, *Goals for Dallas* (Dallas, 1967); See also *Goals for Dallas: Economic Potentials Handbook* [no author listed], (Dallas, 1970); Juanita Craft, interview with Stricklin and Tomlinson, March 20, 1979.
57. Juanita Craft, interview with Egerton, June 10, 1968.
58. "Campaign issues," 1975, Juanita Craft Collection, Box 4.
59. *Dallas Morning News,* December 24, 1975, 5.
60. Juanita Craft, interview with Stricklin and Tomlinson, February 20, 1979; *Dallas Morning News,* December 24, 1975, 5.
61. Kenney, "The Struggle," 140.
62. *Dallas Morning News,* October 12, 1984, 21.
63. Juanita Craft, funeral program, August 10, 1985, Juanita Craft Collection, Box 52.
64. Juanita Craft, interview with Egerton, June 10, 1968; *Dallas Weekly,* February 15–22, 1995, 9.

Growing Up Black in East Texas

Some Twentieth-Century Experiences

WILLIAM H. WILSON

THE EXPERIENCES OF GROWING UP BLACK IN EAST Texas could be as varied as those of Charles E. Smith and Cleophus Gee. Smith's family moved from Waskom, Harrison County, to Dallas when he was a small child to escape possible violence at the hands of whites who had beaten his grandfather. Gee matured in comfortable circumstances on the S. H. Bradley place near Tyler, a large farm owned by prosperous relatives. Yet the two men lived the larger experience of blacks in the second or third generation removed from slavery, those born, mostly, in the 1920s or early 1930s. Gee, too, left his rural setting for Dallas, although his migration occurred later and was voluntary. As Lawrence Levine has noted, post-emancipation blacks moved into direct participation in society, and despite segregation and discrimination, "new channels of mobility and communication were created," bringing "changes and new potentialities."[1]

Joining the rural-to-urban migration was not, however, the most significant common denominator among eight East Texas African Americans who, during the 1950s, built homes in the new all-black community of Hamilton Park in Dallas.[2] The shared foundation of their childhood, youth, and young adulthood consisted of the socialization in the accepted, traditional values: family, work, and education. Given their adult commitment to church activity, religion could be considered central to their lives, but few mentioned it while reminiscing about their earlier years. It is likely that as youngsters they viewed religious activity simply as an extension of family life. All, however, stressed the centrality of family, work, and education.[3]

Parents set the example in an atmosphere of loving family discipline. Charles Smith's mother stayed home to raise eight children while his father worked, but both parents "always stressed the necessity of work." His brother, Willie F. Smith, credited their mother and "some teachers" with inculcating the value of work. Willie B. Johnson remembered that her sharecropper father "was a darned good father. He used to plow. . . . He didn't like for us girls to do that, and there was only one boy in my family." Sadye Gee, born in Dallas, recalled that she could not go to the nearby Hall-Thomas commercial district because "[m]y daddy was so strict I dared not leave the premises," except to go to the YWCA.[4]

Parents expected their children to follow their example. Charles Smith mowed yards and shined shoes in Dallas to buy clothes for school. If Willie Johnson's father disliked having his daughters plow the land he farmed near Kaufman in the 1930s, he had no such compunction about their picking cotton. He insisted that they work steadily and well. One day he saw Mrs. Johnson's sister "looking at birds just flying around, and he said, 'I didn't bring you out here to count them damned birds! Go to work!' She said, 'My back is hurting!' He said, 'You don't have no damned back! Get to work!'" Curtis J. Smith was expected to stay with his aged grandmother, providing company for her and help as needed in her home near Longview. Later, he earned money during his high school years by tractor disking farmland. Doris Robertson, who grew up in Dallas, worked there to help support her mother; she left college before taking a degree because of the "need for finances."[5]

Sadye Gee's father, a skilled carpenter, found employment only intermittently during the Great Depression. The family survived by keeping chickens and a garden and by working hard. Whites delivered their dirty laundry by the bundle to the future Mrs. Gee's home on Mondays. The mother and three children washed the clothes in a big black kettle set up under fruit trees in the back yard. Then they starched and ironed, using old-fashioned flatirons heated over a small portable charcoal furnace. On Thursdays the customers picked up their laundry, "washed and ironed and folded, for $1.50 per week." Le Verne Fields's father operated a truck farm near Tyler for several years, often selling the produce in town himself. She and her siblings dug, sorted, and loaded potatoes on truck or wagon for the trip to town.[6]

Vivid memories of schools, schooling, and teachers dominated these recollections of youth. Black East Texans who went to rural schools remembered inadequate materials, indifferent buildings, concerned teachers who labored to overcome those deficiencies, and parental and community support. "Mother was very protective of us girls," Willie Johnson recalled, but nevertheless her parents sent her trudging off to school each day from outside Kaufman to the "Egypt" section of town, where she "would be so *tired*" after her long walk. The school was dilapidated, "but you talk about somebody who thought she was important—when I got to the sixth grade, I went upstairs . . . I'd pass those little kids and go up the stairs to that raggedy-looking place where I was going."[7]

Curtis Smith walked three miles to elementary school but when he began high school he rode the bus. "The bus would come by and pick us up about 7:00 in the morning, and I imagine we had somewhere around a thirty-five or forty-mile route to get to school," arriving just in time for the beginning of class at 8:45. The segregated high school was operated under the "separate but equal" doctrine, but with no pretense of equality. "I think we had some pretty good teachers, and they taught the best they could with what they had to teach with. Most of the books were passed down, of course." That is, when the white high school acquired new editions, the outdated, worn books were "passed down" to the black schools. Similarly, "all of our football equipment was used equipment. I played football for about three years in high school and all of our equipment was handed-down equipment."[8]

Le Verne Fields began her education at the one-room Lindale elementary school in Smith County. Teachers solved the problem of mutual distraction by moving classes to separate sections of the big room. "You walked into individual corners. Sometimes the teacher would even take you, depending on the weather, outside for classes. Then, the other kids would really be upset because everybody wanted to go outside and have their class. . . . If the weather was really nice, we always had several classes outside. We'd sit around on the ground, and the teacher would teach us there." When the weather confined the children indoors, "we didn't know if we were disturbing each other, because we never knew any other way." On cold days members of the community made certain that "there was always someone coming by" to put firewood in the wood-burning heater. "We never had no problem. There was always somebody that came by to bring some wood to make sure the kids was warm at all times."[9]

When the future Mrs. Fields moved to Tyler with her family she continued to attend elementary school, but not the black school nearest her, for it was overcrowded, and certainly not the white school. Her school received "handed-down" books, yet the students were expected to do their best despite the adverse circumstances. "We would cry sometimes because a page would be missing out of the book, and the pages would not be missing out of the teacher's book. The teacher would have the best book." Teachers and parents were suspicious of excuses for a lack of preparation. "Back then," students without completed lessons "would get a whipping from the teacher and from your parents, too." Woe to the pupil whom the teacher suspected of tearing out a page to avoid a lesson, because of the emphasis on student honesty.[10]

When the Bethlehem, Upshur County, school would not or could not pay for basketball uniforms, Streetman Watson remembered that new uniforms arrived anyway, because "somebody in the community raised money. The school never had that much money. Somebody in the community raised money to buy uniforms and whatever equipment we had." Members of the community sponsored box suppers and other fund-raising projects, which were so well supported that it "wasn't very hard" to have uniforms and equipment.[11]

East Texans who migrated to Dallas or were born there attended Lincoln or Booker T. Washington high schools, but the atmosphere of discipline and high expectations was no less than in the rural or small city settings. Students were expected to behave and to learn. Sadye Gee, who attended Booker T. Washington in the late 1930s, never forgot Jerry Towns, an instructor with a unique method of punishing infractions. Towns sent students after school to the detention room, where they would copy the United States Constitution, crossing "t's" with red ink, and dotting "i's" with blue. The number of copies depended upon the seriousness of the offense. "Then when you would have done that, he would tear it up before your very eyes, . . . so we avoided going to the detention room." Mrs. Gee remembered her task, three copies of the Constitution for an unexcused tardy. She was careful not to be tardy again.[12]

Willie Smith, a graduate of Lincoln High School, valued the education he received. "In the years that I went to school, . . . and before all of the sophistication and all of the hundreds and hundreds of millions of dollars of sophisticated equipment, before all of the modernization came along, no one graduated from school who couldn't read. We didn't have kids graduating from high school and they couldn't read. I mean, we could work math problems in our heads. Now, kids graduating from high school, if they don't have a calculator, they can't even divide. I think it's a sad commentary."[13]

Discipline and hard work should not suggest that growing up was devoid of fun. Streetman Watson and Curtis Smith played in organized sports. Sadye Gee recalled coming from Dallas on the interurban rail car for Sunday and holiday family excursions. With her parents and siblings she left the car at the Vickery community, then far north of Dallas in what was known as the White Rock area. "Then we were met by our cousins who owned a T-Model Ford. . . . It was a thrill to ride in an automobile." Sometimes her family would visit relatives in the Upper White Rock section, where Hamilton Park was later established. "We would play and go up and down the cotton fields and just explore the rural area. . . . We lived in the city, and everything was so fascinating to us." Doris Robertson remembered her high school senior year hayride to the black-owned Anderson farm in the same general vicinity.[14]

The family influences on these East Texans were not transitory or confined to youth, but continued through life. Backgrounds of land ownership and home ownership were reflected in their desire for owned homes in Dallas, even though Dallas blacks in the late 1940s and early 1950s faced significant barriers to home ownership. The barriers included white violence against blacks moving into houses previously owned by whites, and generally successful white opposition to new black subdivisions in outlying areas. When a coalition of black and white leaders was able to establish, in 1953, a suburban-style black subdivision in what was, at the time, far North Dallas, the East Texans gravitated to the new Hamilton Park. Asked if she and her husband could have rented instead of buying in Hamilton Park, Sadye Gee replied: "No way! Daddy wouldn't have that."[15]

Curtis Smith was dubious about pouring his savings into a house that he might not be able to pay for, but family influences inclined him toward home ownership. His father instilled the idea of thrift. When Smith was young, he was provided with some necessities, but everyday clothing and extras were to come from his earnings if he worked, and he was expected to work. Smith began saving early. His father's requirements "taught me to be dependent on myself." The older man later squelched the idea that home owning would compromise financial independence. While Smith and his family were living in an apartment in Dallas, his father came to visit. Smith recalled that he "talked to me and said, 'Every time you pay rent on this place, you don't own any more of it than you did before you paid the rent. If you made a payment on a home, that means you're closer to owning it.' I said, 'Dad, I'm not making enough money.' He said, 'Well, you're making enough money to pay your rent and live here, and you could live in your own place.' "[16]

Their parental commitment to education was so powerful that all but one of the eight East Texans considered here did at least some post-secondary work. All of them formed stable nuclear families, and expected their children, in turn, to obtain good educations. Their children graduated from high school and most pursued college or university studies. The children were also expected to make their way in the world, as their parents and grandparents had done.[17]

The intergenerational commitment of black East Texans to family, work, and education refute white racists' assumptions of black indolence or shiftlessness. Such black identification with traditional American values shames those white Texans who refused to recognize the full humanity and citizenship of blacks. Whites' arbitrary distinctions of segregation and discrimination burned into the consciousness of Charles Smith when as a child of eight he left Waskom by train to join his family in Dallas. More than fifty years later he recalled the Jim Crow section "up front," near the locomotive. "When we got off the train and got on the streetcars to go home, you got in the back. There were signs designated for 'colored' and 'white.' Right then I realized that there is a difference."[18]

At the same time the barriers of segregation were not so impermeable as to prevent friendly interracial cooperation. A white friend of Willie Johnson and her husband intervened with the Hamilton Park sales office to secure an application blank for the couple after an initial refusal. "They wouldn't let us fill it out because they said my husband was too old at that time, and he wouldn't have been able to finish paying for [a house]." Doris and Lincoln Robertson bought a home in Hamilton Park because

Mr. Robertson's white employer, "furious" over the rejection of their application for a Veterans Administration loan, appealed to the local VA office to reconsider. Even before the relatively racially enlightened era of the 1950s, a sympathetic white loaned Sadye Gee's father the money to retire the mortgage on his house and stave off foreclosure.[19]

The experiences of these twentieth-century black East Texans suggest that American values know no racial boundaries; that a commitment to family, work, and education transcends racism, discrimination, and segregation. Their experiences also suggest that the values are durable, surviving geographical migration and generational change. The tall sycamore trees in Sadye and Cleophus Gee's front yard in Hamilton Park symbolize that durability. When the Gees moved to Hamilton Park they brought with them "switches" from the Gee home place in Smith County. The sycamores grew from those cuttings.[20]

Notes

1. Lawrence W. Levine, *Black Culture and Black Consciousness: Afro-American Folk Thought from Slavery to Freedom* (New York, 1977), 139–140. For Smith, see Charles E. Smith, interview by William H. Wilson, Aug. 24, Oct. 24, 1989, interview OH 793, Oral History Collection, University of North Texas, 1–4, hereinafter cited as Charles Smith interview.
2. About thirty closed or unprocessed interviews in the Oral History Collection support the conclusions presented here, which are based on the available interviews. For aspects of Hamilton Park, see William H. Wilson, "Private Planning for Black Housing in Dallas, Texas, 1945–1955," in Laurence C. Gerckens, comp. and ed., *Proceedings of the Second National Conference on American Planning History* (Columbus, 1988), 67–84; and "Desegregation of the Hamilton Park School, 1955–1975," *Southwestern Historical Quarterly* (July 1991), 43–63.
3. The rural-to-urban migration during the lifetimes of the interviewees may be traced in the following Bureau of the Census publications: *Fifteenth Census of the United States: 1930,* Vol. 1 (Washington, D.C., 1932), 1081; *Census of Population, 1950,* Vol. 2, pt. 43 (Washington, D.C., 1952), 43–11, 43–12, 43–14, and 43–31; and *Census of Population 1960,* Vol. 1, pt. 45 (Washington, D.C., 1963), 45–27, 45–37, 45–38, 45–40, 45–41, 45–462, 45–469, 45–477, 45–480, 45–490, 45–492. See also Gilbert C. Fite, *Cotton Fields No More: Southern Agriculture, 1965–1980* (Lexington, 1984), 113, 156, 161, 169, 170–171. For a socio-historical survey of black religion, see C. Eric Lincoln and Lawrence H. Mamiya, *The Black Church in the African American Experience* (Durham, 1990).
4. Charles Smith interview, 6; Willie F. Smith, interview by William H. Wilson, May 31, June 14, 1990, OH 829, Oral History Collection, University of North Texas, 3, hereinafter cited as Willie Smith interview; Willie B. Johnson, interview by William H. Wilson, Feb. 9, 22, 1990, OH 819,

Oral History Collection, University of North Texas, hereinafter cited as Johnson interview; Sadye Gee, interview by William H. Wilson, March 7, 1990, OH 820, Oral History Collection, University of North Texas, 89, hereinafter cited as Gee interview; Curtis J. Smith, interview by William H. Wilson, Feb. 2, 23, March 30, 1990, OH 826, 7–8, Oral History Collection, University of North Texas, hereinafter cited as Curtis Smith interview.

5. Charles Smith interview, 6; Johnson interview, 38; Doris Robertson and Lincoln Robertson, interview by William H. Wilson, Jan. 7, 21, 1990, OH 817, Oral History Collection, University of North Texas, 8, hereinafter cited as Robertson interview.

6. Gee interview, 4–6 (quotation, 4); Le Verne Fields, interview by William H. Wilson, July 9, 16, 1990, OH 835, Oral History Collection, University of North Texas, 2–4, hereinafter cited as Fields interview.

7. Johnson interview, 2–3.

8. Curtis Smith interview, 9–10.

9. Fields interview, 4, 5–6.

10. Fields interview, 8.

11. Ruby Watson and Streetman Watson, interview by William H. Wilson, March 14, 16, 1990, OH 825, Oral History Collection, University of North Texas, 4 (quotation), 5.

12. Gee interview, 110 (quotation), 111.

13. Willie Smith interview, 50.

14. Gee interview, 33; Robertson interview, 13.

15. Gee interview, 21. For a discussion of black property ownership in the twentieth century, see Loren Schweninger, *Black Property Owners in the South, 1790–1915* (Urbana, 1990), especially 207–216, 226–232.

16. Curtis Smith interview, 20 ("taught me" quotation), 38–39 ("talked to me" quotation).

17. Citations to individual interviews in support of the statements would be tedious and cumbersome. The conclusions emerge from a complete reading of each of them.

18. For white depreciation of blacks, see Levine, *Black Culture and Black Consciousness,* 268–269; James A. Burran, "Violence in an 'Arsenal of Democracy': The Beaumont Race Riot, 1943," *East Texas Historical Journal* 14 (Spring 1976), 39–51; and Bruce A. Glasrud, "Child or Beast? White Texas' View of Blacks, 1900–1910," *East Texas Historical Journal* 15 (Fall 1977), 38–44; Charles Smith interview, 5.

19. Johnson interview, 69; Robertson interview, 21; and Gee interview, 39–40.

20. Gee interview, 27.

Preserving Rosenwald Schools in East Texas

The Sand Flat and Richland School Project

JAMES CONRAD
AND THEODORE M. LAWE

Inspired by the Civil Rights Movement of the 1960s and the popularity of the television mini-series *Roots,* an intense effort to preserve African American heritage is sweeping Texas and the nation. More than 100 African American museums have been established in the last forty years.[1] Numerous preservation groups have been organized and have actively worked to protect African American cultural sites, structures, and history in Texas. Over the past decade, several county historical commissions have acquired Texas Historical Commission markers for African American churches, schools, and communities. Even more impressive, a handful of organizations and individuals have embarked on ambitious projects such as setting up African American archives and libraries, cleaning up cemeteries, conducting oral history projects, and opening historical museums. These endeavors receive support from various organizations, including the Texas Historical Commission (THC), the National Trust for Historic Preservation (NTHP), and a host of county historical commissions and societies.

Perhaps the most impressive East Texas African American historical institution is the A. C. McMillan African American Museum in Emory. The museum displays historical artifacts and authentic African American and African art and sculptures.

To ensure new attractions for returning visitors, the curator changes the non-permanent exhibits annually. In addition to its permanent exhibits, the museum follows a comprehensive plan to collect local African American family histories and preserve local African American historical sites and buildings, including the Rosenwald School at Sand Flat.

Rosenwald schools possess a unique history. In 1912 Booker T. Washington, founder and president of Tuskegee Normal and

Industrial Institute in Alabama, and Julius Rosenwald, multimillionaire president and CEO of Sears and Roebuck, partnered to upgrade African American education in the South. They financed the construction of new, modern school buildings with support from local black communities and public school systems.[2] The need for modern school buildings for rural blacks was great indeed. While traveling through the lower South around the turn of the century, Washington had witnessed firsthand the need to revolutionize rural education for African Americans. Almost without exception, schools for blacks were smaller and understaffed compared to white schools. Black schools in the South possessed grossly inferior facilities; many held classes outdoors under brush arbors, in one-room log cabins, or in churches that generally lacked adequate furnishings and supplies. Not only were the African American schools physically inferior, but the length of the school term was shorter than that in white schools. Put simply, equality did not exist in Texas public schools. According to historian William Brophy, the total value of the furniture in white schools in Texas exceeded the total value of all the black schools in Texas. Washington and Rosenwald sought to address this disparity with the Rosenwald Fund, a philanthropic foundation.

Rosenwald Schools were common in rural East and Central Texas well into the middle of the twentieth century. The Rosenwald Fund, along with local African American communities, joined forces to build classrooms, industrial shops, and teachers' houses between 1920 and 1932. Eventually, however, two forces made the school buildings obsolete. First, desegregation of public schools as mandated by the Supreme Court decision in *Brown v. Board of Education* forced school consolidation. Second, massive population shifts from rural to urban areas following World War II resulted in a loss of rural population. A recent survey found only a handful of school buildings still intact, though undoubtedly others exist. Something so common only five decades ago—Texas once boasted 527 Rosenwald Schools—now appears to be a rarity. Rosenwald Schools improved rural African American education, and the story of the schools is essential to understanding the necessity to preserve and document the remaining structures.[3]

Rosenwald Schools were excellent examples of public-private cooperation. Following the example of other philanthropic organizations, the Rosenwald Fund contributed a matching grant that would pay about one-third of the costs of building a school. The remaining expenses would be shouldered by local African American communities and county and state governments. The terms of the grant required that the school be in continuous session for more than five months per academic year; that the building and property be deeded to local authorities; and that the local public school system assume responsibility for staffing and maintenance.[4] Historians refer to the Rosenwald School Program as the most successful effort at enhancing education undertaken by private efforts in the history of the United Sates. The record is astonishing. Rosenwald-funded schools first appeared in Texas in 1920 and continued to be built until 1932, when the Fund ceased to support rural school construction. During that period, the Rosenwald Fund had erected over 5,300 buildings in southern states. Texas' 527 school buildings ranked it third only behind North Carolina and Alabama. Bowie, Cass, and Smith counties in far northeast Texas accounted for the largest number of schools in the state, while a few Texas counties with large African American populations, such as Dallas County, had no Rosenwald Schools. Such absences perhaps resulted from prejudice, since some participation by white residents was required for a Rosenwald School to be built.

The Rosenwald Fund provided primary financial support; other northern philanthropic organizations contributed substantial sums as well. The John H. Slater Foundation funded teacher training schools, trained rural teachers, and supplemented teachers' salaries. Yet another foundation, the Anna T. Jeanes Fund, supported "Jeanes supervisors" to recruit rural teachers, present home demonstration programs, and organize fundraising rallies at Rosenwald Schools. In a 1935 report on African American education, the Texas Department of Education summarized the purpose of the Jeanes Fund field agents: "The Jeanes Supervisors were agents to help with supervising programs for the education of Negro children and the welfare of the Negro people."[5] The Jeanes supervisors first appeared in Texas after World War I. Twenty-two counties employed Jeanes teachers by 1930, the peak year of the program.

A third private foundation, the General Education Board, financed state agents for African American schools, conducted county training programs, and provided summer school for

African American teachers. According to the Texas Department of Education, "the General Education Board provided all salaries and official travel expenses for the State Agents and Assistant State Agents for Negro Education. The Fund also defrayed the expense of State Agents to several national conferences on education." These three funds, along with others, played vital roles in the success of Rosenwald Schools. In Texas, they were administered through the Texas Department of Education in conjunction with Prairie View State College, which acted as the site for program coordination and training.[6]

Rosenwald Schools were built according to standardized architectural plans that incorporated the latest in layout, furnishings, and sanitation facilities. An almost universal feature of the two- and three-room schools was a sliding partition between classrooms which, when opened, created a large auditorium for special programs, public meetings, county agent demonstrations, church programs, and Juneteenth celebrations. The school buildings also included kitchens, industrial shops, and space on the grounds for baseball fields, basketball courts, and gardens. In an era before rural electrification, large banks of windows on the east and west sides of the buildings maximized available natural light.

The small but growing movement to preserve Rosenwald Schools is a new initiative to maintain for future generations a part of the African American heritage. At the national level, the NTHP coordinates "The Rosenwald Initiative," funded in part by a $100,000 grant from the Rosenwald family foundation and matching private donors. This initiative is designed to set up a network to share information and generate public interest among state and local organizations interested in preserving Rosenwald Schools. Recently, the NTHP has sponsored several national conferences and workshops that focused attention on the historic significance of Rosenwald Schools and discussed strategies for saving the extant school buildings.[7]

The Texas Humanities Council, the National Trust for Historic Preservation, municipal governments, and museums like the A. C. McMillan African American Museum are in the forefront of Rosenwald School preservation in Texas. To date, the most impressive steps at the state level came in 2001, when the NTHP sent historian Karen Riles into the field to identify surviving Rosenwald Schools in Texas, an endeavor that resulted in a lengthy report and the identification of twenty-five existing buildings.[8] Riles's work generated numerous newspaper stories about Rosenwald Schools and their importance to African American education and communities.[9] Following up on the Riles report, the NTHP office in Austin launched a campaign to encourage nominations of Rosenwald Schools for listing on the National Register. To date, four Rosenwald Schools in Texas have been listed—Lockhart Vocational School (Caldwell County), Sweet Home Vocational and Agricultural School (Guadalupe County), Garland Community School Teacherage (Bowie County), and Pleasant Hill Rosenwald School (Cass County).[10]

At present, several community based groups and organizations are working to document and restore Rosenwald Schools in Texas. Their intent is to have these buildings recognized as Historical Landmarks by the THC and/or listed on the National Register. Acquisition of state markers and National Register listings enhances the prestige of historic properties by conferring state and national recognition, thereby improving the chances for raising money for repairs and restoration. In addition, those applying for markers and NTHP listing must undergo a rigorous process of collecting and evaluating documents related to the history of the school building, the students, the teachers, and the community. If nothing else is accomplished, this alone is a worthwhile endeavor, for it provides a permanent record for future historians and researchers.

Restoring a Rosenwald School is a much more complex and expensive enterprise than simply securing historical markers. Without question, the major challenge facing preservationists is locating adequate financial resources for professional restoration and modification for adaptive use. Philanthropic foundations do not generally offer grants for private restoration, regardless of the intended use of the structure. Municipalities, counties, states, and the federal government, along with corporate and individual donors, provide the bulk of the funding. The process of restoration is expensive if done by expert architects and contractors, while amateur and volunteer work usually results in diminished historical integrity.

Aside from raising money, the most problematic aspect of preserving a building often is finding an appropriate use for it once it has been restored. Since Rosenwald Schools tend to be found in isolated rural areas or in Freedom Colonies (all black rural communities) away from centers of population, they are subject to vandalism. Furthermore, the buildings, with few exceptions, are of wood frame construction, subjecting them to accidental fire or arson. Some preservation groups solve this dilemma by moving the buildings to nearby cities or historical parks. This, however, renders them ineligible for Texas Historical Landmark designation and for listing on the National Register. Removing a building from its original setting decreases its historical significance, although in some cases removing an historical structure is the only way to save it. A review of past successful projects indicates that options for future adaptive use do exist for Rosenwald Schools. Restored structures throughout the South have become private schools, day care centers, community centers, museums, residences, businesses, and visitor centers. Modifying the interior to suit a new function does not usually preclude acquiring or keeping an historical marker, but the exterior must retain its original appearance. Schools that are to be used as museums should be preserved in their original condition inside and out, or returned as nearly as possible to their original condition. Several examples of rural schoolhouse museums exist; one of the best is in Old City Park in Dallas, in a fully equipped, restored rural school building.

The A. C. McMillan African American Museum is mobilizing the African American community in Rains County for the purpose of documenting, restoring, and planning for future adaptive use of the Sand Flat Rosenwald School just outside of Emory, which was built in 1921 and 1922 on land donated by the Murray family.[11] Rains County once boasted two Rosenwald Schools—the Richland School and the Sand Flat School. The Richland School, located outside of Point in north Rains County, was destroyed by fire in 2002. Plans are being made to have a marker placed at the site of the former school.

Preserving Rosenwald Schools preserves an important yet often-forgotten part of Texas' history. During the decades after the Civil War, African American desire for education was so strong that, against all odds, 678 African American schools were operating in Texas in 1877. Education for African Americans in Rains County can be documented back at least to 1895.[12] According to Gwendolyn McMillan Lawe, four public schools for African Americans operated in the county between 1896 and 1898—Emory #1, Chapel Hill #5, Richland #9, and Isaiah Bunkley #19.[13]

One of the first black teachers in Rains County was Dora McMillan, a mulatto. She was the grandmother of A. C. McMillan, the last principal of the Sand Flat School who became the principal at Rains Junior High School after desegregation. The local A. C. McMillan African American Museum was named in his honor.[14]

According to *The Forgotten Texas Census of 1887–88*, white teachers were paid $49.55 a month and black teachers were paid $41.26 in Rains County.[15] The schools' programs were "separate and unequal." Interviews with several graduates and former teachers of the two Rosenwald Schools reveal that the students had only second-hand books, supplies, and equipment handed down from the white schools. Most of those interviewed, however, generally believed that the school fostered a family environment in the community.[16] Doris Washington, a former teacher of first- and third-grade students, remembers the multiple roles that teachers played, such as bus driver, kitchen helper, and fundraiser.[17] Another teacher, Terecia Carraway, remembers the close working relationships among the schools, the families, and the church at Sand Flat. She credits her being hired as a teacher with her being hired as a church musician. Because there were no available houses or apartments for rent, teachers, most of whom were recruited from outside the community, were boarded with local families. The teachers were college educated, certified, and registered with Rains County.[18]

Many of the students who attended the two Rosenwald Schools in the 1920s and 1930s had children who also attended the same schools. Lois Lane is one such second-generation Rosenwald graduate now employed by the City of Dallas. She remembers Professor C. C. and Mrs. Oma Wesley, a husband-and-wife team that taught all grade levels at Richland School.[19] She credits them with her going to college and her success in life.

The Rosenwald students, many of whom desegregated Rains County public schools in 1965, vividly recall the cultural shock of going from an all-African American school environment to an all-white school environment. Mrs. Audie Shiflet, a business teacher at the integrated school, played a major role in helping newly arrived African American students adjust and feel comfortable in their new surroundings. She later became a charter volunteer when the A. C. McMillan African American Museum opened in Emory in 2000. She accepted the invitation to volunteer from her former student, Gwendolyn McMillan Lawe, museum co-founder and director. Mildred Garrett, former Mayor Pro Tem of Emory and a graduate of Sand Flat, remembered that the school stressed high academic standards but also emphasized values, perfect attendance, and social etiquette. Her son, Howard Garrett, had perfect attendance from the first through the eighth grade.[20]

Desegregation of public schools in Rains County began with the transfer of African American students from St. Paul High School, also a Rosenwald School in Neylandville, located in Hunt County between Greenville and Commerce. These students were residents of Rains County, but because there was no high school for them in Rains County, they were bused approximately forty miles each way to Hunt County. Public education for African Americans in Rains County before 1965 was limited to the eighth grade.

In both the Sand Flat and Richland communities the Rosenwald School buildings, along with the local churches, were the centers of community activity and the entities that defined the communities. Many graduates of these schools have gone on to become teachers, principals, government workers, health care professionals, career military men and women, and business owners. As was the case in other communities with Rosenwald Schools, African American residents of Rains County enthusiastically supported education and thirsted for knowledge. They recognized the value of education to improving their economic and social status.

The plans for restoring and reusing the Sand Flat School building acknowledge the necessity for a broad-based collaborative partnership and financial and technical support from local, regional, state, and national agencies. Museum personnel have formed a relationship with the NTHP, attending national conferences and requesting technical assistance. Once the origins and history of the Sand Flat School are documented and the building restored into a museum, the community will have a location for cultural enrichment, civic programs, and networking. The Sand Flat preservation group realizes that this is a long and tedious project. Such undertakings are essential for the preservation of African American heritage.[21]

The preservation of buildings and sites related to African American history and culture reaches far beyond Rosenwald

Schools. For example, additional research and attention needs to be focused on the origin and development of African American neighborhoods and communities in medium and large cities in Texas. These were once thriving centers of business, culture, and social life for African Americans, but have now largely fallen into disrepair. While the history of African Americans in Texas is less familiar and tends to be more fragile than other, better-known parts of our collective past, it must be preserved. Rosenwald Schools are a vital element in preserving the saga of African American education in Texas.

Notes

1. *Official Museum Directory* (Washington, D.C., 2004).
2. Thad Sitton and James Conrad, *Freedom Colonies* (Austin, 2005), 135–136; Louis R. Harlan, *Booker T. Washington: The Wizard of Tuskegee, 1901–1915* (New York, 1983), 197.
3. Karen Riles, "Texas Rosenwald Schools Survey," National Trust for Historic Preservation, Austin, Texas, 2001.
4. Sitton and Conrad, *Freedom Colonies*, 135–136.
5. *Negro Education in Texas, 1934–35*, Bulletin, Texas State Department of Education, Vol. XL, No. 3, Austin, Texas, March 1935, 20.
6. *Negro Education in Texas*, 26.
7. "Restore America: Communities at Crossroads" National Preservation Conference, Louisville, Kentucky, September 28–October 3, 2004, http://www.rosenwaldschools.com; "Trust Me," *Preservation*, November/December 2004, 9.
8. Riles, "Texas Rosenwald Schools Survey." The surviving schools identified by Riles are: Hopewell School, Bastrop County; St. Mary's School, Bastrop County; Lot Canada School, Beeville, Bee County; Garland School Teacherage, Bowie County; Lockhart Vocational High School, Caldwell County; Linden School, Cass County; Pleasant Hill Vicinity Community School, Cass County; Ashbury High School, Yoakum, Dewitt County; Mount Vernon School, Franklin County; Anderson School, Grimes County; Sweet Home Vocational School, Seguin, Guadalupe County; York Creek School, Guadalupe County; Dayton School, Liberty County; Mt. Pilgrim School, Matagorda County; Davilla School, Milam County; Kerens School, Navarro County; Sand Flat School, Rains County; Calvert School, Robertson County; Sagamore Hill School, Tarrant County; Lillig School, Travis County; Pilot Point School, Travis County; El Campo School, Wharton County; Wharton County Training School, Wharton County; Coupland School, Williamson County; Hopewell School, Round Rock, Williams County.
9. "Texas Rosenwald Properties on 11 Most Endangered List," Texas Historical Commission News Release, July 1, 2002; Donald E. McLeod, "Rosenwald Schools Served Blacks in South," *The Bryan-College Station Eagle*, February 26, 2004; Lonnie Mabin, "Schools Symbolize a Legacy," *The Detroit News*, January 9, 2000; Dionne Victory, "Rosenwald Schools

Marked Turning Point in Black Education," *Texarkana Gazette*, February 29, 2004.

10. "Texas Rosenwald Properties," Texas Historical Commission News Release, 2; Communications from Gregg Smith of National Trust for Historic Preservation, Austin, Texas, to James Conrad, November 29, 2004.
11. Memorandum from Gwendolyn M. Lawe, Director of the A. C. McMillan African American Museum, to Reverend Willie Byrd, Pastor, Prairie Grove Baptist Church, July 16, 2004.
12. Gwendolyn McMillan Lawe, "From Wolf to Wolfwood: An Autobiography and Historical Study of the McMillan and the African American Families of Emory, Texas, 1833–2004," unpublished manuscript.
13. Lawe, "From Wolf to Wolfwood."
14. Rains County Treasurer, Rains County School Account Register, 1897, Rains County Courthouse, Emory, Texas.
15. L. L. Foster, editor, *Forgotten Texas Census: First Annual Report of the Agricultural Bureau of the Department of Agricultural, Insurance Statistics and History, 1887–88* (Austin, 2002), 183–194.
16. Interview with former students Hella Mayberry, Harold McMillan, Dock Mayberry, Modis Mayberry, and Lois Lane, December 2 and 4, 2004.
17. Interview with former teacher Doris Washington, December 2, 2004.
18. Rains County Treasurer, School Accounts.
19. Interview with former student Lois Lane, December 2, 2004.
20. Interview with former student and teacher Mildred Garrett, December 2, 2004.
21. Memorandum from Lawe to Byrd, July 17, 2004. This memorandum argues for the restoration of the Sand Flat School and proposes plans for its reuse.

APPENDIX

Articles on Black History from the *East Texas Historical Journal*

Barr, Alwyn. "Advancing from History's Hollow to History's Mountain: Sources on African American History in Texas." *East Texas Historical Journal* 38.1 (2000): 28–34.

Beil, Gail K. "James Leonard Farmer: Texas' First African American Ph.D." *East Texas Historical Journal* 36.1 (1998): 18–25.

———. "Melvin B. Tolson: Texas Radical." *East Texas Historical Journal* 40.1 (2002): 26–36.

Blyth, Lance R. "Fugitives from Servitude: American Deserters and Runaway Slaves in Spanish Nacogdoches, 1803–1808." *East Texas Historical Journal* 38.2 (2000): 3–14.

Brick, Blanche H. "William Morris Ford, Pastor of First Baptist Church, Longview, Texas, and the Southern Baptist View of Race Relations." *East Texas Historical Journal* 41.1 (2003): 53–60.

Burran, James A. "Violence in an 'Arsenal of Democracy': The Beaumont Race Riot, 1943." *East Texas Historical Journal* 14.1 (Spring 1976): 39–51.

Cain, Jerry Berlyn. "The Thought and Action of Some Early Texas Baptists Concerning the Negro." *East Texas Historical Journal* 13 (spring 1975): 3–12.

Campbell, Randolph. "Slaveholding in Harrison County, 1850–1860: A Statistical Profile." *East Texas Historical Journal* 11 (Spring 1973): 18–27.

Christian, Garna L. "The Violent Possibility: The Tenth Cavalry at Texarkana." *East Texas Historical Journal* 23.1 (1985): 3–15.

Conrad, James, and Theodore M. Lawe. "Preserving Rosenwald Schools in East Texas: The Sand Flat and Richland School Project." *East Texas Historical Journal* 43.2 (2005): 50–57.

Cravens, John N. "Felix 'Zero' Ervin: Louisiana Slave and East Texas Freeman." *East Texas Historical Journal* 10.2 (1972): 125–30.

Crouch, Barry A. "Hesitant Recognition: Texas Black Politicians, 1865–1900." *East Texas Historical Journal* 31.1 (1993): 41–58.

Crouch, Barry A., and Donaly E. Brice. "Dastardly Scoundrels: The State Police and the Linn Flat Affair." *East Texas Historical Journal* 37.1 (1999): 29–38.

Decker, Stefanie. "Women in the Civil Rights Movement: Juanita Craft versus the Dallas Elite." *East Texas Historical Journal* 39.1 (2001): 33–42.

Devereaux, Linda Ericson. "William Goyens: Black Leader in Early Texas." *East Texas Historical Journal* 45.1 (2007): 52–57.

Durham, Kenneth R., Jr. "The Longview Race Riot of 1919." *East Texas Historical Journal* 18.2 (1980): 13–24.

Gaither, Gerald. "Blacks and the Southern Farmers' Alliance Movement." *East Texas Historical Journal* 14.1 (Spring 1976): 24–38.

Glasrud, Bruce A. "Child or Beast? White Texas' View of Blacks, 1900–1910." *East Texas Historical Journal* 15.2 (1977): 38–44.

Gower, Patricia E. "The Price of Exclusion: Dallas Municipal Policy and Its Impact on African Americans." *East Texas Historical Journal* 39.1 (2001): 43–54.

Kibbe, Tina M. "School Desegregation in Port Arthur: The Battle between the Community, the Board, and the Justice Department." *East Texas Historical Journal* 44.2 (2006): 3–16.

Kossie-Chernyshev, Karen. "Constructing Good Success: The Church of God in Christ and Social Uplift in East Texas, 1910–1935." *East Texas Historical Journal* 44.1 (2006): 49–55.

———. "A 'Grand Old Church' Rose in East Texas: The Church of God in Christ (COGIC) in East Texas." *East Texas Historical Journal* 41.2 (2003): 26–36.

McKenzie, Fred. "The Kellyville Incident." *East Texas Historical Journal* 37.1 (1999): 39–41.

Marten, James. "Slaves and Rebels: The Peculiar Institution in Texas, 1861–1865." *East Texas Historical Journal* 28.1 (1990): 29–36.

Moore, Richard. "Radical Reconstruction: The Texas Choice." *East Texas Historical Journal* 16.1 (1978): 15–23.

Moretta, John. "The Censoring of Lorenzo Sherwood: The Politics of Railroads, Slavery, and Southernism in Antebellum Texas." *East Texas Historical Journal* 35.2 (1997): 39–52.

Neal, Diane, and Thomas W. Kremm. "'What Shall We Do with the Negro?': The Freedmen's Bureau in Texas." *East Texas Historical Journal* 27.2 (1989): 23–33.

Obadele-Starks, Ernest M. B. "Ralph Yarborough of Texas and the Road to Civil Rights." *East Texas Historical Journal* 32.1 (1994): 39–48.

Palm, Rebecca W. "Protestant Churches and Slavery in Matagorda County." *East Texas Historical Journal* 14.1 (Spring 1976): 3–8.

Petrovich, Alisa V. "The Jacksons of Brazoria County: The Life, the Myth, and the Impact of a Plantation Family." *East Texas Historical Journal* 36.2 (1998): 42–49.

Phillips, Edward Hake. "The Sherman Courthouse Riot of 1930." *East Texas Historical Journal* 25.2 (1987): 12–19.

Phillips, Michael. "White Violence, Hegemony, and Slave Rebellion in Dallas, Texas, before the Civil War." *East Texas Historical Journal* 37.2 (1999): 25–35.

Pitre, Merline. "Building and Selling the NAACP: Lulu B. White as an Organizer and Mobilizer." *East Texas Historical Journal* 39.1 (2001): 22–32.

———. "The Evolution of Black Political Participation in Reconstruction Texas." *East Texas Historical Journal* 26.1 (1988): 36–45.

Rabe, Elizabeth R. "Slave Children of Texas: A Qualitative and Quantitative Analysis." *East Texas Historical Journal* 42.1 (2004): 10–24.

Richter, William L. "The Army and the Negro during Texas Reconstruction, 1865–1870." *East Texas Historical Journal* 10.1 (1972): 7–19.

Robbins, Fred. "The Origin and Development of the African Slave Trade in Galveston, Texas, and Surrounding Areas from 1816 to 1836." *East Texas Historical Journal* 9.2 (October 1971): 153–62.

Robertson, Robert J. "Slavery and the Coming of the Civil War, as Seen in *The Beaumont Banner*." *East Texas Historical Journal* 34.1 (1996): 14–29.

Sapper, Neil G. "Aboard the Wrong Ship in the Right Books: Dorie Miller and Historical Accuracy." *East Texas Historical Journal* 18.2 (1980): 13–24.

Smallwood, James M. "The Black Community in Reconstruction Texas: Readjustments in Religion and the Evolution of the Black Church." *East Texas Historical Journal* 16.2 (1978): 16–28.

———. "Black Education in Reconstruction Texas: The Contributions of the Freedmen's Bureau and Benevolent Societies." *East Texas Historical Journal* 19.1 (1981): 17–40.

———. "Black Texans during Reconstruction: First Freedom." *East Texas Historical Journal* 14.1 (spring 1976): 9–23.

Sturdevant, Paul E. "Black and White with Shades of Gray: The Greenville Sign." *East Texas Historical Journal* 42.1 (2004): 25–33.

Williams, Milton H., III. "Romeo M. Williams: Tuskegee Airman and Civil Rights Lawyer." *East Texas Historical Journal* 43.1 (2005): 7–13.

Wilson, William H. "Growing Up Black in East Texas: Some Twentieth-Century Experiences." *East Texas Historical Journal* 32.1 (1994): 49–54.

Contributors

Cary D. Wintz is a professor of history at Texas Southern University, where he has taught since 1971. Wintz is the author/editor of more than a dozen books, including *Black Culture and the Harlem Renaissance* and, most recently, *Harlem Speaks*. Wintz is a native Houstonian, fifth-generation East Texan, and past president of the East Texas Historical Association.

Bruce A. Glasrud is professor emeritus of history, California State University, East Bay, and retired dean, School of Arts and Sciences, Sul Ross State University. He is coeditor of *The African American West: A Century of Short Stories* and of *The African American Experience in Texas: An Anthology*.

Archie P. McDonald teaches history at Stephen F. Austin State University and serves as executive director of the East Texas Historical Association and editor of the *East Texas Historical Journal*. He is the author/editor of books on Civil War and Texas history subjects, is past president of the Texas State Historical Association, past chairman of the Texas Committee for the Humanities, and past vice chairman of the Texas Historical Commission.

Alwyn Barr is a professor of history at Texas Tech University and a former chair of the Department of History. His publications include *Black Texans: A History of African Americans in Texas, 1528–1995*, and *African Texans*. Barr is a past president of the Texas State Historical Association and past member of Humanities Texas.

Elizabeth R. Rabe is completing law school at Cornell University and serves as executive editor of the *Cornell International Law Journal*. She holds undergraduate and master's degrees from Hamilton College and University of West Indies, where she was a Fulbright Scholar.

James Marten is a professor and chairman of the Department of History at Marquette University and a former Fulbright Lecturer at Northeast Normal University, Changchun,

People's Republic of China. He is the author of a dozen or more books, primarily on the history of children.

JAMES M. SMALLWOOD is a retired professor of history at Oklahoma State University. He also has taught at Trinity Valley College, Texas A&M University–Commerce, the University of Texas–Tyler, and the University of Kyoto, Japan. He is the author of sixteen books, including *Time of Hope, Time of Despair: Black Texans during Reconstruction.* Smallwood is a member of the East Texas Historical Association and a recipient of the association's C. K. Chamberlain and Ralph W. Steen Awards for outstanding contributions to the association.

MERLINE PITRE is a professor of history and dean of the College of Liberal Arts & Behavioral Sciences at Texas Southern University. She is the author of *Through Many Dangers, Toils, and Snares: The Black Leadership of Texas, 1868–1900*, and *In Struggle against Jim Crow: Lulu B. White and the NAACP, 1900–1957.*

GARNA L. CHRISTIAN has been a professor of history at the University of Houston–Downtown, since 1971. He also has taught at Texas Tech University and Texas Woman's University, Houston. Christian received the East Texas Historical Association's Ottis Lock Outstanding Educator Award in 1985, and his article titled "The Making of George Sessions Perry" received the C. K. Chamberlain Award for best article to appear in the *East Texas Historical Journal* in 2002. Christian also authored *Black Soldiers in Jim Crow Texas, 1899–1917.*

KAREN KOSSIE-CHERNYSHEV teaches history, geography, and economics at Texas Southern University. She holds master's and doctoral degrees from Rice University and received the C. K. Chamberlain Award in 2007 for her article, "Constructing Good Success: The Church of God in Christ and Social Uplift in East Texas, 1910–1935."

GAIL K BEIL, independent researcher and historian in Marshall, Texas, is a past president of the East Texas Historical Association and the Harrison County Historical Commission. She is coauthor of *The Texas and Pacific Depot in Marshall,* a monograph in the Ann and Lee Lawrence East Texas History Series, and is working on a book about James Leonard Farmer Sr.,

Texas' first African American Ph.D., and his son, James Farmer Jr., founder of the Congress of Racial Equality.

STEFANIE DECKER received a doctorate in history at Oklahoma State University, teaches United States history at Amarillo College, and is a specialist in Southern women's history.

WILLIAM H. WILSON earned a doctorate in history from the University of Missouri and retired as Regents Professor from the University of North Texas. He is a Fellow of the William P. Clements Center for Southwest Studies and past president of the Society for City and Regional Planning History. Wilson authored *Hamilton Park: A Planned Black Community in Dallas*.

JAMES CONRAD is an oral historian, librarian, and archivist at Texas A&M University–Commerce, and coauthor with Thad Sitton of *Nameless Towns: Texas Sawmill Communities, 1880–1942*. He is a Fellow of the East Texas Historical Association.

THEODORE M. LAWE is curator/archivist/historian at the A. C. McMillan African American Museum in Emory, Texas. He holds academic degrees in political science, African American history, and urban planning and serves as vice president of the East Texas Historical Association.

Index